Agricultural Trends in India, 1891-1947 :
Output, Availability, and Productivity

Agricultural Trends in India, 1891-1947: Output, Availability, and Productivity

George Blyn

Philadelphia

University of Pennsylvania Press

7387
Printed in the United States of America

Preface

THE ORIGINS OF this research date back to questions raised by Professors Daniel Thorner and Simon Kuznets concerning the nature of economic development in the modern period of India's history. During this period of the rooting of western institutions and industries in India, was per capita output improving, or was it declining, despite the rise in total output? When this question was raised the available data were inadequate, and are still too incomplete to give a conclusive answer.

Professor Thorner sought to narrow the void in knowledge by initiating a research project aimed at discovering long-period trends in the agricultural sector. The project was supported by the South Asia Regional Studies Department, and the writer, then an undergraduate in the department, interested in Indian economic history, served as research assistant under Dr. Thorner. In 1951 the findings of this research were presented as the writer's baccalaureate thesis. This work, subsequently published in India, was a product of the friendly encouragement of Dan Thorner. In the years which followed, from positions at Bombay and Paris, Dan promoted the author's crop trend study and encouraged its further research, which was ultimately presented in 1961 as a doctoral dissertation for the Economics Department of the University of Pennsylvania. It has been my pleasure and benefit to have corresponded with him over these years.

Professor Kuznets was consultant advisor for the initial crop study and an important influence on the later work. The method of deriving long-run trends by averaging the short-segment trends of a series, used in this study, is an outgrowth of graduate training under him. The use of moving averages as a means of avoiding certain procedural problems was adopted after his suggestion. He also contributed to perspective in fitting the present study into the problem of determining long-run trends in per capita national income.

The crop trend research lay largely dormant until the fall of 1957 when I met Professor Bert F. Hoselitz. Under his stimulus, and with financial aid from the Research Center in Economic Development and Cultural Change, the present study began to materialize. I am very grateful for the interest which he showed in my work.

It was my fortune that Professor Richard A. Easterlin accepted the supervision of the dissertation. His suggestions deepened the application of economic theory to the analysis of the trends. The study, and I personally, have gained much in the direction of analytical rigor from his criticism. Professor Wilfred Malenbaum was supervisor during the closing phase of the dissertation work; his contribution to it was especially valuable in clarifying the exposition.

I am glad to have the opportunity to acknowledge also my debt to others in the Economics Department at Pennsylvania. From Dr. Sidney Weintraub I gained an attachment to economic theory and greater interest in its applications to the present problem. Dr. Irving Kravis served as my advisor and helped in the formative stage of the thesis. Dr. Rhoads Murphey, now of the Geography Department, University of Michigan, provided a receptive and helpfully critical ear at a time when I was working out the broadening of the present study as compared with the earlier work. Dr. Donald S. Murray resolved certain of my problems when I was trying to work out a system for correlating yield per acre with other variables. The late Professor Lester E. Klimm developed my appreciation for the usefulness of regional analysis and provided provocative stimulation for these parts of the study.

I am also grateful to many others for their aid. The late Dr. Harold H. Mann, formerly Director of Agriculture for Bombay Province, and a contributor to Indian economic research since before the turn of the century, gave both advice and encouragment. Professor John Brush of the Geography Department, Rutgers, the State University, read the chapters on productivity and tendered criticisms which sharpened this section of the work. Dr. Kshiti Mukerji of the Gokhale Institute of Economics and Politics, Poona, India, has been particularly helpful on questions concerning work on long-term trends in Indian national income. Villanova University lightened the burden of computational work and provided the services of capable research assistants, Charles Santangelo and J. Harry Klemm. The Research Council of Rutgers, the State University, shouldered the burden of professional artwork on charts and maps. Several libraries have been particularly helpful, especially the South Asia Section, Library of Congress, Walter H. Maurer, Librarian, also the Philadelphia Commercial Museum Library, Carolyn Milheim, Librarian, and the Joint Bank-Fund Library, Martin Loftus, Librarian.

The present work is changed in several respects from its version as a dissertation. Part A remains the same in form and substance though it was rewritten. Part B is a considerable rearrangement of the substantive portion of the work. The regional analysis has been integrated into the whole of Part B rather than being confined to mainly one chapter. Likewise the separate discussion of half-century trends and first-last period trends has been eliminated so that a given trend is discussed in its regional and historical aspects at each point. The analysis of changes in productivity has been broadened by the separate chapter on acreage, and deepened in the chapters on yield per acre. Statistical series for crops and the main findings on trends remain the same as in the dissertation, but the modified series for Greater Bengal and British India discussed in the concluding chapter are slightly changed.

George Blyn

Contents

List of Tables

List of Charts and Maps

I

Views on Crop Production Trends in India

1. Significance of crop production trends : consumption, production. 2. Past views on crop trends in India : popular views in the period before independence, research studies on crop trends. 3. Plan view of crop trends.

1. Significance of Crop Production Trends

THE TRENDS IN production of crops in India and Pakistan are representative of change in agriculture as a whole, and agriculture remains the largest single sector of the economy. About eighty-five percent of agricultural output in India, in a recent period, consisted of crops;[1] in Pakistan, however, animal products would presumably have had somewhat greater relative importance. Total agricultural output accounted for about fifty percent of national income[2] and provided employment for about seventy percent of the work force in this same period.[3] The relative importance of agriculture was probably even greater in the period of about a half century ago.[4]

[1] India, Ministry of Finance, Department of Economic Affairs, *Final Report of the National Income Committee February, 1954,* pp. 45, 51, giving net output data for 1948/49–50/51.

[2] *Ibid.,* p. 106; national income as net output at factor cost.

[3] Daniel and Alice Thorner, *The Working Force in India, 1881–1951* (Bombay : Indian Statistical Institute, 1960), Part Two, Table 3.

[4] Difficulties in statistical comparison of recent and earlier census data on the work force are discussed by Thorner, *loc. cit.* Inadequacies in earlier measurements of national income are taken up by Thorner in "Long-term trends in output in India," *Economic Growth: Brazil, India, Japan,* ed. S. Kuznets *et al* (Duke University, 1955).

19

Important changes occurred in the economy of India in the half century preceding independence. Commercialization, which had been promoted by trading elements and encouraged by greater need for cash payment of land revenue, was given further impetus by the spread of the railroad network.[5] Industrialization grew appreciably in the recent decades though it did not reach major proportions.[6] Population expansion, slow up to the first world war period, tripled in percentage rate of growth, up to about one percent per year.

India's lands, however, had been settled since ancient times and farming practice became dominated by custom during that period. How then was agriculture to respond to the marked changes occurring in the economy? The crop trends reveal the nature of change in production and provide the main basis for estimating changes in consumption.

Availability of crops for consumption depended largely on output but also on foreign trade and several other possible influences. The effect of trade on domestic availability of crops can be estimated; it is conceivable, however, that even if domestic availablity was reduced by trade, the economy might have nonetheless benefitted from the imports of non—crop commodities. Change in the proportion of gross output wasted, or used for seed or fodder, could also have influenced availability for consumption, but it is doubtful that such changes were appreciable. It is also unlikely that change in age or occupational structure of population had sufficient bearing to affect the significance of output for consumption.

[5] Rail freight increased from about 20 million tons to 120 million from 1890 to 1930. Daniel H. Buchanan, *The Development of Capitalistic Enterprise in India* (New York: The Macmillan Company, 1934), p. 196.

[6] "Average number of persons employed under the factory act" increased from about 0.3 million to 1.3 million from 1895 to 1930; *ibid.*, p. 297. Output of factory establishments, excluding "small enterprises," was about six percent of national income according to the *Final Report*, *op. cit.*, p. 106.

With knowledge of the crop trends certain aspects of the trend in national income can be explored. For instance, if the magnitude of agricultural output relative to total output can be approximated, it is then possible to determine the growth rate which would have occurred in the nonagricultural sector, if, as one possibility, per capita income had remained constant. Whether per capita income was constant, rising, or falling, thus depends on whether this suggested growth rate for the nonagricultural sector is viewed as likely, low, or high.[7]

Production could have increased only through expansion of acreage or raising the acre productivity. It would seem that there was little opportunity for the former inasmuch as India's population was already over two hundred million a half century before independence. If land were available for expansion the expectation would be that it was submarginal, low in productivity. The potential for increasing yield per acre was great (considering its initial low levels), but there would appear to have been a lack of the material requirements for doing so. Change in both acreage and yield per acre are examined in the later portions of this study.

Yield per acre, under the conditions of the law of diminishing returns, which seems within the realm of applicability for the India of this period, would be expected to increase, but

[7] Using data from my 1951 study, discussed later in this chapter, Surendra J. Patel, "Long-term changes in output and income in India: 1896–1960," *Indian Economic Journal*, V, 3 (January 1958), built up a series of national income estimates with crop output as the base and percentage additions to it to represent "other agriculture," and "small enterprises." To these were added known data on output of mines and factories. "Commerce, transport, etc." was projected as a percentage addition to the total output of agriculture, mines, and factories.

H. C. Arora and K. R. R. Iyengar, "Long term growth of national income in India, 1901–1956," *Papers on National Income and Allied Topics*. Indian Conference on Research in National Income (Bombay: Asia Publishing House, 1960), p. 210, used the index of agricultural output from the 1951 study in conjunction with indexes of business activity of other sectors to estimate national income.

the rate of increase would be diminishing,[8] resulting in lower average output per agricultural worker. Diminishing returns assumes that the proportion of agricultural labor to land increases, that technology and capital per worker remains relatively unchanged, that additional land brought under cultivation is not generally more fertile than previously cultivated land, all conditions which appear as though they might have been satisfied; but whether additional labor had positive marginal productivity or was merely redundant, is a question which cannot in general easily be answered. If yield per acre is aggregated for all crops, however, and if the rate of increase in yield per acre is found to have been decreasing, then, although it cannot be proven that diminishing returns was in effect for the reasons postulated in the law, it would suggest the possibility that these conditions might have held. With available data, it is at least possible to explore whether the conditions required by the law of diminishing returns were in force, and, if so, whether yield per acre was increasing in the manner which the law leads us to expect.

2. Past Views on Crop Production Trends in India

2.1 Popular views in the period before independence. There was relatively little concern up to the 1930's over the trend in crop output. Political and academic leaders at that time believed that total crop output was growing faster than population, and that food crop output was keeping pace with population growth.[9] Poverty was attributed by many leaders

[8] It is conceivable that the rate of increase in total yield or output could be rising if acreage expansion were large, even though the ratio of labor to land was increasing and there was diminishing returns in yield per acre.

[9] Vera Anstey, prominent economic historian, claimed that, though agricultural output was inadequate, it was rising faster than population.

to inequitable distribution rather than to inadequate production.

R. Palme Dutt, the influential communist leader, asserted that growth of production outstripped that of population.[10] Between 1891 and 1921, he claimed, population (for all India) increased 9.3% and foodgrain acreage (for British India) rose 19%. The latter figure was based on the government's *Agricultural Statistics of India* series. In 1891, however, 12% of the area reported by the later date (mostly in Madras Zamindari areas and Assam) was not yet included in the crop statistics; a large part of the increased foodgrain acreage apparently resulted from expanded coverage of the crop statistics. The favorable growth of production compared with population continued into 1921–31, Dutt further claimed, citing Professor P. J. Thomas, according to whom population increased 10.4% and agricultural output by 16%[11]

Dutt also cited Professor Radhakamal Mukerjee's *Food Planning for Four Hundred Millions,* according to which the increase between 1910/11 and 1932/33 was 17% for population and 34% for crop output.[12] Had the change been measured between 1920/21 and 1932/33, however, then, according to Mukerjee's data, population would still have shown a 17% increase, but food production would have shown a 3%

"Economic Development," *Modern India and Pakistan,* ed. L. L. O'Malley (London: Oxford University Press, 1941), pp. 291–292, 297. Her view was based on the D. B. Meek index which is discussed below.

[10] R. Palme Dutt, *India Today* (2nd rev. ed.; Bombay: People's Publishing House, 1949), pp. 51–52. The first edition, published in England in 1940, was banned in India, though it did circulate there illegally.

[11] *Indian Journal of Economics,* April 1935. Dr. Thomas was Professor of Economics at the University of Madras; his 1935 study covered only those British India provinces for which data had been available for the earlier decades.

[12] London: Macmillan, 1938. Dr. Mukerjee was head of the department of economics and sociology at Lucknow University and a prolific author.

decrease. Comparison of isolated years may give misleading results. For other reasons also, indicated below, Mukerjee's study probably overestimated growth of output.

In the Nationalist movement through most of the 1930's, poverty was ascribed to British rule and the inequitable distribution of income with which it was allegedly associated. Ghandi wrote in 1930 that divine law gives man his daily bread and that, if distribution was equitable there would be no poverty[13] The 1931 Congress Meeting (Sardar Patel, president) adopted a Fundamental Rights Resolution which vigorously held that political freedom must include real economic freedom, but its twenty-point economic program made no explicit reference to the need for increasing output.[14] Nehru's presidential addresses to the 1936 Congress Meeting emphasized the need for reducing inequality and spurring industrialization, but the Agrarian Program adopted that year had no specific suggestions for increasing output.[15] Subhas Chandra Bose showed greater awareness of the economic problem; his presidential address to the 1938 Congress called for greater use of science and agricultural capital in order to increase output. He also raised the question of need for birth control.[16]

With the entrance of Congress into provincial government offices between 1937 and 1939, the need for increasing agricultural output was widely recognized. In some provinces, especially United Provinces, Congress tried various direct aids

[13] Mohandas K. Ghandi, *The India of My Dreams,* ed. R. K. Prabhu (Bombay : Hind Kitabs, 1947), pp. 22–23. His 1946 viewpoint, in *Food Shortage and Agriculture,* ed. B. Kumarappa (Ahmedabad : Navijivan Publishing House, 1949), continued this theme but recognized the need and difficulty of expanding crop output.

[14] *The Indian Annual Register,* ed. N. N. Mitra, 1931, I, 278. Patel was party chief and Home Minister for India after independence.

[15] *Ibid.,* 1936, II, 189, 206, 230, 250.

[16] *Ibid.,* 1938, I, 341. Bose headed the Indian National Army of Liberation sponsored by Japan during the war. He was reported lost in a plane crash.

to production.[17] The National Planning Committee meetings of 1939/40, though originally concerned with industry, broadened their scope, under Nehru's influence, to plan for better distribution and increase of agricultural output.[18]

The Central Government's interest in crop output became more prominent after Japan's occupation of Burma.[19] A Grow More Food Campaign, with specific plans for increasing output, was started in 1942.[20] The Bengal famine of 1943 spread awareness of the "terrible urgency of the production problem as well as that of distribution."[21] Virtually all groups acknowledged the problem by this time and the various early plans for economic development all gave agriculture an important place.[22]

2.2 Research studies on crop trends. Studies of India's crop trends are discussed below, grouped according to their treatment of the government source data.

2.21 Virtually complete revision of government data. There appears to be only one such study, K. L. Datta's *Report on the Enquiry into the Causes of Rise of Prices in India,* covering 1894–1912. Datta revised or replaced published government data with first hand reports obtained under his direction in various parts of British India (excluding Burma). His conclusions were that toward the end of the period foodgrain output

[17] Indian National Congress, Central Elections Board, *27 Months of Service* (Bombay: n.d.).

[18] For the history of the NPC and Nehru's role in it, see K. T. Shah, *National Planning, Principles, and Administration,* 1948.

[19] Congress held no office in the Central Government at that time.

[20] *Report of the Foodgrains Policy Committee, 1943* (Delhi: 1943).

[21] J. Nehru, *Discovery of India* (New York: The John Day Co., 1946), pp. 510, 511, 513.

[22] *A Brief Memoir Outlining a Plan for Economic Development for India* (Bombay: 1944), sponsored by Tata, Birla, and other industrialists; *People's Plan for Economic Development of India,* by M. N. Roy for the Radical Democratic Party (Delhi: 1944); S. N. Agarwal, *The Ghandian Plan* (Bombay: Padma Publications, 1944), endorsed by Ghandi.

was growing slower than population, but that nonetheless, the standard of living was rising.[23]

2.22 *Little or no adjustment of government data.* British India, and especially all-India studies, which did not adjust for expanded crop report coverage, exaggerated output growth. Meek's index of crop output, probably the most widely known, was based on the "readily available" level of data for thirteen crops in all-India (including Burma) during 1909/10–35/36; agricultural output growth was found to be 0.65% per year as compared with 0.60% for population.[24] Radhakamal Mukerjee's study covered almost the same period as Meek, 1910/11–37/38, and reached a similar conclusion— population growth did not outpace food supply, whether the latter was measured at the production or consumption level; he observed a gradual worsening in the closing years. The inferior cereals, Mukerjee also noted, were becoming more important relative to the superior cereals, rice and wheat.[25]

Professor Thomas concluded, in two separate studies, that population was increasing less rapidly than crop production. One of these studies, previously cited, analyzed the change between 1900/01–04/05 and 1925/26–29/30 for the limited part of India in which crop report statistics were geographically uniform; the agricultural output growth was said to be

[23] The above remarks on Datta are based on the very informative work of Kshiti Mohon Mukerji, "Planning and the Public Sector in an Underdeveloped Economy" (Unpublished Ph. D. dissertation, Department of Economics, University of Calcutta, 1958), pp. 46–48. Mukerji discusses several other recent studies of output trends which are not available in the United States.

[24] D. B. Meek, "Some Measures of Economic Activity in India," *Journal of the Royal Statistical Society,* Vol. C—new series (1937), p. 364. Indexes of industrial output and aggregate economic activity are also given.

[25] *Op. cit.,* pp. 20–21. In his later Oxford Pamphlet on Indian Affairs, No. 8, *The Food Supply* (2nd ed.; London: Oxford University Press, 1944), p. 10, the worsening in per capita food ratio is said to have taken place since 1930/31. The change is then said to have brought about a "striking deterioration" of the food supply.

29% while population growth was 13.5%.[26] His study for 1911/12–34/35, during which time the change in geographical coverage of crop reports was considered negligible, included all-India (and Burma), and found that food supply had kept pace with population. If poverty worsened, he held, it was because of poor income distribution.[27]

Two other studies may be included in this group. *Technological Possibilities of Agricultural Development in India*, by William Burns, gave series for 1911/12–43/44 as background for the Grow More Food Campaign. Burns observed that fluctuations in output and acreage of subsistence crops stemmed mainly from seasonal weather fluctuations, whereas the variations for cash crops were largely the result of price changes.[28] Dr. Baljit Singh, using Burns' British India series, found that foodgrain output per capita declined in the two decades of 1921–41. Output fluctuations had become more affected by rainfall variations, Singh claimed, because cultivation had been extended to marginal inadequately irrigated lands. Higher price induced greater output of cash crops, he agreed, but lower price did not reduce normal output because the cultivator required a certain cash income to meet money-payable obligations.[29]

2.23 Revision to correct for lack of comparability in the government data series. In the few such studies K. J. Kham-

---

[26] *Op. cit.*, cited in G. B. Jathar and S. G. Beri, *Indian Economics* (9th ed.; Madras: Oxford University Press, 1949), I, 62.

[27] P. J. Thomas and N. Sundarama Sastry, *Indian Agricultural Statistics* (University of Madras, 1939), pp. 87–98. This volume is an excellent guide to the agricultural data, written to recommend improved methods in the crop report statistics.

[28] Lahore: Superintendent of Government Printing, 1944. I followed Burns' method for separating out the provincial component in the crop series where Indian States were included in the British India Province reports.

[29] *Population and Food Planning in India* (Bombay: Hind Kitabs, 1947), p. 62.

bata was the pioneer. To obtain a measure of income which was comparable over 1900/01–21/22 for all-India (including Burma), each region was accounted for either by government reports or his own estimates where necessary. His method of estimating for unreported regions was the main basis for my own 1951 crop study, discussed below. The difference in trends when the series are used in their "readily available" state and when they are refined in this manner may be appreciated by comparing rice output trends obtained from the Meek and Khambata data for 1909/10–21/22, 0.85% per year increase contrasted with 0.96% per year decrease.[30]

R. C. Desai's thorough study, "Consumer Expenditure in India, 1931/32 to 1940/41" is better constructed than any of the previous studies, but unfortunately, it is only one decade in length. Total food consumption was found unchanged despite the population growth. There was a decline in food consumption per capita and in per capita expenditure on all goods and services.[31]

K. M. Mukerji's recent work explores the relationship between certain economic variables and the net income generating activity of government. To obtain an overall index of economic activity he developed crop output series extending from 1900/01 to 1944/45 for all-India (excluding Burma) and to 1952/53 for the Indian Union. Mukerji used the same methods as in my 1951 study, except for one improvement, discussed below; his series differed little from my own despite the improvement in method.[32]

[30] K. T. Shah and K. J. Khambata, *Wealth and Taxable Capacity of India* (Bombay: D. B. Taraporevala Sons & Co., 1924).

[31] *Journal of the Royal Statistical Society*, CXI, Part IV (1948), pp. 261–307. The full study was later published as *Standard of Living in India and Pakistan* (Bombay: Popular Book Depot, 1953). His evaluation of source materials is very useful.

[32] K. M. Mukerji, "Planning and the Public Sector in an Underdeveloped Economy" (Unpublished Doctoral Dissertation, Department of Economics, University of Calcutta, 1958).

My own 1951 work, "The Agricultural Crops of India, 1893–1946 : a Statistical Study of Output and Trends," was the most comprehensive research in geographical coverage and length of time series. Virtually all of British India was included as well as the Indian States for which data was at least available by the end of the period. The main findings are summarized in the following tables.

Table 1.1

ALL-INDIA ESTIMATES OF FOOD CROP, COMMERCIAL CROP, AND TOTAL CROP PRODUCTION, 1893/94 TO 1945/46, ACCORDING TO BLYN'S 1951 STUDY

	Index of Average Annual Crop Output			Non-food to Food Crop Output Ratio
	Food	Commercial	Total	
1893/94 to 1895/96	100	100	100	0.22
1896/97 to 1905/06	96	105	98	0.24
1906/07 to 1915/16	99	126	104	0.28
1916/17 to 1925/26	98	142	106	0.32
1926/27 to 1935/36	94	171	108	0.41
1936/37 to 1945/46	93	185	110	0.44

Source : Thorner, "Long-term Trends", *op. cit.*, p. 122.

Table 1.2

ALL-INDIA ESTIMATES OF THE AVERAGE ANNUAL PER CAPITA FOOD OUTPUT AND ALL-CROP OUTPUT, 1893/94 TO 1945/46, ACCORDING TO BLYN'S 1951 STUDY

	Output in Index Units Per Capita	
	Food Crops	All-Crops
1893/94 to 1895/96	100	100
1896/97 to 1905/06	95	97
1906/07 to 1915/16	91	97
1916/17 to 1925/26	90	98
1926/27 to 1935/36	78	90
1936/37 to 1945/46	68	80

Source : Thorner, "Long-term Trends," *op. cit.*, p. 123.

Annual indexes of all-crop and foodgrain crop output according to the 1951 study are given in Appendix Table 1A.

Aggregate crop output is seen to have gradually increased over the period, but the pace was slower than population growth, especially after 1921. Food-grain output declined so that per capita output fell markedly. Commercial crop output increased rapidly, nearly doubling over the period.

Several shortcomings of the 1951 work are relevant to an understanding of methodology of the present study and to the qualifications in the above conclusions. Emphasis in the earlier study was on describing the trends and explaining the methodology; causes of the trends—acreage and yield per acre changes—and their regional differences were not analyzed. The trends were not summarized statistically except by index numbers. Although the data were adjusted to be geographically uniform, no adjustments were made to overcome deficiencies in certain of the yield per acre series.

Certain biases were injected into that study because of methods used to adjust the data for geographical uniformity. One occurred where and when crop acreage was available, but not yield per acre (or output); yield per acre was then estimated for each year as the average for all reported yields per acre for that crop. Earlier reports tended to come from more important, more productive, regions; later reports included less productive regions. Trend in average reported yield per acre was biassed downward and consequently so also were the yields per acre for the aggregate of unreported regions. Since output was a function of yield per acre, as well as acreage, its growth was made to appear smaller.[33] For

[33] This is discussed in the 1951 study, Blyn, *op. cit.,* pp. 40, 45, 50. The criticism is repeated by A. K. Biswas, "A Note on the Trend of Agricultural Production in India, 1893–1946," Memorandum of the Center for International Studies (Massachusetts Institute of Technology, 1953), pp. 5–6.

example, combined rice yield per acre for early-reporting Bengal and Madras was about 40% and 70% higher than later-reporting United Provinces and Central Provinces, respectively; later-reporting Bombay, however, had a slightly higher yield per acre than Bengal-Madras.[34]

A second bias resulted where and when crop acreage was not available and estimated area was taken as average crop acreage for the first ten years reported for the given region. This device was principally used for the Indian States since crop acreage was reported in most of the British Provinces. Inasmuch as overall crop acreage did increase, though not rapidly, this method exaggerated output in the earlier unreported years, and hence understates growth. This is discussed in my 1951 work and the view is expressed that this bias is likely to be small.[35]

Mukerji's improved method aimed at avoiding this bias. Acreage of the non-reporting state is taken as a fixed proportion of acreage for each year in a similar nearby reporting region. The proportion is from the average relationship of the first ten years in which both state and other region were reported. The results of his work, however, were substantially the same as mine, as he points out, so the bias was evidently not large.[36]

A third aspect of method in the earlier study may not involve bias, and if it does, its direction is not easily apparent. When there were no yield per acre (or output) reports available for a given crop from any part of India, the yield per acre used was the average of the first ten years of the combined reporting regions. If there actually had been an upward

---

[34] Percentages based on difference in average yield per acre during first ten years of reported data, starting with 1911/12 for U.P., 1912/13 for Bombay, and 1913/14 for C. P.; 1951 study data were used.

[35] Blyn, *op. cit.*, pp. 39, 43.

[36] Mukerji, *op. cit.*, pp. 67, 69, 76.

or downward trend in yield per acre during the unreported years, then the view of growth would have been either inhibited or exaggerated. This bias, if present, is likely to be small.[37]

3. Plan View of Crop Trends

The present study is a descriptive analysis of the trends by crops and groups of crops, by regions as well as for British India, and by decade-length periods in addition to longer periods. Output, at the gross level, and its determinants, acreage and yield per acre, are analyzed in the same time-regional framework. Population trends are analyzed similarly, both to indicate change in consumption and to serve as a measure of change in farm labor.[38] At the regional level the analysis is generally by groups of crops rather than individual crops. Several influences on yield per acre are also analyzed but this is in a simple twofold division of the whole period.

All trends are measured in annual percentage rates of change so as to facilitate comparisons and bring out relationships. The method of trend measurement, described in chapter four, in general follows that of Professor Arthur F. Burns in *Production Trends in the United States Since 1870.*[39]

Time coverage of the study, in crop years,[40] extends from 1891/92 to 1946/47, fifty-six years. The beginning year is the first for which crop output was reported in the main government series, and the closing year takes the study up to formation of the independent governments of India and Pakistan.

[37] Blyn, *op. cit.*, pp. 34, 53. Another bias is described in the last footnote to this chapter.

[38] Agricultural labor data in the six or seven censuses over the period are not sufficiently comparable to be used for this purpose.

[39] New York: National Bureau for Economic Research, 1934.

[40] The crop year ends on June 30th for most crops.

There is virtually no possibility of extending coverage into earlier years. Starting with 1947 the changes in reporting were so great that it would not be feasible in this study to push coverage beyond that year.

The time span has been divided into ten equally spaced overlapping "reference decades." Five of the reference decades span the census years, i.e. 1891–1901, and the other five are centered on the census years, i.e. 1896–1906. Reference decades are grouped into historical periods in part B.

Geographical coverage includes almost all the British India Provinces, but excludes the former Indian States, which were administered by their traditional rulers. Burma Province became a separate colony in 1937 and has been excluded throughout this study. Desolate British Baluchistan, for which almost no crop data were available, is the only province not included. British India, excluding Baluchistan, contained 76% of the population and 51% of total area of all India in 1941. Figure 1.1 shows the British India Provinces and Indian States as they were constituted at the close of the period.[41]

Incompleteness of data for Indian States discouraged their inclusion in this study, although methods were devised to include them in the 1951 study. Complexity of research is considerably increased and firmness of findings reduced by their inclusion. One of the larger Indian States, Mysore, could have been included since its agricultural statistics were comparable to those of the provinces; Mysore comprised about 4% of Indian States area and 8% of their population. The main shortcomings in the Indian States data are the multiplicity of reporting units, fragmentary output reports, and general paucity of acreage data for years when output reports were not given.

[41] Orissa, formed in 1935, included parts of Madras and Central Provinces; these parts were added back into those provinces in this study.

Figure 1.1
Regions of This Study, Provinces of British India,
and Major Indian States

Numbered Areas:

1. Baluchistan
2. Kashmir and Jammu
3. Rajputana
4. Ajmer-Merwara
5. Goa
6. Hyderabad
7. Mysore
8. Coorg
9. Central India
10. Assam

Scale: 1" = 420 miles

Broken lines within Provinces
enclose Indian States, not part
of British India.

Boundaries as of 1931

The regional plan makes it possible to test the meaningfulness of average findings for British India as a whole, and is helpful in suggesting reasons for differences in trends. Regionalization adopted for this study follows the boundaries of large provinces as they existed earlier in the period, prior to division into smaller provinces. In this way the problem of disentangling earlier-reported data for sections of large provinces is avoided.[42] United Provinces, Central Provinces, and Madras are retained as separate regions. Bengal, Bihar, and Orissa are combined as Greater Bengal. Punjab, North West Frontier, and Delhi are combined in Greater Punjab. Bombay and Sind, because of their extreme differences in rainfall (see figure 6.2), make the least suitable combination of provinces. Assam and Ajmer-Merwara are included in the British India aggregates but not in the regional plan. (Area of the regions is given in Appendix, Table 1 B; regional populations are given in Appendix, Table 4 C. The plan of regionalization is also discussed in Chapter IV, 2.)

Eighteen crops, all the major crops, are included in this study—rice, wheat, jowar, bajra, ragi, maize, barley, gram, sugarcane, sesamum, rape and mustard, linseed, groundnut, cotton, jute, indigo, tobacco, and tea—all the crops for which there were sufficient primary data to obtain continuous series over the whole period. These crops occupied 82% of total cultivated area in British India in 1940/41. Over half the remaining area was under "other foodgrains"; fodder constituted most of the remainder, followed by fruits and vegetables, other oilseeds, and spices.[43] Output data were not available for

---

[42] District level data required for doing this are generally not available in this country.

[43] In my 1951 study "other foodgrains" were included and also castor (oilseed) and coffee. Foodgrains were thus given greater representation in total output than was justified by their importance. Since foodgrain output growth was slow, this contributed an additional downward bias in the aggregate output series.

all years in all regions for the crops included, as shown in Chapter II, but adjustments were devised, as explained in Chapter III, to fill in these gaps in the data.

The following chapters are divided into two parts. Part A is methodological and deals with the nature of the primary data, methods used for adjusting them, and measurement of crop trends. Part B describes and analyzes the British India and regional crop trends derived from the data developed in Part A.

PART A

*Methodology of Treating Data
and Measuring Trends*

II

Nature of Crop Data

1. Main sources of crop data. 2. Comparability of coverage in the *Estimates* series. 3. The government estimating method and its scope for error and bias : estimating formula and estimators, crop acreage, standard yield per acre and seasonal condition. 4. Tests of *Estimates* reliability : rationality and internal consistency of primary data, comparison with independent data. 5. Conclusion.

1. Main Sources of Crop Data

STATISTICS OF INDIAN AGRICULTURE have been collected for centuries because most rulers assessed taxes against either the land or its product.[1] The kind of data varied regionally depending on the form of land revenue assessment. Toward the close of the nineteenth century, government interest in famine control and commercial needs for information led to central publication of coordinated agricultural series for British India and provinces.[2]

Agricultural Statistics of India was the first of these publications;[3] it gives details of land use in terms of area. Annual data are provided for districts, provinces, British India, and certain of the Indian States. By the middle of the period under

[1] For an interesting general and historical account of Indian statistics, see Lord Meston, "Statistics in India," *Journal of the Royal Statistical Society*, XCVI (1933), 1–20.

[2] Hereafter referred to as *Agricultural Statistics*. Issued by the Department of Commercial Intelligence and Statistics.

[3] District totals were not published for the years 1920/21–29/30.

39

study, twenty-five crops and ten categories of "other crops" were covered, in addition to other aspects of land utilization. The series started with the crop year 1884/85, and by 1891/92, all provinces, except sparsely settled Baluchistan, were reported. Returns for Bengal were not complete until 1893/94.

Virtually the entire series of *Agricultural Statistics* is available in the United States, but there are some gaps in the data for 1939/40–45/46. For some of these years the data for areas which became part of independent India was cast in a different regional mold than the system of British Provinces, and regional data for areas which became part of Pakistan were not available.

Estimates of Area and Yield of the Principal Crops in India,[4] issued annually from 1891/92, contains most of the data used in this study. *Estimates* gives output as well as acreage data for the reporting provinces and states, British India and all-India; states and provinces were not always separated, however, until 1921/22. District level reports were given in *Season and Crop Reports* issued by provinces.

Output and acreage data are estimates of the standing crop at harvest time, the final forecast in the succession of several forecasts issued during the growing season and published either in the weekly *Indian Trade Journal* or separately. Final forecasts were sometimes revised, however, when more complete data was available. This was partly occasioned by later release of the *Agricultural Statistics* acreage, which was considered more reliable.

The whole *Estimates* series is found in the United States, but only fragments of the provincial *Season and Crop Reports*

[4] Hereafter called *Estimates*. Issued by Department of Commercial Intelligence and Statistics. Annual average yield per acre series were given starting with 1912/13.

are available here. It may be, however, that the latter were not published for all regions during the entire period. Absence of this data was a handicap in securing uniform coverage of the regions in this study.

2. Comparability of Coverage in the Estimates Series

Coverage in the *Estimates* series broadened over time, both in number of crops and reporting regions. Reports for earlier years tended to cover commercially important crops and the regions producing most of their supply.[5]

The broadening of crop coverage is shown in Table 2.1.

TABLE 2.1

FIRST REPORTING YEAR FOR CROPS IN ESTIMATES

1891/92 Rice, Wheat, Cotton, Jute, Tea, Indigo; Linseed, Rape and Mustard, Sesamum (oilseeds)
1897/98 Groundnut (peanut)
1898/99 Sugarcane
1911/12 Barley, Maize; Jowar, Bajra (millet grains); Gram (bean)
1917/18 Castor (oilseed)
1919/20 Coffee, Rubber, Tobacco
1936/37 Ragi (millet grain)
Source : *Estimates*.

Nine crops were reported in the first issue, and two more crops followed shortly. Five minor cereals were added to the reports twenty years after the first issue; these crops were of much less commercial importance than rice or wheat, but their output was almost half of rice and wheat combined. The last five

[5] Earlier *Estimates* covered ". . . those tracts where the respective crops were grown on an extensive or commercial scale. Tracts of minor importance have been added gradually." *Estimates*, 1940/41, p. 1.

crops brought into the *Estimates* occupied much less acreage than the ones reported earlier.

The broadening of *Estimates* reports in terms of regions is seen in Table *2.2* to be more gradual than the change in crop

TABLE 2.2

PROVINCE'S FIRST YEAR OF REPORTING IN ESTIMATES CROP SERIES

	Aj	As	Be	Bi	Bo	Cp	Co	De	Ma	Nw	Or	Pu	Si	Up
Barley	15		15	11	11	19		12		12	x	11	11	13
Bajra	15		15	15	11	19		12	12	12	x	11	11	11
Cotton	03	03	92	x	91	91		x	91	x	x	91	91	91
Gram	15		12	11	11	11	20	12	12	12	x	11	11	11
Groundnut					97	31		04			38	42		40
Indigo			92	x	12			91				91		91
Jowar	15		15	15	11	11		12	12	12	x	11	11	11
Jute		95	91	x							x			
Linseed			92	x	91	91					x	13		91
Maize	15		12	11	11	19		12	17	11	x	11	11	11
Ragi				36	36				36		36			
Rape-Mustard		91	92	x	91	31				x	x	91	91	91
Rice		05	91	x	12	13	08	91			x	39	12	11
Sesamum	13		94	x	91	91		91			x	91	91	91
Sugarcane		05	98	x	07	13		21	01	x	x	99	33	98
Tea		91	91	x			25	91				91		91
Tobacco		27	25	19	27	27		27	19	36	x	26	30	26
Wheat	13		91	x	91	91	x			x	x	91	91	91

NOTES

Years are crop years, *i.e.,* 91 stands for 1891/92. Provinces abbreviated above for Ajmer-Merwara, Assam, Bengal, Bihar, Bombay, Central Provinces, Coorg, Delhi, Madras, North West Frontier Province, Orissa, Punjab, Sind, and United Provinces. "x" indicates reports for province started with original province : Nw was formed 01 and De 11 out of Pu; Si reported with Bo 21–32; Bi and Or reported with Be til 11; Or reported with Bi til about 35; As reported with Be 05–11.

Source : *Estimates* series.

coverage. For example, the initial year reports of the rice series covered Bengal and Madras, about two-thirds of average output, but the coverage expanded in 1905, 1908, 1911, 1912, 1913, and 1939. The last province added, Punjab, was of small importance in total rice output, but the value of the crop there exceeded the value of linseed output from the whole of British India. A summary view of the enlargement of *Estimates* coverage is seen in the changing proportion of acreage reported by *Estimates* to that reported by *Agricultural Statistics.* From 1891/92 to 1904/05 the proportion is about 42%, from 1905/06 to 1910/11, about 44%, in 1911/12 up to 67%, in 1912/13 up to 73%, and from 1916/17 on, it is about 77% and increasing slightly. In Chapter III, crop estimating procedures are established for provinces unreported in early years.

Parts of certain provinces were not included when the province was first reported in *Estimates.* "Minor" producing districts, where output was relatively small, were not included in certain provincial reports until about 1912/13. Zamindari areas of two provinces, where revenue assessment was fixed permanently or for long periods of time, were another type of omission, involving Central Provinces up to 1897/98 and a large part of Madras up to about 1906/07. Adjustments for these omissions are discussed in chapter three.

It may be noted that there are many blanks in Table *2.2,* indicating no *Estimates* reports for crops in certain provinces. Output was usually nil or negligible in these cases because of unsuitable physical conditions for the particular crops. The blanks in the larger provinces for groundnut, jute, and tea are examples of this. Omissions for Ajmer-Merwara, Coorg, and Delhi are of little significance since these provinces were very small. Wherever there was unreported output, however, it is accounted for in the estimates of Chapter III.

3. The Government Estimating Method and Its Scope for Error and Bias

The reliability of *Estimates* for the crops and regions which were covered in the reports is examined in the following sections. Reliability may partly be gauged by examining the method with which the government reports were formulated, as follows in this section. Tests of reliability of *Estimates* data based on their internal consistency and comparison with independent external data are considered in another section.

3.1 The estimating formula and estimators. The government's[6] estimating formula was: Output = Crop Acreage x Standard Yield per Acre x Seasonal Condition of the Crop. The first and last factors varied annually; the standard yield factor was a constant in each district, at least for five years at a time. Acreage was area sown, regardless of whether the crop came to maturity, unless another crop was planted in its place. The standard yield per acre was not well defined, but was supposed to be the yield on land of average quality in a year of average weather conditions. Seasonal condition was the proportion of current yield to standard yield.

Village officials supplied the reports on acreage. The condition factor was determined on the basis of village reports as well as judgement of the district official. The district standard yield was based on a variety of information, such as settlement reports, crop cuttings, and again the judgement of the district official. Provincial officials could alter or originate the standard yield figure and condition factor.

The accuracy of village reports depended on the position of the village official who supplied the information and the kind of information recorded in the village. Where there were accountants or recorders, often called *patwaris*, the reports were better than where they were supplied by village watch-

---

[6] Estimates of output for plantation crops were obtained from the plantation managers. Methods used by the latter for crop estimating are not given in the sources used for this study. Tea and indigo are plantation crops included in this study; rubber and coffee are other plantation crops reported in *Estimates*. Coffee estimates were discontinued in 1909 because they were judged unreliable; in 1919 they were re-established, apparently on better basis.

men, sometimes called *chaukidars*. The kind of crop statistics kept in the village largely reflected the nature of the land revenue assessment system. Where the assessment was fixed permanently, there was less need for agricultural records, or recorders, and the information generally came from the *chaukidar*. In other places where assessments were revised periodically records were better. The fixed form of revenue assessment was prevalent mainly in Greater Bengal. Rao has pointed out, however, that some permanently assessed lands had *patwaris,* and in some of the other lands reports were provided by *chaukidars,* so that the line dividing qualities of *Estimates* reports does not conform completely to the line separating types of land revenue assessment systems.[7]

3.2 Crop acreage. The crop area data are generally considered quite reliable. In most parts of British India the data were obtained by field-to-field enumeration of the village official, whose work was supervised by the district officials. Most of the land had been professionally surveyed so that an accurate outline of boundaries and dimensions existed.[8]

Some of the *patwari* reports are said to have ". . . become conventional in the sense that year to year fluctuations are not always recorded and the estimates of area under any crop, therefore, tend to become serially correlated to a large extent."[9] This would not seriously affect measurement of secular trend, provided that longer period changes were reflected in the reports.

A portion of the Punjab crop area reports is affected by a similar qualification. Starting with 1913/14 the *Estimates* crop area reported for less important producing districts was the average acreage in the previous five years. In *Agricultural*

[7] *Op. cit.,* p. 4.
[8] Of British India's 512 million acres, 97 million were unsurveyed, but crops were reported from these lands.
[9] *Final Report of the National Income Committee,* 1954, *op. cit.,* p. 25.

Statistics, on the other hand, crop acreage reported prior to 1906/07 was not actual area shown but a greater or lesser amount depending on how the seasonal condition compared with normal. Trend measurements are not likely to have been much affected by these circumstances. In the North West Frontier Province reported acreage was similarly qualified.[10]

3.2 Standard yield per acre and seasonal condition factor. There was no uniform wholly objective system for setting the standard yield per acre and the concept did not lend itself to easy or accurate measurement.[11] In a typical district of two million acres, average soil, average weather and water supply would be difficult to ascertain. Accumulated past records of stratified samplings based on detailed district soil and water maps would have been required. Crop cuttings from plots selected as typical became increasingly important in setting

[10] *Estimates,* 16th issue, 1915, Appendix II; *Agricultural Statistics,* 28th issue, for 1908/09, p. 115. Areas from the latter were used to estimate output of crops not reported in *Estimates* for Greater Punjab regions.

[11] The full definition of the standard was "That crop which past experience has shown to be the most generally recurring crop in a series of years; the typical crop of the local area; the crop which the cultivator has a right (as it were) to expect, and with which he is (or should be) content, while if he gets more he has reason to rejoice, and if less he has reason to complain; or in other words, it is the 'figure which in existing circumstances might be expected to be attained in the year if the rainfall and season were of an ordinary character for the tract under consideration, that is, neither very favorable nor the reverse.' Briefly, it is stated to be 'the average yield on average soil in a year of average character.' This normal or average yield will not necessarily correspond with the average of a series of years' figures, which is an arithmetical average." *Estimates,* 1940/41, p. 46. The average envisioned is apparently the mode, not the mean.

Of this definition it was said, "I need not repeat the same soul-stirring and mouth-filling formula which has hitherto done duty as a definition of the term 'normal,' as it is well known to all who have anything to do with forecasts. I can imagine that the official who evolved it had the satisfaction of feeling that he had done a good day's work, but one thing is certain and that is that a normal crop is the one which is least often reported." Board member G. A. D. Stuart, *Proceedings of the Board of Agriculture,* 1919, p. 24.

the standard. In some districts the standards were reset every five years from the average of crop cuttings regardless of seasonal character in those years.

The standards were in general set higher than the average of reported yields per acre.[12] For two similar reasons this did not necessarily engender erroneous yield per acre estimates. First, this relatively high standard conformed better to the village official's concept of the standard or normal upon which he based his estimate of the seasonal factor.[13] Second, both standard and seasonal condition factor were ultimately set by the same district or provincial officers. It would seem likely that exaggerated standards would be offset by lower condition estimates in that circumstance.

The seasonal condition estimate was based completely on judgement. It was therefore more susceptible to bias than the other two factors. The Royal Commission on Agriculture observed, however, ". . . that it is easy to take an exaggerated view of the consequent inaccuracy."[14]

Condition estimates were expressed in annas of the rupee, sometimes called *annawari* estimates. The crop would be estimated, for instance, as 8 annas (out of 16 in the rupee) if it were 50% of a normal crop; a 20 anna crop would be 125% of normal. The normal crop was not always equated to 16 annas; in most of British India it was less than 16. If 12

[12] Indian Council on Agricultural Research, *Sample Surveys for the Estimation of Yield of Food Crops, 1944–49,* 1951, p. 5.

[13] "The *patwari* or *chowkidar* being . . . pessimistic by nature . . . his idea of a normal crop is that which he longs to see but rarely sees and the result is that the standard with which he compares a crop is really something above the normal. Consequently, his estimates generally fall below the mark." D. B. Meek, cited in Desai, *Standard of Living, op. cit.,* p. 12, from *Evidence,* Royal Commission on Agriculture, Vol. I, Part II.

[14] Great Britain, *Report of the Royal Commission on Agriculture in India,* 1928, p. 608.

annas were normal then an 8 anna crop would be 67% of normal.[15]

Since the condition could only be expressed to the nearest anna, there is an inherent error in the estimates; human judgement, however, might not be capable of greater accuracy. Estimates to the nearest anna could be as much as a half anna out, which would be 6% of an 8.5 anna crop or 3% of a 16.5 anna crop. Some preference for even numbers was shown, and this could have doubled the error.[16] Since there would be slight variations in actual yields per acre in the district and among the districts of the province, this type of error could be averaged out in either the district or provincial office. An actual 8.1 anna crop, for example, would be underestimated as 8 annas, but a 7.9 anna crop would be overestimated at 8 annas.

Apart from error due to the inaccuracies described above, there were at least two reasons to expect bias. One reason was the association of land revenue assessment with crop condition. That this affected the estimates is clearly seen in the warning of the Board of Agriculture[17]

. . . against the danger of estimates prepared for statistical purposes being coloured by questions of suspension and remission of revenue. We consider that there has too frequently been in the past a tendency on the part of both primary and other reporting agencies to report an incorrect crop, when the crop approaches a point at which questions of suspension and remission appear likely to arise.

Whether the downward-expected bias of the village official

[15] Provincial anna normals were: 12 annas—Madras, Bombay, Bengal, Assam; 16 annas—United Provinces, Punjab, North West Frontier Province; Bihar and Orissa—12 districts at 12 annas, 7 at 13 annas, and 2 at 14 annas.

[16] A. L. Bowley and D. H. Robertson, *A Scheme for an Economic Census* of India (New Delhi: Government of India Press, 1934), p. 37.

[17] *Proceedings of the Board of Agriculture*, 1919, p. 32.

or perhaps an upward-expected bias of the district official dominated, is not apparent. A downward bias could have been offset in the district office by raising the condition factor, or as Desai points out, by setting a lower anna valuation for the standard crop, or by keeping the standard yield per acre high. Desai concluded that ". . . on those grounds alone the direction or the extent of bias could not be determined."[18]

A second reason for expecting bias was that the village officials were "pessimistic by nature." This could, of course, have been offset in the manner described above. A conservative attitude has also been attributed to the village official, leading him to overestimate bad years and underestimate good years.[19] Fluctuations would then have been toned down, but trend would not have been affected.

4. Tests of Estimates Reliability

4.1 Rationality and internal consistency of primary data. One test for reliability of data is its rationality. If behaviour of a given time series is not consistent with knowledge of the change in its underlying determinants, or if it is inconsistent with changes which are known to have occurred in series which depended on the given series, and if the relationships between the series are properly understood, then the given series may be considered unreliable. Unfortunately, this ultimate test for reliability cannot be applied until after the trends of the given series, their causes and consequences, have been studied.

Behavior of a series should also be rational in its relative changes; it should be internally consistent. An element of unre-

[18] *Standard of Living, op. cit.,* pp. 12–13.
[19] *Final Report of the National Income Committee 1954,* p. 27. The same view is held by Dr. V. G. Panse, "Trends in Areas and Yields of Principal Crops in India," *Agricultural Situation in India,* VII, 3 (June 1952), cited in Mukerji, *op. cit.,* p. 64.

liability was observed, in this respect, in a number of yield per acre series which show distinct change in level before and after certain years, as is seen in table 2.3; trend lines through the data before and after the change in level are widely discontinuous. Since there appeared to be no real basis for the radical jump in yield per acre for those years, it was assumed that the changes were due to a difference in the nature of the government's crop estimation starting in those years. Six of the changes were in Madras starting with 1916/17, a seventh in Madras began in 1915/16. All these changes resulted in higher yield per acre levels and suggest that earlier yields per acre were underestimated. Three other changes—in Madras, Unitd Provinces, and Bombay—came at different later years and indicate that earlier yields per acre were overestimated. The adjustment for these series is described in section 3.2 of the next chapter.

TABLE 2.3

CHANGES IN YIELD PER ACRE LEVELS FOR SELECTED CROPS OVER CERTAIN YEARS (PERCENT)

Province	Crop	Year of Change	Change from Previous Year	Difference in First Five Years After Change and Preceding Five Years	Difference in Later and Earlier Trends for Year of Change
Madras	Rice	1916/17	30	17	20
	Jowar	1916/17	30	36	29
	Bajra	1916/17	33	40	35
	Cotton	1916/17	36	50	41
	Sugarcane	1916/17	20	43	35
	Sesamum	1916/17	58	51	42
	Groundnut	1915/16	79	44	25
	Tobacco	1937/38	−19	−28	−17
Bombay	Groundnut	1923/24	−46	−33	−61
United Prov.	Tobacco	1942/43	−23	−57	−57

Source : Calculated from yield per acre data of *Estimates*.

4.2 Comparison with independent data. There are few means of checking the reliability of *Estimates* with sources which were independent of the government's agricultural statistics. Since much of the crop was not marketed,[20] the records for transportation[21] or processing of crops—even if obtainable —would not include all output. Two collections of independent data are available, however; one is for annual totals of exports and estimated domestic use, in factories and elsewhere, of cotton and jute. Another set of data for several of the closing years of the study is provided by the random sample surveys of the Indian Council on Agricultural Research and the Indian Statistical Institute.

Both cotton and jute, according to the exports-domestic use data, were underestimated in the government's output reports. Average output of cotton, 1915/16–39/40, was apparently underreported by 16%. Much of this underestimate appears attributable to non-reporting Indian States among the Deccan States, States of Western India, Central India States, parts of Rajputana State, as well as others. The extent of underestimate, if there was any, for British India Provinces must have been much less than the underestimate for All-India.[22]

Jute output, 1919/20–40/41, was 15% less than exports-domestic use, and little of this appears attributable to non-

[20] Estimates of village retention of crops are given in Chapter IV, Section 2. 2.

Foreign marketing of most crops was relatively small compared to total output. In a group of 10 years or periods of years from 1909/10– 43/44 Jathar and Beri, *op. cit.*, I, 164, found that tea exports were highest relative to output, 96% in the quinquennium preceding World War I, but this fell to 77% by 1936/37. For wheat the proportion exported fell from 14% to 2% in the same periods. Reliability, therefore, cannot be tested by merely comparing exports with reported output.

[21] Some data of this type is given in the government's *Inland Trade by Rail and River of India* series, published up to 1920/21, and again starting with 1933/34.

[22] Home consumption, outside the factories, is estimated at 750,000 bales per year during these years, according to the industry's figures.

reporting States. This apparent underestimation in *Estimates* seems high, however, since total exports of raw jute, and raw jute equivalent of exported jute yarn, cloth, and gunny bags, calculated from the trade series, is nearly equal to the reported output.[23] Underestimation was indicated by another source, however, at least for acreage during several recent years, 1943-46, in Bengal, where random sample surveys of jute acreage reported that total acreage exceeded *Estimates* by 29%, 25%, 25%, and 52% in the respective years.[24]

The I.C.A.R. Sample Surveys,[25] 1944-49, for rice and wheat, found output generally underestimated in the government figures for Indian Union regions, but there was considerable regional variation, including over-estimation. For rice, Uttar Pradesh (United Provinces) showed slight overestimation, Assam estimates were close to the survey, Bombay and Madras slightly underestimated, but in Coorg, Madhya Pradesh (Central Provinces), Orissa, and especially Bihar, there was sizeable underestimation. The underestimates varied annually up to about 20%, except for Bihar where it was about 30%. The error in all states except Bihar and Orissa was due to yield per acre estimation; in the latter states, however, acreage underestimation, revealed by complete enumeration, contributed to the error, and in Bihar this accounted for a majority of the error. In Bengal, 1944/45, complete enumeration showed overestimation of 11% for acreage.[26] Desai combined the various regional errors, weighting them by provincial

[23] Exports obtained from *Annual Statement of the Sea-borne Trade of British India* series. Gunny bags estimated at 1,044 per ton, gunny cloth at 3,671 yards per ton, and waste in processing raw jute into yarn at 10%.
[24] According to Professor Mahalanobis' Area Surveys, cited in Desai, *Standard of Living, op. cit.,* pp. 7–9.
[25] Indian Council of Agricultural Research, *Sample Surveys for the Estimation of Yield of Food Crops, 1944–49,* 1951, pp. 39–42. Some *Estimates* were influenced by the Surveys; the two sources are therefore not completely independent.
[26] Desai, *op. cit.,* pp. 7–9.

output, and came to an overall underestimate of 3.5% for rice in British India.[27]

Output reports for wheat were overestimated in Bombay, ranging from 5% to 40%, for the several years of the sample survey, and in Uttar Pradesh, up to about 15%. No uniform tendency was seen in Madhya Pradesh, but in Bihar and Punjab there was underestimation up to about 20%. The Bihar underestimation resulted from very large underestimation in acreage and somewhat less overestimation of yield per acre.[28] The average error for wheat output reports for British India, according to Desai, was only about 1.1% underestimate.[29]

5. Conclusion

The nature of the crop data indicates two kinds of problems confronting their use for analysis of trends. One involves more or less remedial types of shortcomings which would affect the trend measurements, particularly the broadening of coverage, and also the instances of trend discontinuities in yield per acre. Adjustments to eliminate these shortcomings in the raw data are described in the next chapter. The second problem concerns reliability of the basic core of statistics on which the adjustments and measurements have been built. In general, how reliable are the reported statistics for the crops in regions which they did cover, and how does this affect the significance of the measured trend rates?

The extent of the underestimation was apparently less than 15% for cotton and jute over a long period, and, according to Desai's estimates, very low for rice and wheat in British India in the closing years of the study. It is true, however,

[27] *Ibid.,* pp. 16–17.
[28] I.C.A.R., *op. cit.,* pp. 42–44.
[29] Desai, *op. cit.,* pp. 16–17.

that regional variation in extent of underestimation (or over-estimation) was substantial. Relatively recent national income measurement in India assumed a 20% margin of error in net value of crops and animal products for the former provinces and states combined.[30] The error for crops alone, apart from error in valuation of netness, and for the provinces only, must have been substantially less. For foodgrains, V. K. R. V. Rao, in a government study of food statistics, assumed that the error was not more than 10%.[31] Much of this error, again, may be attributable to Indian States for which approximations were made in that study.

Whatever the error, however, it is possible that the meas-ured trend rates represented the actual change with perfect reliability. Three cases of this are conceivable : the first would be if the percentage of error or underestimation remained constant over the period, as was believed by Professor Thomas.[32] In this case the height of the trend line would be affected, but not the rate of change. The second would be the case where both upward and downward actual fluctuations were moderated[33] to leave trend unaffected by the reported statistics. A third case would be where the percentage error fluctuated over time in a random fashion above and below the trend line, again leaving trend unaffected.

It is also possible, however, that the fluctuation in error was not self-cancelling over time, and in this case the extent of error may have an appreciable effect on the trends. If the range of error was 20%, then an overestimate of 10%, fol-lowed by underestimate of 10% at opposite ends of the period,

[30] Final Report of the National Income Committee, op. cit., p. 146.

[31] India, Department of Food, The Food Statistics of India, 1946, p. 7.

[32] Thomas and Sastry, op. cit., p. 89.   Professor Thomas believed that ". . . the errors were more or less systematic . . . whatever error there is, is common for the whole period."

[33] As believed by Dr. V. G. Panse, cited in Mukerji, op. cit., p. 64.

would give the measured trend a downward bias. Over a half-century period, an error distribution of this type appears quite unlikely. In a given ten year period, this type of bias in trend could be large, but in an average of ten such short periods the effect can be expected to be much reduced.

A realistic variant of the case where errors do not cancel over time is the possibility that over the years there was a gradual reduction in the percentage of error. If over fifty years the aggregate error was reduced from 20% under-estimate to 10%, this would give the measured trend a maximum upward bias of somewhat less than 0.2% per year.[34] It is not likely, however, that if there were a reduction in error, it would be so perfectly gradual. If the theory of declining underestimate percentage is subscribed to, a bias effect of 0.1% per year would seem more realistic.

There appears to be little basis for choosing between these possibilities of how the error might have been distributed over time. Whether the case was one of chronic underestimation or of moderating the extremes, there seems little reason for expecting that either pattern would have changed over the period. The greatest likelihood would seem to be that there was some improvement in the accuracy of the *Estimates*. Some of the bias which would have resulted from this was removed, however, by adjustment of the yield per acre series where changes in the parameters of estimation evidently occurred. It does seem that neither the degree of error, nor the likelihood

[34] Raymond Goldsmith, "The Economic Growth of Tsarist Russia, 1860–1913," *Economic Development and Cultural Change*, IX, 3 (April 1961), p. 447, considered the effect of possible secular change in the degree of understatement of official crop statistics on trends in Russia during that period. The fifty year average rate of growth was estimated at 2% per year, but if, he suggested, underestimation was reduced by half from 20% to 10%, it would raise the growth rate only slightly to less than 2.2%. The average output growth rate for India, however, was much less than 2%, as will be seen in chapter five.

of an error distribution making for maximum bias, was sufficiently large to significantly affect the British India trend rates
for aggregates of crops over the full period.

III

Methods Used for Adjustment of Crop Data

1. Minor adjustments : inclusion of minor producing districts, allowance for seed deduction, composition of *Estimates* reports for regions. 2. Major adjustments : unreported *zamindari* lands, discontinuities in yield per acre trends. 3. Provinces where output was unreported : choice of independent variable for correlation, method of correlation and effect on trend estimates. 4. Conclusion.

As INDICATED IN PRECEDING CHAPTERS, various shortcomings in the primary data cause unwarranted impressions concerning the agricultural trends. These data have been adjusted to give uniform coverage over time in order to obtain comparable trends over the whole period. The methods used for making these adjustments are described in this chapter. Appendix Table *3A* gives the adjusted series and special notes for each crop.

The adjustments may be divided into two groups : the minor adjustments have relatively little effect on trends and the methods of adjustment presented no large difficulties. The major adjustments have marked effects on the series, mostly during the first twenty years. Great difficulties were encountered in making many of these adjustments.

1. Minor Adjustments

1.1 Inclusion of minor producing districts. Estimates' notes state that up to 1912/13 only certain major producing districts within the provinces were included in some of the crop reports. It seemed possible that the subsequent inclusion of other districts might have affected trends during the period. Crop acreage in the minor districts was obtained from *Agricultural Statistics* for each year and multiplied by the provincial yield per acre for the districts reported in *Estimates*. When the adjustments were completed, for sugarcane in United Provinces, and oilseed crops in Punjab, their effect was found to be small. Output of minor districts for other crops was found negligible and no changes were made.

1.2 Allowance for seed deduction. The *Estimates* measure output at the gross level and contain no deductions for seed or other purposes. *Estimates'* notes state, however, that deductions for seed were made in certain instances, sugarcane in United Provinces prior to 1917/18 and indigo in several provinces. Trend for the given series would not be affected by this condition, but the series would have less weight in the aggregate trend because of this deduction.

For sugarcane, using Desai's data, the seed requirement for United Provinces was taken as 2333 pounds of cuttings per acre from the previous harvest.[1] *Estimates* for cane, however, are in gur form, liquid extracted from the crushed cane; the gur equivalent of 2335 pounds of cane is 0.105 tons. The reported gur harvest for each year was raised by the gur equivalent of seed which must have been required for the following year's harvest, 0.105 times that output.

The indigo adjustment applied to United Provinces and Bombay, where *Estimates* reported that 10% of acreage was reserved for seed production, and to Punjab, where varying percentages of sown acreage were used for seed. Output was raised by 10% to conveniently make this adjustment. Area

[1] *Standard of Living, op. cit.,* p. 127.

sown should have been similarly raised, but instead the yield per acre was mistakenly raised. Since indigo was the least important of crops, this mistake is not serious.

1.3 Composition of Estimates *reports for regions. Estimates* reports for given regions changed in two ways; boundaries of certain provinces shifted, and Indian States, which had been included in some provincial reports, were completely removed after 1921/22. Both types of change affected the view of regional trends and the States change also affected British India trends in reported data. The methods of correction for these changes were, for the most part, relatively simple.

There were three important boundary changes. Two involved Assam and Bengal, in 1905–10 and 1941–46, and the third was formation of the separate Orissa Province in 1935, which included parts of Madras and Central Provinces.

The short-lived Eastern Bengal Province, including Assam, was reported in combined form in *Estimates* output, but the acreage was given separately in *Agricultural Statistics;* sugarcane yield per acre in Assam, 1905/06–10/11, was estimated from the average proportion of Assam to Assam plus Greater Bengal yield per acre in 1911/12–20/21 applied to the Eastern Bengal reported yield per acre. Assam output, acreage times estimated yield per acre, was subtracted from Eastern Bengal output to obtain Greater Bengal output, and yield per acre for the latter region was obtained by dividing output by acreage.

Since rice is the important crop in both regions, a more elaborate method was employed to make this adjustment. Yield per acre was estimated for each year in the Greater Bengal region from the simple linear regression of Greater Bengal yield per acre on that of Greater Bengal plus Assam combined during 1911/12–28/29. The equation gave results averaging only one percent away from yield per acre for

Greater Bengal based on *Estimates* for those years. Greater Bengal output was taken as estimated yield per acre multiplied by acreage.

Starting with 1941/42 separation of Assam and Bengal data was again a problem because some agricultural statistics for the last years were not published until after independence, and were then given in the regional framework following partition into India and Pakistan. Part of the Assam district of Sylhet was joined with East Bengal in Pakistan, and consequently when East and West Bengal are added to obtain the original Bengal Province, a part of Assam is added in also. Crops which were sufficiently affected to merit adjustment were tea, jute, and rice.

Estimates data for the original Assam and the smaller Assam without the Sylhet area are available in different issues for the same two years, 1939/40–40/41. The average difference in acreage between the two Assams was taken as the Sylhet area for tea and jute from 1941 to 1946, deducted from Bengal and added to Assam. Output was adjusted by using the tea yield per acre in Assam and the jute yield per acre in East Bengal during each of the years 1941 to 1946. For rice, the acreage sown in all Assam was estimated annually by using the average proportion of rice area sown in all Assam to that in the smaller Assam during 1939/40 and 1940/41. Yield per acre for all Assam was taken as that of Assam without the Sylhet area, as given in *Estimates*.

The separate Orissa Province received over ten million acres from Madras to form Ganjam and Koraput districts and over a million acres from Central Provinces which were added to Sambalpur district. To maintain comparable regional units over time, the output of Ganjam and Koraput was deducted from Orissa (Greater Bengal) and added to Madras; 30% of Sambalpur output was likewise added to Central Provinces.

Output of the districts for the various crops was estimated from the acreage given in *Agricultural Statistics* and the yield per acre which was assumed to be the same as that reported in *Estimates* for Orissa.

Certain Indian States were included in provincial output reports up to 1921/22. The States component of the reported figures was small and involved few crops in Greater Bengal, Madras, and United Provinces, but in Bombay-Sind, Greater Punjab, and Central Provinces the condition was more extensive. Almost all the adjustments were made by replacing the acreage in *Estimates* with that in *Agricultural Statistics,* for the province alone, and multiplying by the yield per acre reported for the Province–States region. Unfortunately, the *Estimates* notes did not always clearly specify the years when reports were mixed; comparison with *Agricultural Statistics* usually resolved this difficulty. In some cases, too, *Agricultural Statistics* did not give area for crops reported in *Estimates;* the provincial area was then estimated from the proportion of Province to Province-States area reported in later years.

2. Major Adjustments

2.1 Unreported Zamindari *lands.* In Madras and Central Provinces, the zamindari land tenure sections, where revenue was assessed on large estates over long periods of time, were not included in *Estimates* reports up to 1910/11 and 1896/97 respectively. A third of Madras and about a quarter of Central Provinces was in zamindari tenure.

Little change was made in the Central Provinces series, although perhaps a more extensive adjustment should have been made. *Estimates'* notes clearly state that zamindari lands were unreported in these early years. *Agricultural Statistics,* although carrying a note on non-reporting of zamindari lands in Madras, made no mention of zamindari lands being unreported in Central Provinces. It was assumed, therefore, that the *Agricultural Statistics* acreage included the zamindari lands, and that adjustment for affected crops could be made by raising *Estimates* acreage (and output) to be consistent with *Agricultural Statistics*. However, the *Agricultural Statistics* acreage was virtually the same as in *Estimates* for three of the four crops for which output was reported—wheat, sesamum, and linseed—and only slightly larger, about one percent, for cotton. The only adjustment made was to raise cotton acreage (and output) by the excess of *Agricultural Statistics* over *Estimates* acreage.

Inspection of other *Agricultural Statistics* series for Central Provinces leaves some question as to the adequacy of this treatment. Total land area reported in *Agricultural Statistics* rose gradually to about ten percent higher in 1897/98 over 1891/92, followed by another increase of about ten percent from 1905/06 to 1906/07, after which the figure remained stable. This twenty percent increase might have represented zamindari lands added to *Agricultural Statistics* coverage in addition to the zamindari lands (over a third, perhaps, of total zamindari lands) which were reported in 1891/92. At the same time, however, with seeming inconsistency, net area sown, according to *Agricultural Statistics,* showed a downward trend to 1897/98 and only a one to two percent increase from 1905/06 to 1906/07 (or from 1901/02–05/06 to 1906/07–10/11). In retrospect it would seem that a more extensive adjustment might have been made—if a suitable method could have been devised.

All the crop series were adjusted for Madras up to 1910/11. The *Estimates* notes state that up to 1906/07 reports were only for ryotwari lands, but after that certain zamindari lands were included. Examination of *Estimates* crop acreage series shows that a large increase occurred in 1911/12 as compared with 1910/11 and the same is true for a short period of years before and after 1911/12. This suggests that the major change in *Estimates* came in 1911/12 and not in 1907/08. Confirmation of this is gotten by comparing crop acreage in *Estimates* with *Agricultural Statistics* for 1907/08 to 1910/11. The *Agricultural Statistics* notes state that zamindari lands were included in those series from 1907/08 on, and this is confirmed by the sharp increases in *Agricultural Statistics* crop areas from 1906/07 to 1907/08 and in the averages for short periods before and after 1907/08. Acreage in *Agricultural Statistics* series from 1907/08 to 1910/11 are much larger than those in *Estimates*.

For rice, cotton, sugarcane, and sesamum, crops which were reported in *Estimates,* adjustments were made as follows: Between 1907/08 and 1910/11 the *Agricultural Statistics* crop acreage was used in place of that given in *Estimates* for the province. For the years 1891/92 to 1906/07 the *Estimates* acreage was increased by the average proportion of *Agricultural Statistics* acreage to *Estimates* acreage for each crop during 1907/08 to 1910/11. Yields per acre in zamindari lands were assumed to be the same as elsewhere in the province.

The adjustment was made differently for other crops, most of which were not reported in *Estimates* until later years— jowar, bajra, ragi, maize, tobacco, indigo, and groundnut (though the last two were reported in *Estimates*). First, the proportion of zamindari to ryotwari total land in each district was determined from the revenue records in *Agricultural Statistics*. It was assumed that for each crop the zamindari acreage in each district was in this same proportion to ryotwari acreage. The provincial ratio of zamindari to ryotwari acreage was obtained, using 1907/08–11/12 data, by summing the preceding district acreages. Multiplying the ryotwari reported acreage up to 1906/07 by this same ratio gave the estimated zamindari acreage. Yield per acre was assumed to be the same as for the rest of the province.

These adjustments result in large additions to the *Estimates* reports for many crops.[2] but the direct effect on trends is, however, confined to the two overlapping reference decades in which change of coverage occurred. Trends during 1891/92–1901/02 and 1896/97–06/07 were not affected since all acreage and output figures were raised by the same percentage. Trends during 1901/02–11/12 and 1906/07–16/17 were made smaller as compared with trends through the unadjusted data. For example, in 1901/02–11/12 the rice output trend, after raising the *Estimates* reports by 40% for years up to 1910/11, was 0.99% per year as compared with 2.77% through the unadjusted data. The indirect effect of the adjustments and reductions in trend is also spread into trend measurements for groups of decades and the whole period by the process of averaging the decade trends.

2.2 Discontinuities in yield per acre trends. To eliminate the discontinuity for each crop, discussed in Chapter II, 4.1, yields per acre for all years up to the year of change were raised (or lowered) by the percentage required to make the straight-line trend yield per acre of that year equal to the yield per acre of straight-line trend in the following period extended back one year. These percentages are given in the last column of Table *2.3.* The adjustments were mostly in Madras where rates of change for all leading crops during the 1906/07–16/17, 1911/12–21/22, and 1916/17–26/27 reference decades were lowered because of the adjust-

[2] The percentage adjustment for each crop is given in the notes to Appendix Table *3A.*

ment; average rates for groups of decades and for the ten reference decades were also lowered. Groundnut was the most rapidly expanding crop in Bombay-Sind Province; the adjustment accentuated the upward trend rates by lov.ering output of the earlier years. In United Provinces the tobacco crop was of relatively small importance.

3. Provinces Where Output was Unreported

The broadening coverage of provincial *Estimates* reports, described in Chapter II, 2, necessitated the most extensive of all adjustments. Crop acreage reports are provided in *Agricultural Statistics* for these provinces;[3] the remaining problem, therefore, is to estimate yield per acre. An estimated yield per acre which was sensitive to regional conditions in each year was desired, as pointed out in Chapter I, 2.23. In devising a technique for this purpose, the questions arise—what to correlate with, how to correlate, and what effect does the estimating method have on the crop trends?

3.1 Choice of independent variable for correlation. Data in the relevant years are available for variables related to yield per acre, such as rainfall, acreage, price, exports, and yield per acre of other crops. A multiple regression with several variables would give better results than simple regression, but the volume of calculation required to obtain suitable equations for the gaps in Table 2.2 precluded use of more than one variable.

Each of the variables mentioned above was tested to see how yields per acre predicted by simple linear regression compared with actual yields per acre for years in which the

[3] For about a dozen cases of annual crop reports for provinces, mostly in Greater Bengal, no acreage data was given in *Agricultural Statistics* for the first one to three years of the study. Estimates were made for these years on the basis of a variety of conditions.

latter were available in *Estimates*. Rainfall, it might be expected, would show considerable correlation with yield per acre, but this apparently holds mainly for large fluctuations; distribution within the year or season may be more important than total amount.[4] It would not have been feasible, however, to work with monthly rainfall data. The correlation of acreage and yield per acre in the same year showed little correlation, and the same held for yield per acre lagged one year behind acreage. Results using exports and prices were also not favorable.

The yield per acre of other crops in the same region, especially similar crops, may be expected to show much correlation with the yield per acre of the given crop. If soil conditions and efficiency of cultivation were similar for the two crops, and both were exposed to the same weather and market conditions, the yields per acre could be expected to fluctuate similarly. It was found, as will be shown below, that yields per acre of a related crop in the same region gave good results in predicting yield per acre for a given crop. In some cases it was necessary to use the related crop of a nearby region.[5]

The 'similar' crop for estimating each given crop yield per acre was chosen on the basis of certain generally known characteristics, or characteristics observable by simple inspection, and by other characteristics which were tested statistically. The most important general characteristic was that the similar crop be grown in the same time of the year, i.e. a *kharif* crop, grown during the monsoon season, or a *rabi* crop, grown following the monsoon season. Crops are designated as

---

[4] India, Meteorological Department, *Memoirs of the Indian Meteorological Department,* Vol. XXV, Part IV, R. S. M. V. Unakar, "Correlation between weather and crops with special reference to Punjab wheat," 1929.

[5] P. Thomas and N. Sundarama Sastry, *Indian Agricultural Statistics* (Madras: Oxford University Press, 1939), pp. 28–30 discuss the complexity of factors affecting yield per acre and give additional references.

substitutes largely on this basis in the *Indian Crop Calendar,* which gives sowing and harvesting times by provinces for each crop.[6] Preferably the crops were to be similar in product, i.e. grains, oilseeds, which usually meant that the average yields per acre of the two crops would not be much different. Though most crops were annuals, this element in similarity was also considered; tea, for instance, is a perennial, and the amount harvested per acre depended mostly on the market, in contrast to annual crops which are usually completely harvested. In addition, the two crops, as much as possible were to be grown in the same part of the region, as was indicated by the *Crop Atlas of India.*[7] Lastly, from inspection of the yield per acre series, trend in the independent variable was preferably to be small, or at least not incompatible with trend, based on later reports, in the dependent variable. Among *kharif* crops, for instance, yield per acre for jowar would be estimated from sesamum rather than cotton; the great difference in these yield per acre trend rates, at least for British India as a whole, is shown in Table *5.4*

After the preceding conditions were fulfilled, or considered acceptable for a potential 'similar' crop, two statistical tests were employed. The first measured agreement in signs of first differences in the two series for years when both were reported. Preference went to the crop which gave a maximum of "asfd," similarity in direction of change from year to year, movement up or down from the previous year. On the average the "asfd" between crops which were chosen to act as independent variables and the dependent variable crops was about two-thirds of the years for which comparison was possible. Finally, the last and ultimate criterion was to see how well the similar

[6] Issued by the Economic and Statistical Advisor, Ministry of Agriculture, Delhi, 1950.

[7] Department of Commercial Intelligence and Statistics, Revised Edition, Delhi, 1939.

crop served to predict yields per acre for the dependent crop in the period from which the regression equation was derived. The relative mean deviation of predicted yields from actual yields was kept as low as possible. Average "rmd" for the regression equations which were used was very close to ten percent. If the equations served equally well in predicting yields per acre during the years for which no comparison could be made, then the predicted magnitudes were on the average ten percent plus or minus the unknown actual.

3.2 Method of correlation and effect on trend estimates. There are four problems which had to be resolved in order to correlate the chosen series. First, and most important of these in effect on trend estimates, was whether the series were to be correlated in their raw form or whether the correlation would be between deviations from the trend of each series. There is usually no question that the latter is the correct method for correlating time series; otherwise there is the possibility, for instance, that two rapidly increasing series would show much correlation when in fact the deviations from their trends might be behaving oppositely. If, however, there were relatively little trend in the series, then the need for adhering to this rule is correspondingly small. Inspection of yield per acre graphs in the early stages of the research indicated little trend in the relevant series. Because of this, and in view of the time which would have been required to calculate trend deviations for all the series which were tried, and in view, also, of the fact that it would then have been logically necessary to make an assumption concerning trend of the unknown yield per acre series in the unreported years, it was decided to correlate the series in their raw form. It is for this reason that one of the initial criteria in choosing between potential similar crops was that it have little trend, or at least not incompatible trend compared with trend in reported years for the unknown series.

It would have been impossible to study each crop in each region sufficiently well to make an assumption regarding trend in the unknown period. The most feasible possibility was to extrapolate the trend of later years back to early years, but this generally did not give credible results in instances where it was tried, though this might be expected since straight line arithmetic trends were used rather than logical trends.[8] Of course, it might have been assumed that the yield per acre trend rate was zero in all these cases, but this is not less of an assumption than that the trend rose or fell at some particular rate. In effect, then, whatever trend there was in the independent variable series was built into the relevant years of the dependent series. This may be even more realistic than the assumption of a uniform zero trend rate. If there was trend for some crop yields per acre, others might have been changing in about the same way.

When the research reached a later stage it became possible to observe, at least in British India as a whole, the yield per acre trend rates for crops which were estimated in the above manner. Figure 7.1 shows the moving averages for yields per acre of foodgrain crops and Table 7.1 gives the average yield per acre trend rates for the first four reference decades; rates for each reference decade are given in Appendix Table 5A. Rates for the six minor foodgrain crops are generally less than for the nonfoodgrain crops and less than the rate for wheat, which is what one would expect. It would seem, however, that the actual rates, were they known, for these minor cereal crops would be somewhat less than what was evidently built into them.

How much influence did these estimated yields per acre

[8] However, to calculate yields per acre for Madras sugarcane, 1891/92–1900/01, trend in later years was projected back and cyclical variations were added for each year according to the cyclical variations of the Madras rice series from its trend.

have on the aggregate crop trends in British India and the regions? Appendix Table *3B* gives the annual percentage of all-crop output in series included as a result of using these yields per acre. For British India the maximum figure, in 1891/92, was 39%, declining to 25% by 1910/11, and showing marked decline to 13% in 1911/12, 9% in 1912/13, and about 4% in 1913/14. In those years large extensions of coverage occurred in Madras, Bombay-Sind, United Provinces, and Central Provinces. The percentage for each region in 1891/92 was: 73% Bombay-Sind, 64% United Provinces, about 54% in Greater Punjab and Central Provinces, 45% Madras, and 18% in Greater Bengal.

The trend for yield per acre of the all-crop aggregate was influenced by each crop to the extent of the above percentages. Trends for output, however, depended on acreage as well as yield per acre; the acreage data were taken from *Agricultural Statistics*. For the combined group of six crops the acreage trend was responsible for over half the trend in output. The influence of the estimated yield per acre trends might roughly be said to equal half the respective percentages cited above and in Appendix 3B.

The remaining three methodological questions—length of period from which the regression was derived, form of the equation, and fitting—had much less effect on the estimated trends. Usually the first ten to fifteen years of reports for the dependent variable crop were used for the regression analysis. A longer period, twenty years for example, would have meant that conditions as recent as 1931/32 were affecting magnitudes calculated for 1891/92. In delimiting the regression period the span of years was continued up to the year when "asfd" was no longer positive.

Linear type regression equations were employed, except in the case of Bombay-Sind rice, for which the parabolic form was used. In most cases, however, the straight line equation was in the form $y = bx$, omitting the "A" constant of $y = A + bx$.[9] The latter form was used where acreage for the crop was large, generally for the foodgrains. Without the "A", or with "A" implicitly equal to zero, the straight line passes through the origin of a graph, where otherwise it starts at the "A" amount above the origin. Equations with the "A" constant give better predictive results, but much labor can be saved if the constant need not be calculated.

In fitting the equations in the form $y = A + bx$ (and in the one case of $y = A + bx + cx^2$) the least squares method was used. For equations in $y = bx$ form, a very simple method was used to obtain the value of "b", the sum of "y", dependent variable, divided by sum of "x", independent variable, for the years of the regression period. The latter can be computed quickly, and even where the final form of equation was $y = A + bx$, preliminary equations in the form $y = bx$ were used to help in resolving certain questions of choice in order to obtain the best equation.

The two groups of equations differed in the following respects. Those in the $y = bx$ group showed an average of 64.1% "asfd" and were derived from an average 11.2 years of regression period; the average "rmd" for this group was 10.3%. The $y = A + bx$ group had 69.6% "asfd" on the average; the equations were based on an average of 15.3 years in the regression period, and gave results averaging 8.9% in "rmd". Distribution of "rmd" in each group is shown in Table 3.1

[9] Of the equations used, 30 were in the form $y = bx$ and 22 as $y = A + bx$. For each series of years requiring an estimated yield per acre, more than one equation was usually derived, and the one giving best results was finally chosen. Total number of equations tried was therefore much larger than the total used.

TABLE 3.1

FREQUENCY DISTRIBUTION OF RELATIVE MEAN DEVIATIONS OF
PREDICTED YIELDS PER ACRE FROM ACTUAL YIELDS REPORTED
IN ESTIMATES DURING REGRESSION PERIOD

Relative Mean Deviation	Number of Equations	
	$y = bx$	$y = A + bx$
0.0 — 4.9%	3	5
5.0 — 9.9	13	7
10.0 — 14.9	10	8
15.0 — 19.9	3	2
20.0 — 24.9	1	–
	—	—
	30	22

Note : The "rmd" for the one equation in parabolic form
was 3.4%.

4. Conclusion

The major adjustments, described above, affect the results
of this study in a number of ways. First, the absolute magnitudes of data during certain periods of adjustment were raised
(or in a few cases, lowered) by some given percentage—for
crops in the Madras zamindari areas, and for crops affected
by discontinuity in yield per acre trends. Trends derived for
those periods were not affected by the adjustment except in
the case of trends for aggregates of series, where the adjusted
series (usually) had greater weights in the aggregate.

Second, trends for periods of time which overlapped the
years of adjusted data, including, therefore, trend for the
whole period, were generally made smaller because of the
higher magnitudes ascribed to earlier years. Madras was the
region principally affected by these considerations, and to that
extent so too was British India.

Third, in the case of provinces where certain crop output

was unreported, the magnitudes estimated for yield per acre were a function of another, reported, yield per acre series in that province, or a nearby province. Since the crops reported in earlier years were more important commercially, and since yield per acre for such crops might tend to show more favorable trends (as a result of man's controls) than those of unreported, less important, crops, it is possible that the yields per acre so estimated were biassed upward.

There are two circumstances which suggest that this bias, if it existed, was small : a) in the earlier years yield per acre was more influenced by rainfall, which would affect crops in the same region about equally, and less by the controlling influences, which might not have applied to commercially less important crops, and b) the relative mean deviation of estimated from actual yields per acre in the period for which both crops were reported was generally small, (Table 3.1). This leaves the possibility, however, that the annual deviations of estimated from actual yields per acre could have fallen in such a way as to give trends different from those derived, even though the relative mean deviation of the estimated from actual was less than the "rmd" obtained for that series. In any case, it should be appreciated that the output trends were affected by acreage, which was reported, as well as by yield per acre.

IV

Measurement of Trends

1. Aggregation of crops; units; weights. 2. Classification of crops : types and regions. 3. Trend measurement : short and long period trend rates, the terminal year problem, trend rates for population series.

1. Aggregation of Crops

IN ORDER TO AGGREGATE THE physical output series, they must be converted to common units and weighted according to the importance of each crop's unit of output. Caloric units could be used as a common denominator for food crops, but the nutritive importance of foods also depends on protein content, vitamins, and minerals. Arbitrary weights could conceivably be ascribed to the various nutritive qualities, but although such a system would have the advantage of being unaffected by time,[2] certain crops—cotton, jute, tobacco, indigo, and others—would not fit into the system.

Relative importance of crops is indicated by prices, and the monetary unit in which they are expressed provides a com-

[1] An index of foodgrain output weighted by protein content of each crop was given in my 1951 study, *op. cit.,* p. 112. It differed very little from the index of foodgrain output aggregated by physical output.

[2] A system for aggregating food production of crops and animals with a common unit on the basis of weights reflecting ten nutritive values, including calories, proteins, fats, minerals, and vitamins, has recently been developed by Leonard Zobler, "A New Areal Measure of Food Production Efficiency," *Geographical Review,* LI, 4 (October 1961).

mon ground for aggregation. Unfortunately, the structure of prices changes over time, particularly when there are large changes in the general price level, and also when there are changes in quality of some crops. Quality and price are likely to be positively associated, and the weight of the improved crop in the aggregate will therefore depend on whether the structure of weights was taken from prices of a year before or after the improvement. Since rising output is probably associated with improved quality, aggregate trends will be pitched up or down according to the weight given the improved crop. Cotton appears to be the only notable example where this would be a problem.

Ideally, several sets of weights representing different conditions over time might be used, and if aggregate trends were similar despite the difference in weights, then a clear picture would emerge. The extent of calculations for aggregating eighteen crops over fifty-six years in six regions and British India, and the measurement of trend for these series, necessitated a choice for one set of price weights. Years of war, international disturbance, or of unusual seasonal conditions, would not be a representative source of these weights. The character of available data also limits the choice of years from which weights might be taken.

Prices and Wages in India[3] is an available source for the period up to 1921, giving average annual prices in several of the main market towns of important provinces for fifteen of the eighteen crops in this study; a British India average of these prices is not given. The main objection to using these prices is that they are at the wholesale level, presumably including costs of transportation from village to wholesale market as well as the wholesaler's other costs of operation. If transportation and marketing costs were in the same propor-

[3] Issued by the Department of Statistics.

tion to farm prices for all crops, then the wholesale level of prices would be acceptable, but the proportion is not likely to be the same for all crops, in part because of the differences in proportion of crop marketed. Weights at the wholesale level would therefore result in measurement of output of marketing services in addition to farm production.

"Harvest Prices of Principal Crops in India,"[4] available for the period since 1915/16, was desirable to use because it represents prices paid to farmers at the village level.[5] It was also convenient because British India average prices were available for these series.[6] Given this source, the remaining question was—which part of the series would provide the most representative weights? The war years 1915/16–20/21 and 1939/40–46/47, and the depression years 1929/30–32/33 were ruled out because export crop prices were not in their usual relationship with non-export crops. This leaves most of the 1920's and the mid–1930's; average prices during 1924/25–28/29 for each crop were taken for the weight structure. During this time the general level of prices was fairly stable and there appeared to be no unusual foreign trade conditions affecting export crop prices.[7] The same set of weights was also used in my 1951 study; thus, comparison is facilitated between this and the earlier study.[8]

A set of price weights from the mid-1930's would not seem

[4] Published in *Agricultural Statistics* and other publications.

[5] Desai, *Standard of Living, op. cit.*, pp. 173–174, points out that some of the prices were at wholesale level, and that there were inconsistencies in the methods by which the provincial average prices were obtained.

[6] Calculated in Thomas and Sastry, *op. cit.*, Appendix X.

[7] Price changes, although mostly in general level rather than structure, are described in Jathar and Beri, *op. cit.*, II, 315–326, B. A. Patil, *Agricultural Price Problems in India* (Bombay: The Bombay State Cooperative Union, 1959), pp. 123–141, and D. Bright Singh, *Inflationary Price Trends in India Since 1939* (Bombay: Asia Publishing House, 1957), pp. 25–28.

[8] Mukerji, *op. cit.*, also used the same set of weights as in my 1951 study.

to be less acceptable than the set used from the 1920's. Would this alternative set of weights have given different trends for the aggregate series? The provincial *Harvest Price* data were averaged (weighted by output) to obtain British India prices for 1934/35–38/39 comparable with the 1924/25–28/29 prices; both sets are given in Appendix Table *4A.* Change in price structure is indicated by Table *4.1,* which gives the percentage price decline for each crop between 1924/25–28/29 and 1934/35–38/39.

TABLE 4.1

DECREASE IN BRITISH INDIA CROP PRICES BETWEEN AVERAGES
FOR 1924/25–28/29 AND 1934/35–38/39

(Percent)

Tea	19.6	Jowar	42.7	Rice	45.8
Linseed	40.6	Tobacco	43.5	Groundnut	46.1
Cotton	41.0	Bajra	43.7	Sugarcane	46.9
Sesamum	41.0	Wheat	44.4	Maize	49.1
Gram	41.4	Barley	45.2	Jute	56.8
Rape and Mustard	41.9			All Crops	45.7

Source : Computed from Appendix Table 4A.

There was remarkably little dispersion in the percentage decreases in price. Tea, for which the price remained high, and jute, for which price declined the most, were the only major exceptions. The average price decline, obtained by weighting the price decreases by average crop output in the years 1924/25–28/29 and 1934/35–38/39, was 45.7%. Crops which declined more than the average—jute, maize, sugarcane, groundnut, and rice—would have had less weight than the others if 1934/35–38/39 prices had been used. It will be seen in later chapters that sugarcane and groundnut were among the most rapidly expanding crops; their influence on the aggregate series would have been smaller if the later prices were employed. Cotton and tea were the other crops with high growth rates, and they would have received greater weights in the aggregate series. Rice, which had a quite low rate of expansion, would have had almost the same relative importance, or slightly less, according to the above data. It appears in general that there would have been very little difference if the 1934/35–38/39 prices had been used rather than 1924/25–28/29 prices.

Prices for several crops not given in *Harvest Prices* were obtained in the following manner. For ragi (millet) the price was taken as same as for jowar (millet). Groundnut, tea, and indigo prices were estimated by first getting the average export value per unit and then reducing it by a proportion which would bring it down to the village level of price. The latter proportion was obtained by averaging the percentage required to reduce the export value of five crops—wheat, linseed, sesamum, cotton, and jute—to the harvest level reported for these crops. Prices used as weights are shown in Appendix Table 4A.

2. Classification of Crops

There appeared to be several alternative classifications of crops which would help bring out the composition of the aggregate crop trends. A division between food and nonfood crops would place thirteen of the eighteen crops in the former category, and would leave only cotton and jute as major crops among the nonfoods. The food category could be further subdivided between grains and edible oilseeds, with tea and sugarcane as 'other foods.' Additional processing of data required for this classification appeared excessive for the present study.

A division between commercial and noncommercial crops would be convenient for observing whether the market influence had a favorable effect on output of certain crops. The crops do not divide very simply on this line, however; some, like jute, tea, and indigo are wholly marketed, but the proportion of other crops marketed varied, and would be difficult to determine. Exports would be too narrow a measure, as seen from the fact that although only one percent of rice output was exported in the 1930's, a quarter of the output was machine milled in commercial establishments.[9] It has been estimated that toward the close of the period, "gross village retention," for seed and other purposes, was approximately as follows: rice 59%, wheat 49%, barley 71%, maize 80%, jowar and bajra 80%, ragi 90%, gram 55%, sugarcane 13%, tobacco 7%, groundnut 5%, and cotton 12%.[10] Among the oilseeds, village retention of linseed was estimated at about 20%,[11] and 5–10% for rape and mustard, and sesamum.[12]

The foodgrain-nonfoodgrain classification adopted for this study serves as an indicator for two aspects of change. Foodgrains—cereals and pulses—constituted about half of average diet, the remainder being apportioned between meat, milk products, oils, vegetables, sugar, condiments, and other foods;[13]

[9] Baljit Singh, *op. cit.*, p. 83.

[10] Desai, *Standard of Living, op. cit.*, pp. 119–126 on measurement of commercial marketing, and pp. 33, 121, 125, 170 for estimates.

[11] India, Agricultural Marketing Advisor, *Report on Marketing of Linseed,* Delhi, 1938, p. 21.

[12] Desai, *ibid.*

[13] According to average family budgets of industrial workers in about a dozen of the (28) localities surveyed by the Cost of Living Index Scheme of the Department of Labour in India during 1943–47. For these towns the cereals-pulses expenditure relative to total food expenditure ranged from over 40% in Bombay and Punjab to as high as 75% in Assam and Bihar. The representativeness of industrial worker's diet to urban diet as a whole, and to rural diet, should also be considered. Appendix 4B gives the percentage expenditure on each of the above-mentioned diet categories for these towns.

trend for the major group may be readily observed with this classification. The foodgrains were also the least commercialized of the crops studied, as seen in the above village crop retention data for the late 1930's, with only half or less being marketed. Since the crops cannot be perfectly divided on being marketed or village-retained, the foodgrain component may be taken as the mostly noncommercial group of crops.

The representativeness of the foodgrain-nonfoodgrain weighting may now be considered. Average acreage of the eight foodgrain crops in the study was 80% of the total for the eighteen crops during the entire period; whereas, in the more comprehensive *Agricultural Statistics,* foodgrains constituted 78% of total acreage. To improve the balance of weighting, at least for output, the value of cottonseed, as 36% of value of ginned cotton fibre output, was added to nonfoodgrain output.[14] Thus constituted, the foodgrains were 68% of all crop output during 1944/45–46/47, when weighted according to the prices used in this study. In India during 1948/49–50/51 foodgrains and their byproducts were 66% of the value of all crops produced, based on current prices.[15] Comparable figures were not available for Pakistan, but during 1946/47–48/49, foodgrains comprised 75% of crop output,[16] when weighted according to prices used in this study. If the two percentages are combined, weighted by the population of each country, foodgrains constituted 68% of combined total output.

[14] From data of India, Ministry of Finance, Department of Economic Affairs, *Final Report of the National Income Committee February 1954,* p. 36. Byproducts of all the crops ought to be considered. For rice, according to the same source, the value of bran removed in milling was 8% of the value of cleaned rice. However, if this were added to the foodgrain output total in the study it would give further undesirable weight to this component.

[15] *Ibid.*

[16] Pakistan data from Pakistan, Department of Commercial Intelligence and Statistics, *Statistical Digest of Pakistan for 1950.*

The regional form of the study, summarized briefly in Chapter I, 3, is also an aspect of classification. If data were available for the more than two hundred districts, then regionalizations might have been constructed to test for causes of crop trends. Districts in which irrigation expanded, or where transportation was improved, could then have been compared with other districts which did not change in these respects. The general unavailability of district level output data in the United States prevented this type of regionalization.

Given the provincial level data, there was relatively little choice in arrangement of regions. There appeared to be no advantage to making any other combinations of provinces other than in the three multi-province regions—Greater Bengal, Greater Punjab, and Bombay-Sind. The combination of Bombay and Sind was not desirable, but resulted from the combined reporting of the two provinces as one administrative unit during 1921-32. Otherwise it would have been better to include Sind as part of Greater Punjab, since the two areas are more similar climatically, and what is of more direct relevance, crop trends in both were affected by expansion of government irrigation works. About two-thirds of total Sind area was irrigated in 1940/41 and over 90% of irrigation was by government works. In Bombay only about 3% of area sown was irrigated and only about a quarter of irrigation was by government. The increasing government irrigation was a contributing factor to trends derived for Bombay-Sind, but this factor is almost entirely unrepresentative of Bombay. Bombay was about four times larger than Sind in population.

Appendix Table 4C gives annual aggregate all-crop output, foodgrain and nonfoodgrain output, weighted in average prices of 1924/25–28/29, for British India and the six regions. Acreage and yield per acre (in aggregate rupees per acre) are also given for the three groups of crops.

3. Trend Measurement

3.1 Short and long period trend rates. The main structure of crop trend rates[17] was obtained by fitting[18] simple exponential equations to overlapping segments of the series between population census years, i.e. 1891–01, 1901–11, and between population mid-census decade years, i.e. 1896–06, 1906–16, etc. An arithmetic mean of the ten decade rates was taken as the average trend rate over the whole period; because the rates are small, the results so obtained were virtually identical with a geometric mean of the ten decade rates, which would take longer to compute. For British India all-crop output, arithmetic and geometric means are the same.

By fitting the trend to short segments rather than to the entire length of the series, only the data within the given segment determines the trend rate which is derived. If a trend line is fitted to the entire series, then trend in the given segment depends mainly on data of other years. The system of short period trends is consequently advantageous for analyzing

[17] For some purposes, straight line arithmetic or semi-logarithmic trends were fitted to the entire series, and in some cases the geometric mean rate of change was computed between averages of each half of a series.

[18] Equations were fitted by the method of moments using Glover's tables as extended by the National Bureau for Economic Research. Fitting by the method of least squares to the logarithms of the data, which requires more labor, gives almost the same results, as seen in the comparison below for British India wheat output for the ten decades, 1891/92–01/02, 1896/97–06/07, 1901/02–11/12, etc. Percentage rate of change per year is given for least squares (LS) on the top line and moments (M) below.

LS   1.58   2.43   1.96   1.60   −0.98   −0.44   0.07   0.74   1.31   0.08
M   1.63   2.35   2.03   1.56   −0.98   −0.43   0.07   0.74   1.38   0.08

The use of Glover's technique, and other aspects of Arthur F. Burn's (*op. cit.*) method of trend measurement, generally followed in this study, is evaluated in Boris P. Pesek, "Economic Growth and Its Measurement," *Economic Development and Cultural Change,* IX, 3 (April 1961). The methods are not found ideal but give nearly the same results as Pesek's preferred method.

changes within a long series. Variation in short period trend rates may be seen in Appendix Tables *5A* and *5B*.

By overlapping the trend periods, the sampling of rates of change is broadened and the rate obtained from averaging the short period trends is made more representative by being based on ten rather than only five rates. The average trend rate for the five decades between the census years is not always very similar to the average for the decades between the mid-census years, as may be seen in the Table *4.2* examples.

TABLE 4.2

AVERAGE TREND RATE OF CHANGE IN FIVE DECADES STARTING WITH 1891/92 COMPARED WITH DECADES STARTING IN 1896/97

(Percent per Year)

	1891/92 Decades	1896/97 Decades
British India Wheat Output	0.83	0.86
Acreage	0.00	0.98
Yield per Acre	0.79	−0.03
British India Jute Output	0.51	0.01
Acreage	0.44	−0.08
Yield per Acre	0.08	0.20
Madras All-Crop Output	1.19	0.77
Acreage	0.36	0.25
Yield per Acre	0.82	0.48

Source : Appendix Tables 5A and 5B.

The overlapping trends for British India wheat output are shown in Figure *4.1*. Trends for decades starting with 1896/97 are shown in dotted lines, those for decades starting in 1891/92 are drawn solid. For this series there is little difference between the two sets of trend lines. Average trend line slope for the ten decades represents the long ·period rate,

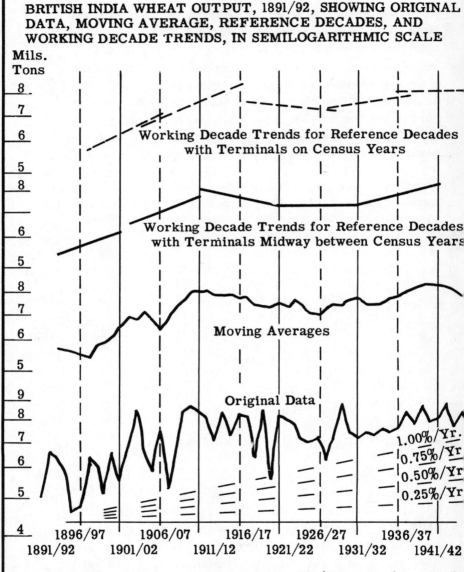

FIGURE 4.1
BRITISH INDIA WHEAT OUTPUT, 1891/92, SHOWING ORIGINAL
DATA, MOVING AVERAGE, REFERENCE DECADES, AND
WORKING DECADE TRENDS, IN SEMILOGARITHMIC SCALE

Note: Reference decades extend from 1891/92 to 1901/02, 1896/9
to 1906/07, etc.

Source: Based on date in Appendix 3A.

which may be gauged between 0.50 and 1.00% per year on the scale at the bottom of the chart.

3.2 The terminal year problem. If the crop series are mechanically divided into the periods delineated above, the results may be undesirable because the beginning and ending, or terminal years, may be at different cyclical stages. Trends derived from such segments would not be homogeneous, and averages of these trends would not be representative of the long period trend. Over many years the difference in terminal year cyclical stages would not have much effect on trend, but in short segments the effect may be considerable.

Two devices were employed to avoid this problem. The first was to transform the data into moving average series, thereby reducing the amplitude of fluctuations and eliminating part of the annual fluctuation. Difference in cyclical stage at opposite ends of the trend period would, as a result, be less serious. Second, the data were divided into working and reference decades so that the terminal years might be brought under closer agreement as to cyclical stage.

The series obtained by adjusting the primary data, as described in Chapter III, were refined into five year moving averages. Each year in the latter series is an average of the five years centered on that year—the given year, the two years before, and the two years after. This greatly smooths out the year to year fluctuations, as is seen in Figure *4.1*

There are several disadvantages, however, in using moving average series. One is that the first and last two years of the 1891/92–1946/47 period is consumed in obtaining the moving averages. As a result the first year in the moving average series is 1893/94 and the last is 1944/45. It is partly for this reason that a span longer than five years was not used, though it would have smoothed out the series even more.

A second disadvantage is that the moving averages for a

given decade period are affected by a few years outside the decade. The five year average of the terminal year is affected by two years beyond the decade, and the next year of the decade is affected by one year outside the decade. In a "decade" of eleven years there are fifty-five weights in the moving average series, of which six come from outside the decade.

A third disadvantage is that the peaks and troughs in the moving average series do not always coincide with those in the original data, although the difference is not likely to be more than one or two years. To avoid this, shorter-spanned moving averages, and weighting systems, were tried, but the results did not appear to merit their use. Examples of the shifting in turning points are seen in Figure *4.1*, where the peak in the data for 1897/98 becomes a trough in the moving average, and the same again in 1906/07. In the first case the trough was shifted by two years, and in the second case it was shifted by one year.

The other device for maintaining similar cyclical stage in the terminal years was to divided the series into working decades, each representing the reference decades. The latter are the regularly intervalled eleven-year segments extending from census year to census year, and from the mid-census decade years. Working decades include most, but not necessarily all, of the reference decade years. Terminal years of the working decades were kept within a range of not more than two years from the reference decade terminal years; length of the working decades was kept within a range of eight to thirteen years. Trend of the working decade was taken to represent trend during the reference decade.

To choose the best sets of working decade terminal years, the moving average series were plotted on semilogarithmic graphs, as in Figure *4.1*.[19] The trend of the series was then more discernible and it was possible to choose the terminal years so that the cyclical stages would be similar. For the reference decades 1891/92–1901/02 and 1936/37–46/47 there was no choice, however, as to working decade terminal years, since 1893/94 and 1944/45, the beginning and end of the moving average series, had to be used, according to the above rules. Working decade terminal years for acreage and yield per acre series were made the same as those chosen for the output series, except for the British India aggregate series—all crops, foodgrains, and nonfoodgrains—for which separate working decade terminal years were chosen.

The extent of correspondence between terminal years of working and reference decades in the moving average series may be illustrated by the example of British India wheat output. Of the twenty working decade terminal years, eleven are the same as the terminal years of the reference decades. Working decade terminal years were shifted by one year from the reference decade terminals at 1896/97, 1901/02, 1906/07, 1916/17, 1936/37, and by two years from the reference terminals at 1906/07 and 1916/27.

The difference in rates which may result from using working decade rather than reference decade terminal years is is indicated by the 1906/07–16/17 reference decade for the above series. Trend for those years was 1.71% per year, but this is measuring from the deep trough in the moving average series at 1906/07, easily apparent in Figure *4.1*, to the level at 1916/17. The working decade was set at 1904/05–16/17, and for these years the rate is 1.56% per year.

3.3 Trend rates for population series. For seven of the ten reference decades the population rates of growth were simply

---

[19] Two-cycle log paper was used on all graphs, including those which are shown on the following pages.

computed as the geometric mean rate between first and last year of the reference decade. The census years were reference decade terminal years for five of the decades, and population estimates for the other reference decade terminal years, 1896/97, 1906/07, etc., were interpolated on the basis of the growth rate between census years, i.e. 1896/97 was estimated as 1891 reported population plus growth for five years at the rate for 1891–1901.

The population data were taken as reported by the census[20] except for two circumstances. Adjustment was made for the substantial overcount which occurred in 1941 for Bengal and Punjab, according to the census review of a decade later.[21] There were difficulties in interpolating 1946 population because the 1951 India and Pakistan Censuses no longer carried the British India classification and because the new states were not all the same as the former provinces. British India population for 1946 was estimated as 1941 population plus growth in five years at the rate of growth for India-Pakistan in 1941–51. Bombay-Sind population was estimated similarly, as the 1941 amount plus growth of the (larger) region in 1941–51. The same procedure was followed for Bengal and Punjab, based on the combined India and Pakistan portions of those regions.

Rates for three of the ten reference decades, those affected

[20] For 1891–1941 the source was *1941 Census of India,* in which, conveniently, the provinces are kept at one territorial size to facilitate comparison.

[21] *Census of India, 1951,* V. 1, Part 1B, pp. 104–105. In Bengal the overcount was about 5.4 million and in Punjab 1.2 million; the British India total was correspondingly inflated.

This had the effect of lowering the decade rates which would otherwise have resulted for the last two reference decades.

[22] The 1891 and 1901 all-India census reports are said to be underestimated by 2.5 and 1.4 million respectively, according to Kingsley Davis, *The Population of India and Pakistan* (Princeton: Princeton University Press, 1951), p. 27. Since most of the underestimate was prob-

by the great influenza mortality of 1918, were computed differently from the above seven reference decades in order to obtain more realistic rates for each decade as a whole. The 1906/07–16/17 rate simply assumed that population grew at the same rate from 1911 to 1916 as it did from 1901–1911, 0.49% per year for British India; this avoided use of the 1911–21 geometric mean growth rate, 0.09% per year, in estimating for 1916, which would have given a decade growth rate of 0.28% per year. The rate for 1911/12–21/22 was estimated from the trend of all eleven years, and assumed that population during 1911–18 grew at about the same rate as 1901–11, and that population for 1919 and 1920 were 1921 census population projected backward according to the rate from 1921–31; for British India this gave a trend rate of no change, 0.00% per year, as contrasted with 0.09% per year as the geometric mean between 1911 and 1921. The 1916/17–26/27 rate was also computed from the trend of the projected data for 1916–18 and 1919–26, giving 0.45% per year contrasted with the 0.52% geometric mean between values simply interpolated for the two terminal years. Population decade rates for each region were computed in the same way as described above.[23]

ably in the Indian States the effect on British India trends is probably negligible.

[23] Appendix Table *4D* gives the British India and regional population data during the period.

PART B

Description and Analysis of Crop Trends

V

Output and Availability

1. Foodgrain output : British India trends for individual crops and aggregate foodgrain output, regional foodgrain output and population growth, trend in availability of foodgrains. 2. Non-foodgrain output : British India trends for individual and aggregate nonfoodgrain crop output, regional nonfoodgrain output, nonfoodgrain output per capita and availability. 3. All-crop output : regional trends and population growth, all-crop availability, all-crop output and national income.

AGGREGATE OUTPUT TRENDS IN British India and its regions are compared with population growth in this chapter and analyzed in terms of the component trends of foodgrain and nonfoodgrain crops. Population growth rates serve as a standard for comparison, the crop rates being considered high or low depending on whether they were more or less than the population rates. Comparison of population and output trend rates is not an entirely satisfactory indication of the trends in per capita consumption since allowance must be made, at least, for the net flow of trade. Consequently the trends in (gross) availability, output plus net flow of trade, are also compared with population trends. Welfare depends on the distribution of crop commodities among population groups, and the availability of nonagricultural goods, which is partly related to exports of crops, but no attempt is made to analyze these aspects of the economy.

The trend rates which are emphasized in this analysis are

93

an average of the ten reference decade trend rates; change in the reference decade rates is given by the trend rate of acceleration or retardation in reference decade rates. Average rates for the first and last four reference decades are also employed to bring out the change in rates over time. In the middle two reference decades unusual conditions caused very low rates which were not typical of either the earlier or later parts of the period.

Description and analysis of the trends in acreage and yield per acre, which brought about the changes in output, are taken up in Chapters VI, VII, and VIII respectively. The emphasis in this chapter is on the crop composition and regional aspects of the output trends, and on their significance.

1. Foodgrain Output

1.1 British India trends for individual crops and aggregate foodgrain crop output. For the half-century as a whole, the very low average rate of increase in aggregate foodgrain output and the decline in rice output stand out strikingly in Table 5.1.[1] Half of foodgrain output, and third of all-crop output, consisted of rice; its decline therefore had a weighty effect in depressing these measures of aggregate output. Besides rice, three other foodgrain crops had low or negative average rates of change in output—jowar, barley, and ragi. The remaining four crops had higher rates of increase in output, and among these the rate for wheat, most rapid of the grain crops, was notable. But even though wheat was the second ranking grain crop, it only comprised about a quarter of foodgrain output, and consequently this high rate was not able to greatly offset the negative trend rate for rice.

[1] Crop output trend rates for each reference decade are given in Appendix Table 5A. In all the tables which follow, crops and regions are ranked in order of their importance in total value of output.

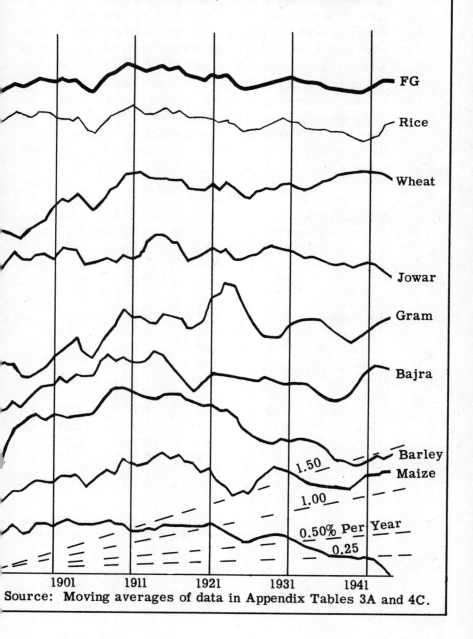

FIGURE 5.1

BRITISH INDIA: OUTPUT OF FOODGRAIN CROPS; FIVE YEAR MOVING AVERAGES; SEMILOGARITHMIC

FG

Rice

Wheat

Jowar

Gram

Bajra

Barley

Maize

1.50

1.00

0.50% Per Year

0.25

1901   1911   1921   1931   1941

Source: Moving averages of data in Appendix Tables 3A and 4C.

An equally important feature of the foodgrain trend rates, revealed by Table *5.1*, is their decrease from moderate or high rates of increase in the early part of the period to lower, generally negative, rates in the later decades. In the most general measure of the change in rates over time, the trend in reference decade rates, all eight foodgrains showed retardation.

The timing of the downturn or slowdown in expansion is indicated in the moving average chart, Figure *5.1*.[2] For aggre-foodgrain output, and for rice and wheat, the critical period was 1911/12. Two crops, barley and ragi, turned down during the preceding decade, and the remaining crops had their downturn during the next decade.

TABLE 5.1

BRITISH INDIA AGGREGATE AND INDIVIDUAL FOODGRAIN CROP OUTPUT : AVERAGE TREND RATE OF CHANGE, AND CHANGE IN REFERENCE DECADE RATES OF CHANGE

(Percent)

Crops	10 RD Av. (Per Year)	Change in RD Rates (Per RD)	First 4 RD Av. (Per Year)	Last 4 RD Av. (Per Year)
Aggregate	0.11	–0.17	0.61	0.03
Rice	–0.09	–0.03	0.35	–0.12
Wheat	0.84	–0.09	1.89	0.57
Jowar	0.05	–0.12	0.50	–0.34
Gram	0.26	–0.34	1.73	–1.15
Bajra	0.72	–0.11	1.86	0.59
Barley	0.02	–0.55	2.03	–1.34
Maize	0.51	–0.17	1.55	0.44
Ragi	–0.37	–0.23	0.24	–0.98
Population	0.67	0.11	0.44	1.12

Source : Computed from individual reference decade (RD) rates given in Appendix Table 5A.

[2] Vertical scales for these charts are omitted so as to group the series as closely as possible, thereby facilitating comparison of trends; slope

During the latter decade there were several unusual circumstances which contributed toward marking this period as a turning point. The years of the first World War brought a drop in grain exports to about 25% less than in the previous quinquennium, a reduction of about two-thirds of a million tons[3] out of approximately fifty million tons of foodgrains then being produced. However, it cannot be stated here whether the loss of trade caused reduced plantings and output or rather resulted in somewhat more grain left available domestically.

Toward the end of the decade there were two unusually depressing years. The main one of these was in 1918/19 when twin misfortunes struck, a catastrophic failure of the monsoons and a calamitous scourge of influenza. The mortality of the epidemic, which killed over ten million, was furthered by the effect of famine which resulted from drought. At the same time, because of sickness and mortality which laid whole villages absolutely desolate, crops in many areas were left unharvested.[4] In 1920/21 the monsoon rains were again very unfavorable. All foodgrain crop series show troughs in both 1918/19 and 1920/21. In the five year moving averages of these series, the effects of the war, the epidemic, and the monsoon failures are spread to two years before and two years after the events.[5]

scales are given for the latter purpose. Two log cycle (per 8½ x 11 sheet) graph paper was used.

[3] Based on data from Department of Commercial Intelligence and Statistics, *Annual Statement of the Seaborne Trade of British India*; Burma exports excluded.

[4] Extract from All-India Census Report, 1921, in *Census of India, 1951*, Volume I, Part I–B, Appendices to the Census Report, 1951, p. 289.

[5] A somewhat parallel situation developed during the second World War. By that time, however, foodgrain exports had fallen to about a quarter of what they had been before the first World War, and consequently the loss of foreign grain markets during the second World War

1.2 Regional foodgrain output and population growth. The regional viewpoint is particularly important in observing the foodgrain output trends because it then becomes apparent that the British India average rate was not typical of any regions, but was, rather, the result of averaging disparate rates of change, as seen in Table 5.2[6] Greater Bengal's steep rate of decline stands alone among the regions; the remaining regions all had rates higher than the British India average. Greater Punjab and United Provinces had average rates about equal to their average rates of population growth. The remaining three regions, however, had rates considerably less than their population growth. For the five regions other than Greater Bengal the combined average foodgrain rate was only slightly less than their population rate (Table 5.2).

The Greater Bengal rate is almost entirely attributable to rice, which constituted 91% of its foodgrain output in the first half of the period, and was still as high as 89% in the second half. For rice alone the average rate of decline was 0.76% per year. Other foodgrain crops, mostly grown in the western portion of the regions, showed no general tendency to offset the rice decline—the three millet crops declined, as also did maize. Output of wheat and barley changed little, but there was a moderate increase in gram.[7]

Since the British India average rate of decline for rice was

was much smaller. In 1942/43 cyclones and floods reduced the Bengal rice crop by about a third; this, coupled with absence of imports from Japanese-controlled Burma, and inadequate relief, led to famine, epidemics (of malaria, cholera, and smallpox) aggravated by widespread starvation which resulted in about a million more deaths than would have been normal for that period; Extract from Inquiry Commission Report on Bengal, 1945, in *Census of India, 1951, op. cit.,* pp. 291–292. These unusual conditions did not, however, spread to other parts of India.

[6] Regional output and population trend rates for each reference decade are given in Appendix Table 5B.

[7] Based on observation of five year moving average graphs of the series given in Appendix Table 3A for Greater Bengal.

0.09% per year, it is evident that the combined rice output trend for the remaining regions was more favorable than in Greater Bengal. In United Provinces the rice output trend was also negative, though not as much as in the Bengal region, about 0.21% per year (geometric mean annual rate between averages of first and second halves of the period). Elsewhere—in Madras, Assam, Central Provinces, and Bombay-Sind—the rice output trends were upward as may be seen in Figure 5.2.

TABLE 5.2

BRITISH INDIA AND REGIONAL FOODGRAIN OUTPUT AND POPULATION : AVERAGE TREND RATES OF CHANGE, AND CHANGE IN REFERENCE DECADE RATES OF CHANGE

(Percent)

Region	10 RD Av., Per Year		Change in RD r's, Per RD		First 4 RD Av., Per Yr.		Last 4 RD Av., Per Yr.	
	FG	P	FG	P	FG	P	FG	P
British India	0.11	0.67	−0.17	0.61	0.61	0.44	0.03	1.12
Greater Bengal	−0.73	0.65	−0.02	0.06	−0.56	0.56	−0.61	0.95
United Provinces	0.35	0.40	−0.23	0.17	1.23	0.00	−0.22	1.07
Madras	0.42	0.80	−0.26	0.06	1.47	0.75	−0.16	1.08
Greater Punjab	1.10	0.93	−0.13	0.16	1.99	0.20	0.92	1.41
Bombay-Sind	0.27	0.71	0.12	0.19	0.34	0.30	0.40	1.45
Central Provinces	0.29	0.58	−0.22	0.10	1.22	0.61	−0.24	0.96
Five Regions	0.47	0.64			1.30	0.34	0.08	1.17

Source : Computed from individual reference decade (RD) rates (r) for foodgrains (FG) and population (P) given in Appendix Tables 5A and 5B. The "five region" rate is a weighted average of regional rates, excluding Greater Bengal, using 1941 populations as weights.

Although the regional trend rates for foodgrain output were generally more favorable than is indicated by the British India average rate, the regions, except for Bombay-Sind, did conform to the British India condition that average rates for the early part of the period were higher than for the later decades. Again this is indicated by the trend rate of change in reference decade rates, negative for all regions except Bombay-Sind, and by the averages of first and last four reference decades. In the earlier decades the regional foodgrain output trends exceeded those of population, except in Greater Bengal where the foodgrain rate was negative. But in the last decades average foodgrain rates were negative in four regions, and even in Greater Punjab and Madras where they were positive, the upward sweep of population rates exceeded the output rates.

The unfavorable disparity between population growth and foodgrain output rates commenced at different times for the various regions, as may be observed from Figure 5.3. Up to about 1911/12 in all regions except Greater Bengal, trend underlying the output series appears to slope upward about as much or more than the population series. In Madras and Bombay-Sind the disparity in trends started about midway during 1911–21; in United Provinces, Greater Punjab, and Central Provinces the turning point was about 1921. In Greater Bengal the disparity is observable almost from the outset, perhaps about 1901/02, and as a consequence, for British India as a whole, the 1911/12 period appears as the beginning of the disparate trends.

What was the extent of decline in per capita foodgrain output in the period of divergent population and output trends? The change in per capita output between the starting year indicated in the above paragraph and 1941 as the end year was computed for each region. Output in the given years was taken as the five year average output centered on those years. Popu-

FIGURE 5.2

RICE OUTPUT BY REGIONS, FIVE YEAR MOVING AVERAGES, SEMILOGARITHMIC SCALE

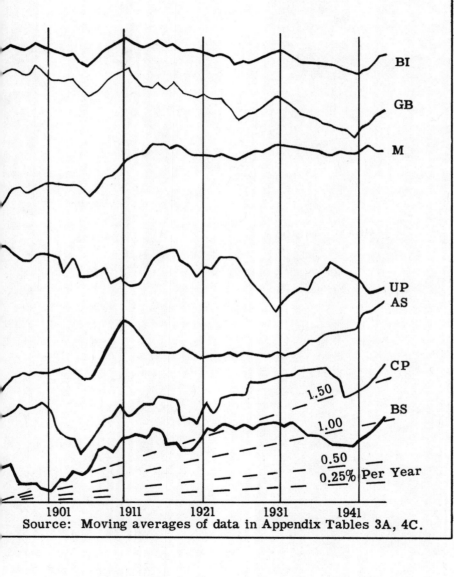

BI

GB

M

UP
AS

CP

BS

1.50

1.00

0.50
0.25% Per Year

1901   1911   1921   1931   1941
Source: Moving averages of data in Appendix Tables 3A, 4C.

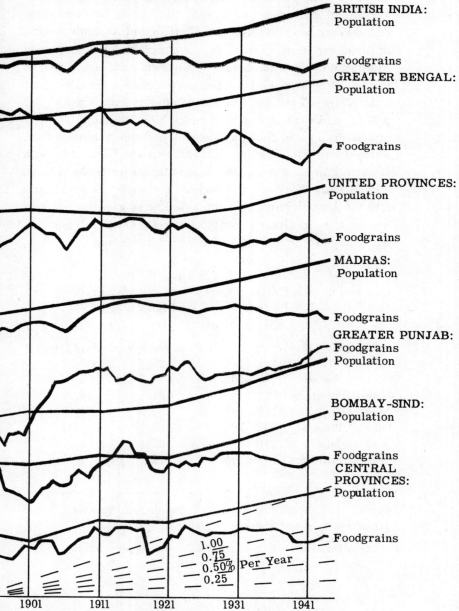

FIGURE 5.3

DECENNIAL POPULATION AND FIVE YEAR MOVING
AVERAGES OF FOODGRAIN OUTPUT FOR BRITISH
INDIA AND REGIONS, SEMILOGARITHMIC SCALE

BRITISH INDIA:
Population

Foodgrains

GREATER BENGAL:
Population

Foodgrains

UNITED PROVINCES:
Population

Foodgrains

MADRAS:
Population

Foodgrains

GREATER PUNJAB:
Foodgrains
Population

BOMBAY-SIND:
Population

Foodgrains
CENTRAL
PROVINCES:
Population

Foodgrains

1.00
0.75
0.50% Per Year
0.25

1901   1911   1921   1931   1941

ource: Population - Appendix Table 4D; foodgrains -
        moving averages of data in Appendix Table 4C.

lation for 1916 was interpolated between 1911 and 1921 using a constant geometric mean rate of growth between these census years. Since in this study, Ganjam and Koraput districts of the newly formed Orissa Province were retained as part of Madras, and since Sambalpur was likewise retained as part of Central Provinces, Greater Bengal population for 1941 was reduced by 4.5 million, Madras population was raised by 3.0 million, and Central Provinces raised by 1.5 million.[8]

The declines in foodgrain output per capita ranged from about twenty to forty percent, as seen in Table 5.3, with Greater Punjab and Greater Bengal at the extremes. On an annual basis, however, the declines were steepest in Madras and the United Provinces. But a decline of even one percent per year, as in Greater Punjab, would seem sizeable, sufficiently large to be noticed within an adult lifetime.

TABLE 5.3

DECLINE IN PER CAPITA OUTPUT BETWEEN SELECTED YEARS,
BRITISH INDIA AND REGIONS
(Percent)

Region	Years	Total Decline	Decline per Year
British India	1911–1941	29	1.14
Greater Bengal	1901–1941	38	1.18
United Provinces	1921–1941	24	1.36
Madras	1916–1941	30	1.40
Greater Punjab	1921–1941	18	1.00
Bombay-Sind	1916–1941	26	1.21
Central Provinces	1921–1941	19	1.05

Source : Foodgrain output (five year average centered on above years), Appendix Table 4C; population, Appendix Table 4D except as noted above.

[8] Rounded figures based on the 1941 census for those districts.

1.3 Trend in availability of foodgrains. The availability of grain for consumption depended on output, the flow of trade, and other factors which are assumed to have been constant over the period—the nutritive quality of the grains, and the proportion of output wasted or used for seed. Exports and imports for each year were aggregated by tonnage, with coastal shipments involving Burma up to 1936 counted as part of foreign trade, in order to determine British India's net flow of grain trade. Trade flow, imports minus exports, was added to output to construct availability series of aggregate food-grain tonnage, given in Appendix Tables *5C* for British India and *5D* for Greater Bengal. Trend rates of change were then obtained for each reference decade in British India and Greater Bengal, both for availability and, for comparative purposes, also for output when aggregated on a similar ton-nage basis; these reference decade rates are given in Appendix Table *5E.*

Trade data were taken from the *Annual Seaborne Foreign Trade of British India* and *Annual Statement of Coastal Trade and Navigation of British India.*[9] However, since all the major seaports of India were in the British Provinces, a part of the reported exports originated in the Indian States and some of the imports were destined for the States. If the State's portion of net flow was the same as their part of India's total population, then about a quarter of the flow added to British India output should be eliminated. It seems doubtful that the proportion would be so high, however, since the States were in general less commercialized than the Provinces. No effort was

[9] Issued by the Department of Commercial Intelligence and Statistics. Overland net foreign trade was not included in the study. Its effect was negligible; during 1925/26–39/40 it amounted to an average inflow of 18,000 tons per year, according to data obtained from the *Statistical Abstract for British India* series issued by the same department.

made to adjust for this complexity, nor for the effect of inter-regional trade between the States and Provinces.

The main conclusion from the comparison of these trends is that the change in availability, after allowing for the international trade flows, was only slightly less unfavorable than the change in output. In British India and Greater Bengal the average rates of change are somewhat more favorable for availability than for output, as may be seen in Table 5.4[10] Since the effect of trade was relatively small, the same pattern of worsened trends in the later decades compared with the earlier part of the period, shown in Table 5.2, is also seen in Table 5.4. India (excluding Burma) had a net outflow of grains up to the first world war and a net inflow thereafter; the first and last four reference decade average rates imply

TABLE 5.4

BRITISH INDIA AND GREATER BENGAL AVERAGE TREND RATES OF CHANGE IN AGGREGATE TONNAGE OF FOODGRAIN OUTPUT AND AVAILABILITY AFTER TRADE
(Percent per Year)

	All 10 Reference Decades		First 4 Ref. Decades		Last 4 Ref. Decades	
	Output	Avail-ability	Output	Avail-ability	Output	Avail-ability
British India	0.10	0.18	0.80	0.83	−0.18	−0.15
Greater Bengal	−0.57	−0.46	−0.14	−0.01	−0.42	−0.36

Source : Computed from rates in Appendix Table 5E.

[10] It is interesting to compare the trend measures obtained when the foodgrain crops are aggregated by using price weights for each crop, as in Table 5.2, and when aggregated by tonnage, as in Table 5.4. The 10 RD average for British India is almost identical, 0.11% and 0.10% respectively, but for Greater Bengal the rates were not so similar, −0.73% and −0.57%. Average first 4 RD rates for British India were 0.61% and 0.80%, and for the last 4 RD's, 0.03% and −0.18% respectively. Greater Bengal 1st 4 RD average rates were −0.56% and −0.14%, and for the last 4 RD's, −0.61% and −0.42%.

that the net outflow was decreasing during the first period and the net inflow during the last period was increasing. The magnitudes of these flows, compared with output, were not large enough, however, to make the availability trends substantially improved over output.[11]

It is interesting to note, however, that when interregional trade within India is considered, as well as international trade, the effect of the trade flows on Greater Bengal appears to have brought a more substantial improvement in the availability trend. Interregional trade flow data were available only up to 1920/21 and for some later years (Appendix Table 5D). When international trade and output are considered for this period, the average of reference decade rates (Appendix Table 5E) was -0.01% per year, but when interregional trade was also included the average trend in availability was 0.11% per year, compared with -0.14% for output. Unfortunately, it should be appreciated that improved interregional trade flow from the viewpoint of Greater Bengal trends must have meant worsened availability trends in some other regions.

To what extent did the small improvement in availability trends as compared with output affect the view of per capita decline (discussed in the previous section)? For British India, from 1911 to 1941, based on the five year averages centered on those years, the decline in per capita foodgrain output (when aggregated on a tonnage basis) was 29%, the same as in Table 5.3, and the decline in per capita foodgrain availability was 26%, or 0.83% per year. For Greater Bengal, from 1901 to 1941, the total decline in per capita foodgrain tonnage of output was 27%, and in per capita foodgrain availability 24%, or 1.04% per year. Change in the grain

---

[11] Declining net outflow in the early part of the period made the availability trend more favorable than the output trend, but grain available in the early years was less than output of grain.

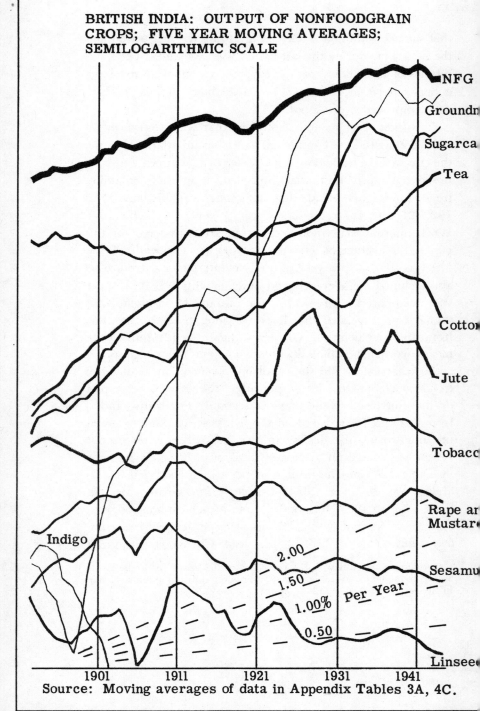

FIGURE 5.4

BRITISH INDIA: OUTPUT OF NONFOODGRAIN
CROPS; FIVE YEAR MOVING AVERAGES;
SEMILOGARITHMIC SCALE

NFG

Groundn

Sugarca

Tea

Cotto

Jute

Tobacc

Rape an
Mustar

2.00

1.50

Per Year

1.00%

0.50

Indigo

Sesamu

Linsee

1901   1911   1921   1931   1941

Source: Moving averages of data in Appendix Tables 3A, 4C.

trade flows clearly did little to offset the adversity caused by decline in per capita foodgrain output.

2. Nonfoodgrain Output

2.1 British India trends for individual crops and aggregate nonfoodgrain crop output. A glance at Figure 5.4 and Table 5.5 shows the diversity of trends among the nonfoodgrain crops: one crop, indigo, plunged rapidly downward; another, linseed, declined more moderately; three—sesamum, rape and mustard, and tobacco—showed scarcely any upward trend; jute increased at a moderate rate; the remaining crops expanded at quite high rates of increase, especially groundnut and tea. Two crops, tea and tobacco, showed almost no fluctuation remaining after the annual series were converted to the five year moving averages, while others, especially jute and linseed, exhibited deep undulations, even in the five year averages. A marked acceleration in rates of increase is apparent for sugarcane, and an even more marked retardation in rates is indicated for groundnut.

Varying conditions of foreign trade affected the crops and account for much of this diversity.[12] The foreign market, and even the domestic market, for indigo was cut away by introduction of German synthetic dye in 1897. Linseed, of which nearly three-quarters of output was exported during some periods, steadily lost foreign markets to Argentina, where yield per acre was double that of India, and price (though also quality) were lower.[13] Sesamum and rapeseed also lost most of their foreign market, which accounted for as much as a

[12] Jathar and Beri, *op. cit.*, I, 137 ff, provide data for part of this section, in addition to the trade series collected for this study.

[13] India, Office of the Agricultural Marketing Advisor, *Report on the Marketing of Linseed in India* (Delhi: Manager of Publications, 1938), pp. 1, 10, 25, 264.

quarter of output in the early part of the period. Tobacco was generally consumed domestically; exports, though less than one percent of output, were rising. Jute, almost all of which

TABLE 5.5

BRITISH INDIA AVERAGE TREND RATES OF CHANGE, AND CHANGE IN REFERENCE DECADE RATES OF CHANGE, FOR INDIVIDUAL NONFOODGRAIN CROPS AND AGGREGATE OUTPUT
(Percent)

Crops	10 RD Av. (Per Year)	Change in RD Rates (Per RD)	First 4 RD Average (Per Year)	Last 4 RD Average (Per Year)
Aggregate nonfoodgrains	1.31	–0.13	1.66	1.08
Sugarcane	1.30	0.42	0.22	3.00
Cotton	1.30	–0.46	2.84	–0.01
Jute	0.27	–0.49	2.13	–0.72
Tea	2.74	–0.27	4.24	2.08
Tobacco	0.03	0.06	–0.29	0.32
Groundnut	6.26	–0.76	8.74	3.24
Rape and Mustard	0.07	–0.04	0.59	0.03
Sesamum	0.09	–0.33	1.22	–0.38
Linseed	–0.47	–0.20	0.52	–1.27
Indigo	–6.19	0.59	–6.02	–6.27

Source : Computed from individual reference decade (RD) rates given in Appendix Table 5A.

was exported, either in raw or manufactured form,[14] expanded rapidly until the first World War, when it lost one of its two

[14] Of the jute manufactured in Indian mills, between 80% to 90% was exported according to data given in the industrial production and foreign trade series for 1936/37 and 1940/41. India, Department of Commercial Intelligence and Statistics, *Statistical Abstract of British India*, 1936/37 to 1940/41, 19th issue, pp. 434, 507.

major markets, Germany; lack of shipping also affected trade but apparently this was not the major factor since cotton exports were not greatly affected by the war.[15] Output fell again, with prices, in the early 1930 depression years.

The remaining four crops were the rapid risers and trade appears to have been a large factor in their expansion. Tea exports, about ninety percent of its output, approximately doubled over the period; the only major competitor, China, probably was not in a position, at least because of disruption, to take advantage of expanding tea consumption, mostly in British markets. The phenomenal advance of groundnut, about a quarter of which was exported in some periods, is called "one of the great triumphs of the Government Agricultural Department,"[16] which successfully introduced disease-resisting varieties from Senegal and Mozambique,[17] and provided a crop for lands "often where practically nothing else will grow."[18] Retardation of the rapid rates of increase for this crop would be expected as the crop came to compete for better lands capable of growing other crops; in addition, exports dropped during the first World War and again in the 1930 depression years. About half the cotton crop was exported in many years, and exports rose rapidly up to the first World War; growth thereafter was slower, partly because of the depression and probably also because of increased competition from other cotton-growing countries, and reduced exports to Japan after the Sino-Japanese war in 1937.[19] The domestic cotton manufacturing industry provided a growing market, however, offsetting some of the export losses. Ex-

[15] According to data in Jathar and Beri, *op. cit.,* I, 163, cotton exports declined 10% from 1909/10–13/14 to 1914/15–18/19.

[16] L. Dudley Stamp, *Asia: A Regional and Economic Geography* (8th ed.; London: Methuen & Co. Ltd., 1950), pp. 219–220.

[17] Jathar and Beri, *op. cit.,* p. 152.

[18] Stamp, *loc. cit.*

[19] Jathar and Beri, *op. cit.,* p. 153.

panded government irrigation works in Punjab and Sind, a reflection of the government's desire to export more cotton, especially to Britain, facilitated the cotton expansion. The upward jump in sugarcane output is directly related to government policy; a protective tariff was levied to discourage imports,[20] which had increased several-fold up to about a third of British India output by 1931, especially from Java, where the yield per acre was four times that of India.[21] By five years after the tariff, imports were almost eliminated. Indian producers quickly expanded domestic output to fill the former import market.

Trade was not the only influence on the crop trends. The deep trough in output for a number of crops between 1901 and 1911, seen in Figure 5.4, may largely be ascribed to the very unfavorable monsoon of 1905, drought in northern and western India and floods in northeastern India. Again in 1918 and 1920 the monsoons had an unusually adverse effect on output. The downturn after the outbreak of war in 1939 was partly caused by reduced exports, and partly, too, by the Grow More Food Campaign, started in 1942, which was, in turn, partly caused by the cutting off of grain imports from Burma.

The average rate of 1.31% for aggregate nonfoodgrain output is almost identical to the rate for sugarcane and cotton, the top two leading crops in value of output. Very high rates for tea and groundnut offset the low rates for the other six crops. Reference decade growth rates in output were slowing down except for three crops, of which only sugarcane had a large effect on the aggregate series; acceleration for the latter crop was not gradual but resulted from the changed trade

[20] Jathar and Beri, op. cit., I, 145.
[21] M. P. Gandhi, The Indian Sugar Industry (Calcutta: G. N. Mitra, 1934), pp. 93, 207.

policy later in the period. The deceleration for indigo meant that the rapid rates of decline were slowing down as the level of output became very small. Retardation for most crops is also indicated by the lower average rates of increase in the last four as compared with the first four reference decades. Despite retardation, aggregate nonfoodgrain output at these rates would have been sufficiently rapid to more than double over the whole period.

2.2 *Regional nonfoodgrain output.* The high average rate for British India aggregate nonfoodgrain output was representative of five regions, Greater Bengal being the exception, as seen in Table 5.6 and as may also be seen in Figure 5.5. In United Provinces and Central Provinces the rate was close to one percent, but in Madras and Greater Punjab it approached two and one-half percent per year. Rates of retardation were slight in Greater Bengal and United Provinces, but in Madras and especially Central Provinces they were sizable.

Regional variation in rates partly reflects the relative importance of the particular nonfoodgrain crops in each region and the British India trend for each crop. In United Provinces sugarcane comprised about half of nonfoodgrain output value and oilseeds, generally declining, most of the remainder. Madras was the major region of groundnut production; output there reached about half of the nonfoodgrain total. Sugarcane, cotton, and tobacco, of about equal importance, expanded considerably in that province. Madras was the leading tobacco-producing region in British India; a high quality was produced there for which there were export markets. Oilseeds were of small importance in Madras. For Greater Punjab cotton and sugarcane, both of which rose rapidly in the region, constituted most of nonfoodgrain output, while oilseeds and tobacco were only about a quarter of the total. Cotton ac-

TABLE 5.6

BRITISH INDIA AND REGIONAL AVERAGE TREND RATES OF CHANGE
IN AGGREGATE NONFOODGRAIN OUTPUT, AND TREND IN REFERENCE
DECADE RATES OF CHANGE
(Percent)

Region	10 RD Av. (Per Year)	Change in RD Rates (Per RD)	First 4 RD Average (Per Year)	Last 4 RD Average (Per Year)
British India	1.31	–0.13	1.66	1.08
Greater Bengal	0.23	–0.02	0.49	0.55
United Provinces	0.92	–0.06	1.29	1.42
Madras	2.37	–0.22	2.86	1.32
Greater Punjab	2.40	–0.14	1.56	1.80
Bombay-Sind	1.44	0.12	2.84	1.80
Central Provinces	0.97	–0.68	3.11	–0.84

Source : Computed from individual reference decade (RD)
rates given in Appendix Tables 5A and 5B.

counted for over half of nonfoodgrain output in Bombay-Sind,
with sugarcane and groundnut as most of the remainder—
all three crops expanded rapidly as was characteristic for
British India as a whole. In Central Provinces cotton dominated with over three-quarters of nonfoodgrain output; the
crop appears, in Figure 5.5, to have just about reached its
maximum level of expansion quite early in the period, and
to have started decline sooner than elsewhere, judging from
Figures 5.4. The extreme difference between averages for the
first and last four reference decades, and the rapid rate of
retardation, as compared with other regions, in Table 5.6,
is remarkable.

In Greater Bengal the main nonfoodgrain crop, about half
of the total, was jute; since virtually all the jute was grown
in this region, the low average rate of increase, 0.27% per

FIGURE 5.5

BRITISH INDIA AND REGIONAL NONFOODGRAIN CROP OUTPUT,
FIVE YEAR MOVING AVERAGES, SEMILOGARITHMIC SCALE

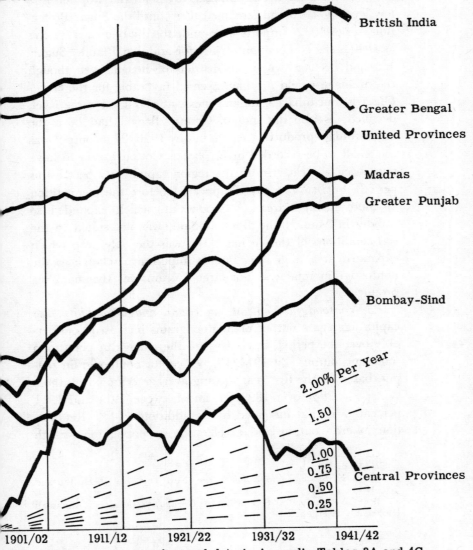

Source: Moving averages of annual data in Appendix Tables 3A and 4C.

year, was almost the same as the rate for British India. Sugarcane, ranking next in importance, increased at 0.42% per
year, less than for British India as a whole; the crop fell to a
low level by 1910 and remained there until the Sugar Protection Act of 1932. Imports were undoubtedly one cause of this
as well as the competition of jute for additional land.[22] Sugar-
can had been grown in all districts of Bengal even though
the drainage would not have seemed favorable for the crop.[23]
Oilseeds and tobacco, ranking next, at about the same level,
declined, as also did indigo. Greater Bengal had been the
largest indigo producing region, but by 1926/27 its output was
too small to be recorded in *Estimates*. Cotton is said to have
once been a great crop in the region (apparently before this
period), but it "virtually disappeared before the competition
of more favored areas."[24] Groundnut, which expanded so
rapidly in Madras and Bombay-Sind, was not suited to the
soil conditions of this region.[25] Tea was the only crop which
expanded at a high rate, but its importance relative to the
nonfoodgrain total was not large (Assam was the main tea
producer.)

2.3 *Nonfoodgrain output per capita and availability.* Per
capita aggregate output of nonfoodgrains increased considerably over the period, in contrast to the change in per capita
foodgrain output. By 1911/12, per capita nonfoodgrain output, based on the five year moving average centered on those
years, was 28% over 1893/94, and between 1911 and 1941
per capita output increased by an additional 14%. Retardation in crop output and acceleration in population growth

[22] Gandhi, *op. cit.*, p. 90.
[23] *Ibid.*, p. 160.
[24] O. H. K. Spate, *India and Pakistan* (New York: H. P. Dutton and
Co., 1954), p. 527.
[25] B. V. N. Naidu and S. Hariharan, *Groundnut* (Madras: Annamali
University, 1941), p. 2.

combined to make the percentage increase in per capita output in the second part of the period much less than in the first.

Welfare of the population, to the extent that it was affected by the consumption of the nonfoodgrain crops, depended on availability, not simply output. Much of nonfoodgrain output was grown for export; these exports helped provide payment for imports of other goods, the availability of which was likewise important to welfare. It is nonetheless revealing to observe the trend in availability of the nonfoodgrain crops since they have an important part in consumption. However, for at least two crops availability does not seem particularly relevant: indigo was not significant because the chemical dyes had largely taken its place, and jute does not seem to be of direct significance either, although some burlap and bagging was needed domestically; almost all this crop was exported whether in raw or manufactured form.

The availability trends in Table 5.7 were constructed in a less refined fashion than for the foodgrains: the period for which trade data were obtained, 1899/00–1946/47, was divided into two halves of twenty-four years each, annual output and net foreign trade of British India in each half was averaged and aggregated by weighting each crop with the 1924/25–28/29 average prices, the geometric mean annual rate between the two averages was taken as the average rate of change in availability. Imports and exports of Burma were taken out of the British India trade series, but coastal trade between Burma and British India Provinces was not considered. Imports of sugar, tea, cotton, and tobacco were included in measurement of the trade flow; for other crops the imports were negligible. Exports of imported foreign commodities were also accounted for, except tobacco, for which re-exports were negligible. Exports of sesamum, rape and mustard, and groundnut do not include shipments in oil form;

TABLE 5.7

BRITISH INDIA AVERAGE LEVELS OF NONFOODGRAIN CROP OUTPUT
AND GROSS AVAILABILITY, AND RATES OF CHANGE, BETWEEN
1899/00–1922/23 AND 1923/24–46/47

	Annual Average 1899/00– 22/23	*Million Rupees 1923/24– 46/47*	*Rate of Change Per cent per Year*
Sugarcane, Output	550	874	2.03
Availability	632	944	1.65
Cotton, Output	441	552	0.94
Availability	223	246	0.42
Tea, Output	416	627	1.85
Availability	9	94	10.55
Groundnut, Output	103	442	6.24
Availability	72	343	6.61
Tobacco, Output	193	232	0.45
Availability	190	210	0.18
Sesamum, Output	93	81	–0.61
Availability	73	79	0.34
Rape and Mustard, Output	239	220	–0.35
Availability	199	205	0.01
Linseed, Output	77	65	–0.73
Availability	19	24	1.06
Above Eight Crops, Output	2121	3116	1.62
Availability	1437	2167	1.73

Notes

See above section 2.3 for methods of construction.

Source : Computed from output data in Appendix Table *3A*
and trade data obtained from *Annual Statement of Seaborne
Foreign Trade of British India* series.

these were not large enough to affect the trends. Cotton availability takes in imports and exports of manufactured cotton converted to raw cotton equivalent, as well as output and trade in raw cotton.[26] As pointed out in the discussion of availability of foodgrains, trade of British India seaports includes exports originating in the Indian States and imports destined for those areas. The output rates in Table 5.7 differ somewhat from those in Table 5.6 because of the difference in methods of computation and because the first eight years are not included in the present table. Comparison of output and availability trends in Table 5.7 probably serves well enough to indicate the difference between these two trends, if not the actual rates.

In aggregate it appears that there was not much difference between the trend in availability as compared with output, though availability improved somewhat faster than output. In both periods availability was much less than output, 67.8% and 69.6% of output for the first and second halves respectively. Despite the large trade flow, it seems surprising that the nonfoodgrain availability trend would be so similar to the output trend.

Availability for three crops—sugar, cotton, and tobacco—was not expanding as rapidly as output. The difference in output and availability trends for cotton is relatively large and in view of the population growth rate it appears that per capita availability of cotton was declining. Trend in oilseed availability was apparently more favorable than was indicated by output. There seems to be no question that output as well as availability of groundnut increased rapidly; exports evidently did not increase as rapidly as output. The large difference be-

---

[26] Yards of manufactured cotton were converted to raw cotton on the basis of 1 yard to 0.25 lbs., from data given in W. S. and E. S. Woytinsky, *World Population and Production* (New York: The Twentieth Century Fund, 1953), p. 1070, which cites U.N.'s F.A.O. data. Ten percent waste was estimated in conversion of cotton to cloth and yarn.

tween output and availability rates for tea is puzzling; if Indian States' output of tea, which rose from about 5% of British India output to about 10% from the beginning to the end of the period, were also included, both output and availability rates would be somewhat larger. The percentage increase in per capita tea availability was apparently very great, but the absolute magnitudes remained small; in the second half it was not much more than a half pound per capita per year.

3. All-Crop Output

3.1 Regional trends and population growth. Trends for the aggregate of all-crop output, given in Table *5.8,* reflect the foodgrain and nonfoodgrain trends, and their weighting, in each of the regions. Two important observations may be made concerning the all-crop output trends.

First, on the average over the whole period, there was relatively little difference between the rates of expansion in all-crop output and population. In five of the regions the ten-reference decade average rate showed either little difference, or more rapid growth in crop output, as in Greater Punjab. The weighty exception was Greater Bengal where the all-crop output trend declined only somewhat less steeply than its foodgrain trend; this influence pulled the British India average rate down considerably below that of population. In most of British India, however, the average output and population rates were in close balance; a crude combination of rates for the other five regions, (Table *5.8*), suggests that the output rate even exceeded that of population. Evidently the high nonfoodgrain rates of expansion were sufficiently large to offset the low foodgrain rates, except in the Greater Bengal region.

The second observation qualifies this long period similarity of output and population rates. All-crop output rates for reference decades were in general decelerating while population growth was accelerating, as seen in the trend rates of change in reference decade rates, Table *5.8*. Similarity in the full

TABLE 5.8

BRITISH INDIA AND REGIONAL ALL-CROP OUTPUT AND POPULATION, AVERAGE TREND RATES OF CHANGE, AND CHANGE IN REFERENCE DECADE RATES OF CHANGE

Region	10 RD Av., Per Year		Change in RD r's Per RD		First 4 RD Av., Per Yr.		Last 4 RD Av., Per Yr.	
	AC	P	AC	P	AC	P	AC	P
British India	0.37	0.67	-0.07	0.11	0.84	0.44	0.35	1.12
Greater Bengal	-0.45	0.65	0.01	0.06	-0.40	0.56	-0.23	0.95
United Provinces	0.42	0.40	-0.15	0.17	1.02	0.00	0.27	1.07
Madras	0.98	0.80	-0.21	0.06	1.71	0.75	0.42	1.08
Greater Punjab	1.57	0.93	-0.10	0.16	2.17	0.20	1.30	1.41
Bombay-Sind	0.66	0.71	0.11	0.19	0.70	0.30	0.79	1.45
Central Provinces	0.48	0.58	-0.37	0.10	1.73	0.61	-0.56	0.96
Last Five Regions	0.80	0.64			1.41	0.34	0.48	1.17

Source : Computed from individual reference decade (RD) rates (r) for all-crop (AC) output and population (P) given in Appendix Tables *5A* and *5B*. The "five region" rate is a weighted average of regional rates, excluding Greater Bengal, using 1941 populations as weights.

period average output and population rates, or higher average output rates as compared with population, results from averaging high crop output rates for the first part of the period with considerably lower rates in the last part, and averaging low population rates in the first part with higher rates in the last part. In the first four reference decades, average rates of

crop output exceeded those of population in all regions except
Greater Bengal. The British India percentage rate of crop
output expansion was about double that of population, and
for the five regions other than Greater Bengal the crop output
percentage growth rate was four times larger than the population rate. But in the last four reference decades the average
output rate was less than the population rate in all regions;
the percentage rate for output was not only much lower than
the average for the first four reference decades, but it was only
half as much as the percentage rate for population. It should
be appreciated, however, that in relative form the differences
in rates appear much smaller; the British India average annual
rate of population increase in the last four reference decades,
1.0112 per year, is only 0.77% larger than the crop rate,
1.0035, in that period.

The chronology of the downturning of per capita all-crop
output in the different regions may be observed from Figure
5.6 by comparing the slope of population change with the
slope underlying the moving average series for output; when
the slopes change from output being steeper or parallel to
population, to output less steep (or downward) compared with
population, per capita output turns downward. In Greater
Bengal this appears to start with the very beginning of the
period, but for the other regions the downturns come much
later. Starting about 1921/22 in United Provinces, Central
Provinces, and perhaps Greater Punjab, the population
growth lines appear to diverge unfavorably from the output
series. But this does not occur in Madras and Bombay-Sind
until about 1931/32. Despite these later downturns, British
India per capita apparently started to decline as early as about
1911/12, reflecting the pull of the Greater Bengal region.
Except for the latter region it thus appears that per capita
output did not turn down until after the middle of the period.

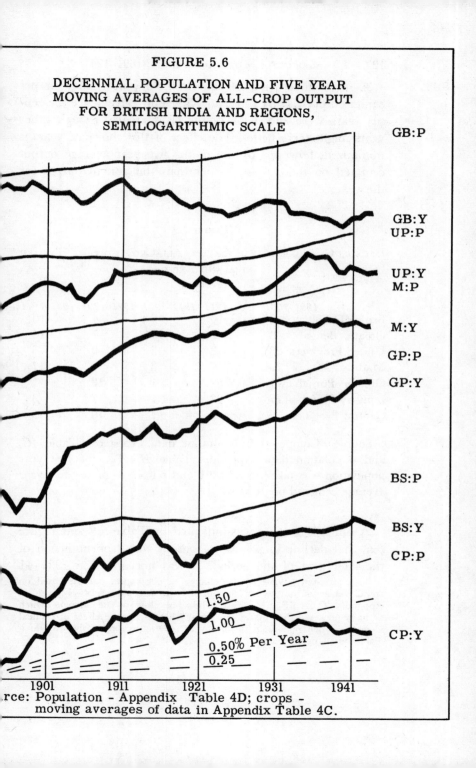

FIGURE 5.6

DECENNIAL POPULATION AND FIVE YEAR
MOVING AVERAGES OF ALL-CROP OUTPUT
FOR BRITISH INDIA AND REGIONS,
SEMILOGARITHMIC SCALE

GB:P

GB:Y
UP:P

UP:Y
M:P

M:Y

GP:P

GP:Y

BS:P

BS:Y

CP:P

1.50

1.00

0.50% Per Year

0.25

CP:Y

1901   1911   1921   1931   1941

rce: Population - Appendix Table 4D; crops -
    moving averages of data in Appendix Table 4C.

A more direct view of the chronology of change in per capita output[27] is given in Table 5.9. For convenience the census years were chosen as points of reference, though other years might serve better. The effect of this choice of years is minimized, however, by use of the five year average output centered on those years, rather than the annual output for the year.

TABLE 5.9

DECADE CHANGES IN PER CAPITA ALL-CROP OUTPUT, BRITISH INDIA AND REGIONS
(Percent)

	1891–1901	1901–1911	1911–1921	1921–1931	1931–1941
British India	2	10	–5	–4	–10
Greater Bengal	–8	2	–15	–7	–14
United Provinces	23	8	3	–8	–6
Madras	19	7	3	3	–17
Greater Punjab	1	42	1	–12	–1
Bombay-Sind	–17	28	1	1	–8
Central Provinces	32	–2	1	–10	–23

Source : Computed from output data, Appendix Table *4C*, and population data, Appendix Table *4D*. For the first year population was taken as of 1891 and output as of the five year average centered on 1893.

Again it is seen, as was indicated by Table *5.8* and Figure *5.6*, that decline in per capita output was a phenomenon of the later part of the period. It was not until the 1931–41

[27] An alternative view of the change in per capita output, based on trend values of output and population at selected years, is given in Appendix Table *5F*. This view, while less close to the changes which actually occurred, has the advantage of eliminating the effect of cyclical elements which remain in the five year moving average series on which Table *5.9* is partly based.

decade that decline occurred in all regions. In the previous decade, two regions, Madras and Bombay-Sind, showed slight increases in per capita output. Up to 1921, except for Greater Bengal, per capita output was generally rising, with the notable exception of the first decade in Central Provinces.

When the major downturns came, their severity was most intense in Central Provinces and Madras, where per capita output declined at rates of 1.78% and 1.85% per year in the period after the downturn. In United Provinces and Greater Punjab the decline was least sharp, 0.67% and 0.63% per year respectively. In Bombay-Sind the decline was 0.83%, and in Greater Bengal over the fifty year period it was 0.91% per year. For British India, during 1911-1941 per capita output declined at 0.72% per year.

3.2 All-crop availability. Little difference between all-crop output and availability trend rates is to be expected, since, as has been seen in Tables *5.4* and *5.7,* the differences were small for both foodgrains and nonfoodgrains. To measure the difference for all-crops, the foodgrain and nonfoodgrain crop groups were combined on the basis of their output weighted by 1924/25–28/29 prices in each half of the 1899/00–1946/47 period. The nonfoodgrain data were taken from Table *5.7.* Foodgrain data from Table *5.4* were made comparable by multiplying aggregate foodgrain tonnage by a weight of Rs. 150.96 per ton (based on giving the rice price a weight of 4 parts, wheat 2 parts, and other foodgrains at Rs. 119.0 also 2 parts). The combined data were averaged for each half of the 1899/00–1946/47 period, and the geometric mean annual rate of increase between the two averages was taken as the all-crop rate of change.

The trend in availability of all-crops, measured as above, turns out to be the same as the trend in output of all-crops, as seen in Table *5.10* below. Availability trends for foodgrains and nonfoodgrain separately showed more improvement than output trends, but when the two crop groups are combined it may seem paradoxical that the result is an availability trend rate which is the same as the output rate. In the availability trend, foodgrains, with their negative trend rate, have a heavier weight, or share of the crops available for home use, than in the output trend. Availability was about ten percent less than output on the average in each period; the proportion of output exported was greater for nonfoodgrains than for foodgrains.

TABLE 5.10

BRITISH INDIA AVERAGE LEVELS OF AGGREGATE CROP OUTPUT AND AVAILABILITY, AND RATES OF CHANGE, BETWEEN 1899/00– 22/23 AND 1923/24–46/47

| | Average Annual Levels, Million Rupees | | Rate of Change per Year |
	1899/00– 22/23	1923/24– 46/47	
All-crop : Output	9813	10447	0.26%
Availability	9009	9595	0.26
Foodgrain : Output	7692	7331	–0.20
Availability	7572	7428	–0.08
Nonfoodgrain : Output	2121	3116	1.62
Availability	1437	2167	1.73

Source : Data from Tables 5.4 and 5.7.

3.3 All-crop output and national income. Change in per capita national income can now be explored. In the period before 1911/12, since per capita agricultural output appears to have been increasing, it seems likely that per capita national income was rising. But in the period after 1911/12 per capita agricultural output is estimated to have declined at 0.72% per year. In that period population increased at about one percent per year. The share of agriculture in total output may be approximated at about 60% for the beginning of this period.[28] Given these conditions, for per capita national income to have been constant in the period from 1911/12 to 1946/47, nonagricultural output would have had to increase at about 2% per year.

Whether this is likely to have occurred is a question which cannot be pursued here, and, indeed, cannot easily be pursued elsewhere in view of the limited data available. A 2% per year increase in total nonagricultural output does not seem implausible if one thinks of the growth of "factory establishments" (large scale) and mining,[29] but this component was only 15% of nonagricultural output in the 1948/49–50/51 national income estimates for India.[30] Small enterprises, including cottage industries, comprised about 20%. Another 35% consisted of commerce, finance (1%), and transportation (railroad transportation 4%). The remaining 30% of nonagricultural output was composed of about equal parts of professional, government, and house property service, plus a small part for domestic service. That these sectors, including 85% of nonagricultural output, grew fast enough to have permitted this 2% average growth rate and constant per capita income in the period after 1911/12 seems questionable.[31]

[28] In the *Final Report of the National Income Committee, op. cit.,* p. 106, agricultural output comprised 48% of national income at the factor cost level; in Pakistan the figure was probably higher. In the earlier years agriculture would have been relatively more important.

[29] According to data assembled by Surendra J. Patel, "Long-term Changes in Output and Income in India: 1896–1960," *Indian Economic Journal, V.* 3 (January 1958), p. 242, this component tripled in output during the period 1906–15 to 1936–45. Per capita income declined from index 105 for 1916–25 to 92 in 1936–45 in Patel's study; the income measure was built up with heavy dependence on my earlier study of agricultural output.

[30] *Final Report of the National Income Committee, loc. cit.*

[31] According to a per capita national income series constructed by K. Mukerji, *op. cit.,* pp. 109–110, for the Indian Union area, 1900/01–

1952/53, average per capita income increased from Rs. 269 during 1911/12–28/29 to 271 during 1929//30–46/47; however, if measured from 1916/17, a slight decline would be registered.

Mukerji's estimate of the nonagricultural sector is based on an index of industrial activity which he constructed with weights as follows: industrial production, weight 53 (cotton manufacturing 9, jute 6, steel ingots 5, pig iron 8, cement 5, paper 3, breweries 1, sugar 5, mining 11); internal trade 23; financial statistics 14; foreign trade 6; shipping 4. The series were also presented at the Second Annual Indian Conference on Research in National Income, in 1962.

VI

Acreage Change

1. Change in British India crop acreage : expansion in all-crop acreage, sources of increased acreage. 2. Regional all-crop acreage : expansion and its sources, regional rates of expansion and the availability of land, the decline in aggregate Greater Bengal acreage. 3. Foodgrain acreage : change in foodgrain aggregate and individual crop acreage at the British India level, regional foodgrain acreage rates. 4. Nonfoodgrain acreage : changes in nonfoodgrain aggregate and individual crop acreage at the British India level, regional nonfoodgrain acreage rates.

CHANGE IN OUTPUT MAY BE attributed to the dual determinants of acreage and yield per acre. The character of acreage change is discussed in this chapter, followed, in the next two chapters, by an examination of the changes in yield per acre.

1. Change in British India Crop Acreage

1.1 Expansion in all-crop acreage. Acreage expansion was the predominant means of obtaining increased output. Its relative importance is indicated by the almost identical (ten-reference decade average) rates of increase for all-crop output, 0.37%, and all-crop acreage, 0.40% per year. If there were no change in average yield per acre the acreage and output rates of change would be identical; since the rates were almost the same it may be expected that the average rate of change in yield per acre was quite small.

The expansion of acreage was slowing down. For the first four reference decades, the average rate, 0.67%, was higher than the ten-reference decade average, and in the last four reference decades the average rate was down to 0.35% per year. The trend rate of decline in reference decade rates of expansion was 0.04% per reference decade. Gradual expansion of acreage is apparent in the five year moving averages of Figure 6.1; a turning point in the rate of expansion may be perceived about midway in the 1911–21 decade.

These findings—widening of cropland area rather than heightening of acre productivity, and slowdown in acreage expansion despite accelerated growth in population—conform to what might be expected in a long-settled tradition-dominated country. Raising the level of yield per acre generally involves use of improved technology, though an increase in the proportion of labor to land may also have this effect. Expansion of acreage is often less dependent on change in technology, and consequently appears as the more likely means of increased output. Much of the acreage expansion, however, was in dry western India where construction of large dams made possible by modern technology (and much capital), opened up vast areas to cultivation. The slowdown in acreage expansion may be attributed partly to the increasingly inferior quality of the remaining sources of additional land, and partly to the low geographical mobility of labor which blocked a more intensive seeking-out of the better lands among those which were still not cultivated.

1.2 Sources of increased acreage. The increase in all-crop acreage may be ascribed to three possible sources: double-cropping of lands already cultivated, transfer of lands from other crops (included in the total area sown as reported in *Agricultural Statistics* but not in all-crop acreage, such as fodder crops, fruits and vegetables, other foodgrains, other oilseeds, condiments, and others comprising about twenty percent of total area sown), and the cultivation of lands not previously used for crops (reported in *Agricultural Statistics* under the headings of not available for cultivation, cultivable waste, fallow, and forest).

The changes in average annual acreage under each of these categories of land use are given in Table *6.1* for the combined six regions between two periods, 1907/08–16/17 and 1936/37–45/46; the first of these periods starts with the first year in which there was not major gap in *Agricultural Statistics* coverage (Madras zamindari areas were not reported until that year) and the closing period is but one year short of the end year of this study because of nonavailability of data.

TABLE 6.1

BRITISH INDIA (COMBINED SIX REGIONS) AVERAGE ANNUAL ACREAGE IN VARIOUS CATEGORIES FOR THE PERIODS 1907/08–16/17 AND 1936/37–45/46
(Millions)

	I 1907/08–16/17	II 1936/37–45/46	II-I Change
All-crop acreage	186.5	196.0	9.5
Total area sown	231.2	241.8	10.6
Area sown more than once	30.0	35.0	5.0
Net area sown	201.2	206.8	5.6
Not available for cultivation	95.6	85.4	–10.2
Cultivable waste	74.4	73.9	–0.5
Fallow	42.1	43.6	1.5
Forest	60.2	63.4	3.2
Above four categories	272.3	266.3	–6.0
Total reported area	473.9	473.3	–0.6

Source : All-crop acreage, Appendix Table *4C;* remaining data from *Agricultural Statistics,* for later years as given in *Estimates of Area and Yield of Principal Crops in Undivided India, 1936–37 to 1945–46* issued by the Economic and Statistical Advisor, Ministry of Agriculture, India. The latter data were adjusted to eliminate the portion of Sylhet District, Assam, from Bengal.

Extension of doublecropping appears to have been the largest single source of increase in all-crop acreage. All-crop acreage increased by 9.5 million acres between these periods, while the total increase in doublecropping (or area sown more than once) was 5.0 million acres during the same period. Some of the doublecropped area may not have been sown with "all-crops," but it seems likely that most of it was.

Lands used for other crops than those included in the eighteen "all-crops" constituted only a minor portion of total area sown but were extensive enough, nearly 50 million acres, to have supplied the remaining part of the increase in all-crop acreage. However, the area sown with these other crops also expanded, though much more slowly than all-crop acreage For British India as a whole the expansion of all-crop acreage was not achieved by reduction of area under other crops.

The other main source of additional all-crop acreage was the reduced acreage of land not previously under cultivation. As Table 6.1 shows, the large decrease in the category of "not available" for cultivation, and the slight decrease in cultivable waste, more than offset the increase in forest and fallow acreage. Decrease in lands not previously under cultivation (net of the small decrease in total reported area) was approximately equal to the increase in net area sown.

Land no longer under the category of not available for cultivation did not necessarily go directly into cultivation. It is possible that land which had been in this category might have been placed under the category of cultivable waste or forest, and that land was taken out of the latter categories into additional areas sown.

2. Regional All-Crop Acreage Change

2.1 Expansion and its sources. The British India rate of all-crop acreage expansion (0.40% per year) was characteristic of four regions, where the rates ranged from 0.30% to 0.44% per year. Rates in the other two regions were extreme opposites— almost no change in Greater Bengal. -0.06%, and very rapid expansion in Greater Punjab, 0.96% per year. In most regions, as in British India as a whole, reference decade rates were slowing down, as is indicated by their negative trend rates of change, and the lower averages for the last four reference decades as compared with the first four, seen in Table 6.2. In the case of Greater Bengal, the exception, reference decade rates were accelerating, and were on the average positive for the last four reference decades.

TABLE 6.2

BRITISH INDIA AND REGIONAL AGGREGATE CROP ACREAGE : AVERAGE TREND RATES OF CHANGE, AND CHANGE IN REFERENCE DECADE RATES OF CHANGE

(Percent)

Regional Crops	10 RD Av. Per Year	Change in RD Rates Per RD	First 4 RD Av. Per Year	Last 4 RD Av. Per Year
British India				
All-Crops	0.40	−0.04	0.67	0.35
Foodgrains	0.31	0.03	0.35	0.39
Nonfoodgrains	0.42	−0.13	0.86	0.03
Greater Bengal				
All-Crops	−0.06	0.10	−0.17	0.28
Foodgrains	0.00	0.10	−0.11	0.34
Nonfoodgrains	−0.41	0.09	−0.48	0.00
United Provinces				
All-Crops	0.44	−0.09	0.85	0.30
Foodgrains	0.41	−0.08	0.74	0.28
Nonfoodgrains	0.60	−0.16	1.43	0.40

Madras

All-Crops	0.31	–0.05	0.53	0.22
Foodgrains	0.04	–0.06	0.34	–0.03
Nonfoodgrains	1.24	–0.11	1.58	0.73

Greater Punjab

All-Crops	0.96	–0.15	1.75	0.44
Foodgrains	0.87	–0.13	1.70	0.39
Nonfoodgrains	1.20	–0.25	1.75	0.50

Bombay-Sind

All-Crops	0.40	0.00	0.46	0.42
Foodgrains	0.31	0.08	0.17	0.56
Nonfoodgrains	0.87	–0.68	1.83	0.05

Central Provinces

All-Crops	0.30	–0.09	0.65	0.07
Foodgrains	0.32	0.08	0.17	0.62
Nonfoodgrains	0.11	–0.48	1.51	–1.35

Source : Computed from reference decade (RD) rates in Appendix Tables *5A* and *5B*.

Change in the rate of change in acreage is also seen in the five year moving averages of Figure *6.1*. It is seen that, with the exception of Greater Punjab, fluctuations in the rate of change in acreage were relatively small, especially for Greater Bengal and Madras.

British India all-crop acreage grew somewhat less rapidly after a turning point between 1911 and 1921. The Madras series shows a turning point at about the same time, but in United Provinces and Greater Punjab the turning points occurred about a decade earlier, while in Greater Bengal the slight upturn after decline appears in the 1921–31 decade. No clear turning point is visible for the other two regions.

Indications of the sources of increased crop acreage in each region are given in Table *6.3*. (In Greater Bengal crop acreage declined slightly.) Extension of doublecropped area was an important source of additional crop area in each region, as

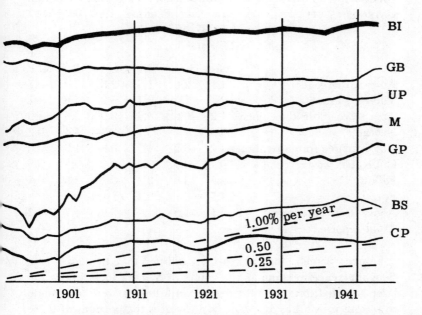

FIGURE 6.1

BRITISH INDIA AND REGIONAL ALL-CROP ACREAGE, FIVE YEAR MOVING AVERAGES, SEMILOGARITHMIC SCALE

Source: Moving averages of data in Appendix Tables 3A, 4C.

it was in British India as a whole. If it is assumed that all the additional doublecropped area was used for the all-crop group, then the portion of increased all-crop acreage from this source ranged from about 20% to 30% in Bombay-Sind, United Provinces, and Greater Punjab, up to about 50% in Madras, and perhaps 100% in Central Provinces.

TABLE 6.3

CHANGE IN THE LEVEL OF AVERAGE ACREAGE OF LAND IN VARIOUS CATEGORIES, BY REGIONS, FOR THE PERIODS 1907/08–16/17 AND 1936/37–45/46

(Millions)

	G B	U P	M	G P	B S	C P
All-crop acreage	–1.1	2.6	1.6	2.8	2.9	0.7
Total area sown	–2.1	1.7	0.7	4.2	4.9	1.1
Area sown more than once	1.2	0.6	0.8	0.9	0.5	1.0
Net area sown	–3.3	1.1	–0.1	3.3	4.4	0.2
Not available for cultivation	–4.2	–0.2	–4.5	0.6	–1.9	0.0
Cultivable waste	0.4	–0.4	2.9	–3.2	–0.5	0.3
Fallow	2.4	–0.8	2.0	–0.2	–2.3	0.4
Forest	4.5	–0.1	0.7	–1.1	0.0	–0.8
Above four categories	3.1	–1.5	1.1	–3.9	–4.7	–0.2
Total reported area	–1.2	–0.7	1.9	–0.5	0.1	–0.1

Source : Same as for Table *6.1*. In addition to reducing Greater Bengal acreage to eliminate the effect of Sylhet's inclusion in the later reported data for that region, adjustments were also made to restore to Madras and Central Provinces the portions of those regions (about 11 million and 1 million acres respectively) transferred to Orissa, Greater Bengal, when that province was formed in 1934/35. Data for the adjustment were not entirely adequate, especially for forest and not available for cultivation categories.

In addition to acreage obtained by doublecropping, in two

regions, United Provinces and Madras, a considerable part of the increase in all-crop acreage was made possible by decrease in acreage under other crops. In these regions, Table 6.3 shows, the increase in all-crop acreage was greater than the increase in total area sown (or net area sown plus area sown more than once), and this excess represents the reduced acreage under other crops.

Large decrease in lands not previously under cultivation made possible the large increases in net area sown in Greater Punjab and Bombay-Sind, and to a lesser extent, also United Provinces. In Greater Punjab the decrease in land considered to be cultivable waste, and also forest, contributed to the increase in all-crop acreage. In Bombay-Sind the major decreases were in the other two categories, fallow and not available for cultivation. In United Provinces there were small decreases in all four of the categories of lands not previously under cultivation.

2.2 Expansion and the availability of land. The extreme difference in rates of change in all-crop acreage between Greater Bengal and Greater Punjab is attributable to the difference in their climates and history of occupance. Greater Bengal, the wettest of the six regions, Figure 6.2, had the densest regional population at the outset of the period. Greater Punjab, the driest of the regions, partly desert, had less than half the population density of Greater Bengal (though it was not the least densely populated region), and had entered into a phase of being 'colonized' at about the outset of the period by settlers moving into areas newly irrigated by permanent canals which led water from storage dams to the high grounds between the rivers. Because these lands received little rain and were difficult to irrigate, they remained until that time, with the exception of some few developments under early Mogul

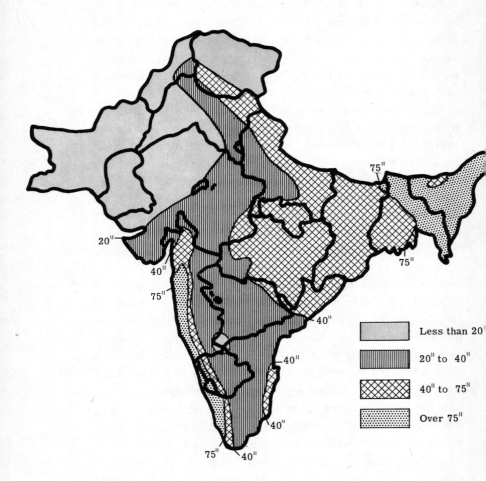

FIGURE 6.2

MEAN ANNUAL RAINFALL AND REGIONS OF BRITISH INDIA

rule, an unutilized potential which was heavily exploited as the period under study developed.

There is no simple measure of potential agricultural acreage, the potential depending on availability of resources needed for development of unused lands and of the return which would be considered economical. Fallow land may be considered part of this potential although in the semi-arid areas it is doubtful that all the fallow land could be cultivated in any given year, because of the scanty water supply and the necessity of fallowing, i.e. dry farming.[1] The category of "cultivable waste" is more difficult to classify; in the later issues of *Agricultural Statistics* this category was titled "other uncultivated land excluding current fallows" (and also excluding forest and land not available for cultivation). In the issues toward the close of this period another category was reported, "culturable area included in other uncultivated land excluding current fallows;" only about ten percent of "other uncultivated land" was considered "culturable," mainly in Central Provinces and Punjab, with small amounts elsewhere only in Bengal and Bombay.

If a generous view of potential acreage is taken, to include fallow, cultivable waste (or other uncultivated land excluding current fallows), and net area sown, then the proportion of potential utilized may be taken as net area sown divided by the sum of the previous three categories. For 1898/99–1902/03, starting with the earliest year for which comparable data were available, the measure stood at 75% for Greater Bengal and 42% for Greater Punjab. It rose in Greater Punjab to 53% by 1907/08–16/17 and 55% in 1936/37–45/46, but in Greater Bengal, due to decline in net area sown and increase in the

---

[1] I am indebted to Professor John Brush, Geography Department, Rutgers, the State University, for this qualification on the use of fallow land.

other two categories, the measure shrank to 70% and 66% respectively for those same periods.

With this measure it can be said that the region with the largest proportion of utilized potential (at the beginning of the period) had the least change in acreage, and the region with the lowest percent of utilized potential had the largest rate of increase in all-crop acreage. In the other regions, where the crop acreage rates of increase were in a narrow range, there was no clear correlation betwen proportion of utilized potential and the rate of increase in acreage.

2.3 The decline in aggregate Greater Bengal acreage. Although the lesser extent of land available for expansion in Greater Bengal is not unexpected, its negative trend in acreage, though quite small, 0.06% per year, seems perplexing. Rice acreage declined at about the same average rate and most other crops also declined with the exception of jute, tea, linseed, and gram.[2]

The decline in all-crop area is not attributable to increase in area of other chops; Table *6.3* shows a decline of a million acres in crops outside the all-crop group (total area sown minus all-crop area). According to this data over 3 million acres of land went out of cultivation (net area sown) between 1907/08–16/17 and 1936/37–45/46. Most of this decrease apparently went into the increase in fallow land.

What explains this general decrease in crop acreage, during a period, moreover, of accelerating population increase? It is conceivable that certain lands became submarginal and were no longer worth the effort or expense of working them, either because of adverse prices or falling productivity. Returns on better lands worked more intensively might have been more

---

[2] For rice the arithmetic mean decline per year between centered averages of the two half-periods during 1891/92–1946/47 was 52,000 acres per year. Similarly measured, jute increased at 3,000 acres per year.

favorable. Another possibility is that the hope of better remuneration in the growing cities might have attracted sufficient labor from rural areas to have in turn led to the decrease in cultivated area. The latter explanation is not adequate, however, because although Calcutta's population nearly tripled during 1891–1941, and Dacca's grew by about fifty percent, and Jamshedpur became a sizeable industrial town, the regional increase in population was far greater than the increase in its urban population.

Is there reason to believe that there was a sufficiently large decrease in productivity to have made cultivation of some lands no longer worthwhile? One possible explanation for this is related to the eastward shift in the main flow of the Ganges waters into the sea. Several districts—Murshidabad, Nadia, and Jessore (Figure *8.4*)—were left with poorly drained malaria-festering channels and were deprived of the annual flood-distributed silts which tended to maintain soil fertility. Population density in these districts remained high but did not follow the general increase which was occuring elsewhere, an indication of the potency of the above changes. Development of the "moribund delta" (discussed at greater length in Chapter VIII) appears to have preceded the period of this study, but its affects, particularly on soil fertility might have continued, ultimately reducing some lands to submarginal status.[3]

Acreage was declining elsewhere in the region, however, apparently for other reasons, at least for certain crops. Jowar, for instance, was grown on less than one percent of the acreage

[3] Spate, *op. cit.*, pp. 524–525, 535–538. I am indebted to Professor Joseph E. Schwartzberg, Department of Geography, University of Minnesota, for calling my attention to the significance of the "moribund delta" for this study, and to Professor Daniel Thorner who also raised this question and suggested many of the references which will be made in Chapter VIII.

in Murshidabad and not at all in Nadia or Jessore, but declined in regional acreage. Maize occupied less than one percent of crop acreage in Murshidabad and Nadia, but this crop, too, declined on a regional scale. Cotton was not grown in these districts, but also showed decline.[4]

A more adequate explanation of the strange phenomenon of declining aggregate acreage in this region is required; it would apparently require analysis at the district level of data.

3. Foodgrain Acreage

3.1 Change in foodgrain aggregate and individual crop acreage at the British India level. The rate of increase in British India foodgrain acreage, 0.31% per year, was slightly less than the rate of all-crop acreage expansion, which implies that the rate for the smaller component, nonfoodgrain acreage, was somewhat greater than for foodgrains. It may be surmised, too, that inasmuch as the foodgrain output growth rate was only 0.11%, average yield per acre was falling as acreage rose. There was virtually no difference between averages rates of increase in the first and last four reference decades, as is seen in Table *6.4*; however, Figure *6.3* indicates a turning-point, a slowing-down in the rate of expansion after the 1911–21 decade.

Among the individual foodgrain crops only two–wheat and gram– appear to have grown more rapidly than the aggregate. The average rate for bajra was also high (Table *6.4*) but this reflects a relatively short span of very rapid growth in the early part of the period (Figure *6.3*). Acreage of the remaining crops expanded at lesser rates, and one, ragi, showed persistent

---

[4] District data from maps in *Crop Atlas of India,* issued by the Department of Commercial Intelligence and Statistics (which is based on *Agricultural Statistics* for 1932/33).

TABLE 6.4

BRITISH INDIA FOODGRAIN CROP ACREAGE : AVERAGE TREND
RATES OF CHANGE, AND CHANGE IN REFERENCE DECADE RATES
OF CHANGE
(Percent)

Crop	10 RD Av. Per Year	Changes in RD Rates per RD	First 4 RD Av. Per Year	Last 4 RD Av. Per Year
All-Crops	0.40	–0.04	0.67	0.35
Foodgrains	0.31	0.03	0.35	0.39
Rice	0.18	0.10	0.03	0.47
Wheat	0.49	–0.02	0.70	0.53
Jowar	0.09	0.03	–0.10	0.24
Gram	0.51	–0.13	1.13	–0.27
Bajra	0.65	–0.04	1.28	0.87
Barley	0.19	–0.25	1.34	–0.25
Maize	0.30	–0.06	0.67	0.47
Ragi	–0.74	–0.14	–0.10	–1.48

Source : Computed from individual reference decade (RD)
rates given in Appendix Tables 5A and 5B.

decline. Three other crops—bajra, barley, and maize—also
showed decline over a long portion of the period (Figure 6.3),
despite the fact that their ten-reference decade average rates
were positive.

Dominance of the rice trend in the foodgrain aggregate
stands out in Figure 6.3. Only during 1911–21, when there
was virtually no change shown in rice acreage, but visible
decline for six other foodgrains, do the series differ noticeably.
The smoothness in the five year moving average series for rice
is also remarkable and is seen to be carried over into the
aggregate series. This relatively small extent of fluctuation,
compared with other crops, may largely reflect the fact that

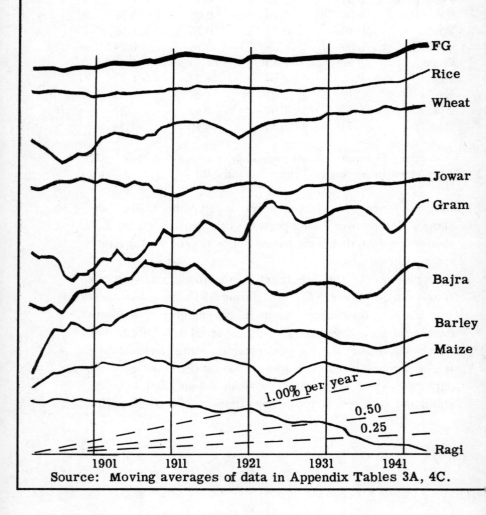

FIGURE 6.3

BRITISH INDIA: AREA OF FOODGRAIN CROPS; FIVE YEAR
MOVING AVERAGES; SEMILOGARITHMIC SCALE

FG
Rice
Wheat
Jowar
Gram
Bajra
Barley
Maize

1.00% per year
0.50
0.25
Ragi

1901   1911   1921   1931   1941
Source: Moving averages of data in Appendix Tables 3A, 4C.

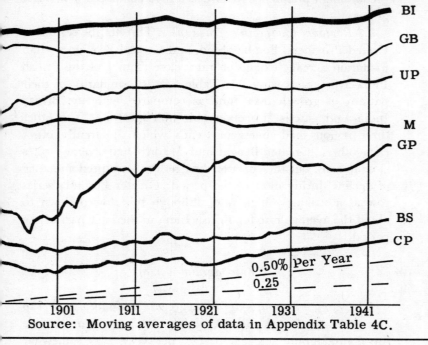

FIGURE 6.4

BRITISH INDIA AND REGIONAL FOODGRAIN CROP ACREAGE,
FIVE YEAR MOVING AVERAGES, SEMILOGARITHMIC SCALE

BI

GB

UP

M

GP

BS

CP

0.50% Per Year
0.25

1901   1911   1921   1931   1941

Source: Moving averages of data in Appendix Table 4C.

most rice is grown on wet lands, and some on irrigated lands, where in either case the annual water supply is dependable enough to maintain the crop acreage, as well as the fact of predominant preference for rice as a food compared with other grains.

3.2 Regional foodgrain acreage rates. Three of the regions— United Provinces, Bombay-Sind, and Central Provinces—had foodgrain acreage expansion rates close to that of the British India average, as is seen in Table *6.2;* the similarity of their pattern of growth over time as compared with the British India aggregate is also observable in Figure *6.4.* The other three regions had divergent trends which apparently offset each other : Greater Bengal and Madras had average rates close to zero, but the chart of their series shows predominance of decline during most of the period; Greater Punjab's series rose at a strikingly high rate, although this slowed down to about the average rate for British India in the later part of the period.

4. Nonfoodgrain Acreage

4.1 Changes in nonfoodgrain aggregate and individual crop acreage at the British India level. The average expansion rate for nonfoodgrain acreage, 0.42% per year, was somewhat more rapid than the foodgrain rate. A notable difference in behavior of the two components is that nonfoodgrain acreage growth was initially rapid, decelerated markedly, and had turned downward by the end of the period (Figure *6.5*), while foodgrain acreage expansion continued at about the same moderate pace throughout the period. The contribution of additional acreage to nonfoodgrain output was also different compared with the foodgrain component, inasmuch as nonfoodgrain output increased at a much more rapid rate than its acreage. This implies that yield per acre contributed a large share to the expansion of nonfoodgrain output while in the case of foodgrains the change in yield per acre tended to pull down output.

TABLE 6.5

BRITISH INDIA NONFOODGRAIN CROP ACREAGE : AVERAGE TREND RATES OF CHANGE, AND CHANGE IN REFERENCE DECADE RATES OF CHANGE
(Percent)

Crop	10 RD Av. Per Year	Changes in RD Rates per RD	First 4 RD Av. Per Year	Last 4 RD Av. Per Year
All-crops	0.40	–0.04	0.67	0.35
Nonfoodgrains	0.42	–0.13	0.86	0.03
Sugarcane	0.60	0.45	–0.86	1.98
Cotton	0.34	–0.50	1.90	–1.34
Jute	0.18	–0.26	1.31	–0.28
Tea	1.29	–0.27	1.98	0.49
Tobacco	–0.17	0.21	–0.94	0.52
Groundnut	6.10	–0.45	8.19	4.10
Rape-Mustard	–0.08	–0.05	0.15	–0.17
Sesamum	–0.17	–0.18	0.45	–0.12
Linseed	–0.27	0.16	–0.64	–0.10
Indigo	–6.65	0.80	–7.59	–5.43

Source : Computed from individual reference decade (RD) rates given in Appendix Tables 5A and 5B.

The much greater diversity of crop acreage trends among the nonfoodgrains as compared with the foodgrains is revealed by comparison of Table 6.4 with 6.5 and Figure 6.3 with 6.5. This diversity would have been additionally underscored on Figure 6.5 had indigo, the pattern of which was the reverse of what is shown for groundnut, been included. Trends for

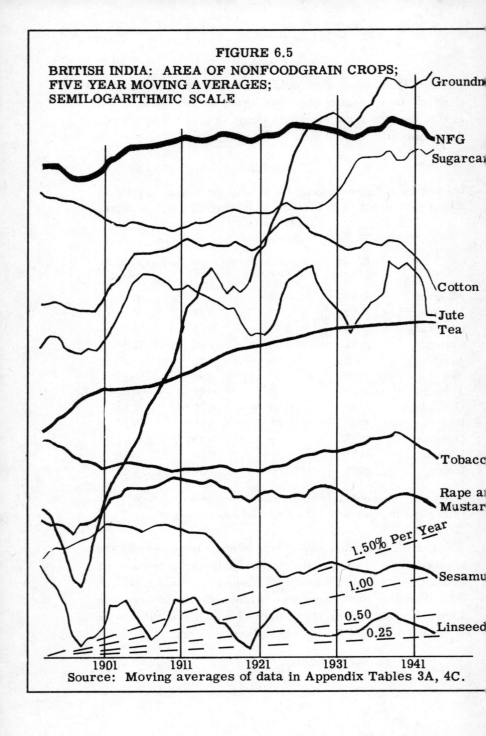

FIGURE 6.5

BRITISH INDIA: AREA OF NONFOODGRAIN CROPS;
FIVE YEAR MOVING AVERAGES;
SEMILOGARITHMIC SCALE

Groundn

NFG

Sugarca

Cotton

Jute
Tea

Tobacc

Rape a
Mustar

1.50% Per Year

1.00

Sesamu

0.50

0.25

Linseed

1901   1911   1921   1931   1941

Source: Moving averages of data in Appendix Tables 3A, 4C.

four other crops—linseed, sesamum, rape-mustard, and tobacco—also showed predominance of decline in Figure 6.5 as well as a negative rate of change in Table 6.5. The rapid risers were groundnut (note, however, its marked deceleration), tea, and sugarcane. Cotton expanded at close to the average rate, but with quite opposite trends in the early and later parts of the period, almost completely the reverse in direction, it may be noted, of what occurred for sugarcane. Jute, with its long periods of steep rise and decline, averaged to a relatively low rate of expansion in its acreage. The contrast between the uneven expansion rate for jute and the smooth ascent of tea is striking, a product of differing developments in world markets.

4.2 Regional nonfoodgrain acreage rates. The British India expansion rate of 0.42% was not typical of the regional rates, as is evident from Table 6.2 as well as Figure 6.6; three of the rates were far in excess of the average, and two were opposite in their effect on the aggregate. Only United Provinces showed resemblance to the British India pattern, both in average rate and deceleration in growth. In the three regions where acreage expanded sharply—Greater Punjab, Bombay-Sind, and Madras—cotton was a leading crop in the expansion; additional irrigation facilities made this possible in the Greater Punjab and Sind area. Groundnut dominated the increase in Bombay and Madras, and was a continuing force for expansion after the mid-period peak for cotton was reached in those two regions. In Central Provinces nonfoodgrain acreage moved with the changes in cotton acreage, the decline of which after the early 1920's was not offset by any other nonfoodgrain crop. The decline in Greater Bengal of oilseeds, tobacco, indigo, and cotton was only offset to a small extent by the increase in tea acreage and the late-period rise in sugarcane acreage; jute, the most extensive nonfoodgrain crop, increased only slightly.

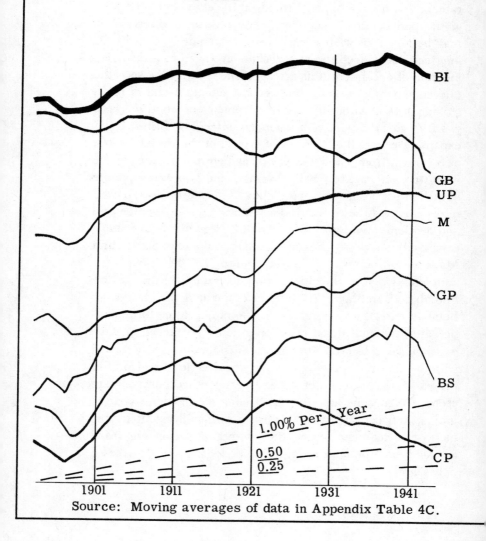

FIGURE 6.6

BRITISH INDIA AND REGIONAL NONFOODGRAIN CROP
ACREAGE, FIVE YEAR MOVING AVERAGES, SEMILOGARITHMIC
SCALE

Source: Moving averages of data in Appendix Table 4C.

In all regions nonfoodgrain acreage was reduced at the close of the period (Figure 6.6) as a result of the war's effect on foreign markets and the Grow More Food Campaign in the last few years. This contributed to the deceleration in nonfoodgrain acreage which characterized all regions except Greater Bengal, where the earlier rate of decline was reduced considerably in the last part of the period.

The British India rate of expansion for nonfoodgrain acreage was somewhat greater than for foodgrain acreage; three regions—United Provinces, Greater Punjab, and Bombay-Sind—exhibited the same characteristic, (Table 6.2, Figures 6.4 and 6.6). In Madras the steep rise in nonfoodgrain acreage contrasted much more sharply with the virtually stationary foodgrain acreage. In Central Provinces and Greater Bengal the nonfoodgrain rates were less favorable than the foodgrain rates.

VII

Yield per Acre Trends

1. British India yield per acre trends : foodgrain crops, non-foodgrain crops. 2. Regional yield per acre trends : comparison with British India trends, leading influences in the individual regions.

THIS CHAPTER ANALYZES yield per acre trends at the British India level, then at the regional level. The analysis moves from trends of crop aggregates to those of individual crops; trends of individual çrops at the regional level, however, were obtained with relatively crude methods compared to those generally used in this study. For some individual crops, analysis of yield per acre trends is pushed back to changes in the influences underlying yield per acre. The study of yield per acre trends is continued into the next chapter, where changes in the underlying influences governing all-crop yield per acre trends are examined, with emphasis, where possible, on the regional level.

1. British India Yield per Acre Trends

The ten-reference decade average rate of change in aggregate yield per acre of all crops was nearly zero, 0.01% per year, a remarkable summary of over fifty years of agriculture up to the middle of the Twentieth Century. It must be asked, however, whether this near-zero rate of change was typical of the conditions it measures, and if not, what is its significance. This chapter will show the variety of yield per acre trends among crops, regions, and time periods. Individual crop rates at the British India level (Table *7.1*) ranged from 1.43% per year to -0.26%; half the crops had rates within plus or minus 0.20% per year, or about 10% total change over a half century. Regional all-crop yield per acre rates extended from 0.65% per year to –0.34,% but only two were within the plus

TABLE 7.1

BRITISH INDIA YIELD PER ACRE OF CROP AGGREGATES AND INDIVIDUAL CROPS : AVERAGE TREND RATES OF CHANGE AND CHANGE IN REFERENCE DECADE RATES OF CHANGE

(Percent)

Crop	10 RD Av. Per Year	Change in RD Rates per RD	First 4 RD Av. Per Year	Last 4 RD Av. Per Year
All-crops	0.01	–0.09	0.47	–0.02
Foodgrains	–0.18	–0.12	0.29	–0.44
Rice	–0.24	–0.15	0.39	–0.57
Wheat	0.38	–0.20	1.25	0.02
Jowar	0.00	–0.17	0.64	–0.63
Gram	–0.26	–0.19	0.52	–0.88
Bajra	0.06	–0.07	0.35	–0.24
Barley	–0.12	–0.30	0.71	–1.11
Maize	0.21	–0.10	0.88	0.10
Ragi	0.12	–0.11	0.29	–0.10
Nonfoodgrains	0.86	0.02	0.81	1.15
Sugarcane	0.73	–0.01	1.03	1.20
Cotton	0.95	0.02	0.98	1.27
Jute	0.14	–0.22	0.86	–0.30
Tea	1.43	–0.02	2.22	1.59
Tobacco	0.17	–0.14	0.72	–0.24
Groundnut	0.23	–0.29	0.73	–0.61
Rape-Mustard	0.19	–0.01	0.48	0.31

Sesamum	0.29	−0.12	0.58	−0.08
Linseed	−0.10	−0.26	1.05	−0.80
Indigo	0.47	−0.28	1.28	−0.89

Source : Computed from individual reference decade (RD) rates given in Appendix Table 5A.

or minus 0.20% per year range. Individual reference decade rates for all crops at the British India level ranged from 0.95% per year to −0.36%, of which only two were in the above range; the trend in reference decade rates was downward at 0.09% per reference decade, indicating, when coupled with the ten-reference decade average rate of 0.01% per year, that in the early reference decades the rates were above zero, and in the later decades below zero. Levels of yield per acre were evidently not changeless over time; in some sectors there was little change (less than 0.20% per year), but in others there were notable upward or downward trends. It happens that these latter trends offset one another so that the British India all-crop yield per acre trend rate of change for the half-century was virtually zero, 0.01% per year.

The near-zero rate of all-crop yield per acre change was not typical of most crops or regions, but does the fact that the divergent rates averaged to nearly zero have some other significance? If increasing yield per acre for some crops entailed sacrifice of yield per acre of other crops, or if increasing yield per acre in some regions caused decreasing yield per acre in others, then the summary rate of nearly zero would indicate the incapacity of the agricultural economy to break out of the confines of its productive conditions.

The proposition that increases must be offset by decreases generally does not apply between regions. An increase in irrigation facilities in one region, for instance, does not mean that facilities elsewhere would have had to be reduced (although conceivably water used in one region might take away from that which is available in another region i.e., Greater Punjab and the Sind). Expanded use of improved seed in one region is not likely to lessen the use of such seed elsewhere.

However, within a given region there may be some tendency for increases in yield per acre to cause offsetting decreases in yield per acre. A progressive exchange of crops planted on poor and rich lands may occur, for instance, with cash crops moving to better soils while subsistence crops take their place on poorer soils. Also, if land and labor were fixed then their increased use for some crops would mean lessened quantities available for other crops. If increases due to such transfers were exactly offset by decreases, then the trend in yield per acre of all crops would be zero percent change per year.

Inasmuch, however, as only two regions had all-crop yield per acre trend rates close to zero, and inasmuch as some technological progress occurred even in these regions, the tendency of offsetting changes in yield per acre should not be taken as a general explanation for the British India zero trend rate of change in all-crop yield per acre. The near-zero rate may be attributed to the combination of low rates for about half the crops and offsetting, but unrelated, trends among the other crops.

1.1 Foodgrain crops. Aggregate foodgrain yield per acre fell at a ten-reference decade average rate of 0.18% per year, and the trend in reference decade rates was, moreover, declining at 0.12% per reference decade. Declining average foodgrain yield per acre was more than offset by increasing foodgrain acreage, but the result, seen in Chapter V, was the small rate of increase in output of foodgrains (0.11% per year).

Eight of the ten reference decade foodgrain yield per acre rates were negative (Appendix Table 5A), including all of the

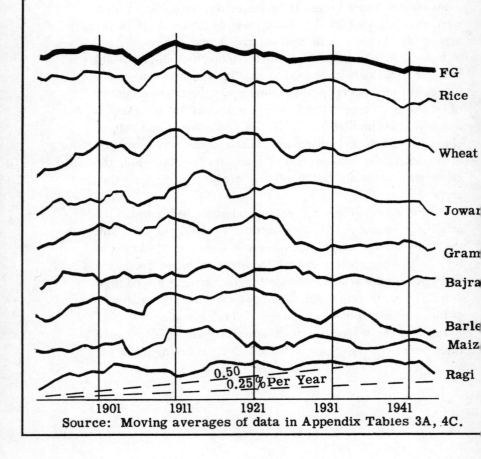

FIGURE 7.1

BRITISH INDIA: YIELD PER ACRE OF FOODGRAIN CROPS;
FIVE YEAR MOVING AVERAGES; SEMILOGARITHMIC SCALE

FG

Rice

Wheat

Jowar

Gram

Bajra

Barle

Maiz

Ragi

0.50
0.25% Per Year

1901   1911   1921   1931   1941

Source: Moving averages of data in Appendix Tables 3A, 4C.

last six. Trend in the first twenty years, judging from Figure
7.1, appears to rise slightly (first four reference decade rate
average was 0.29% per year), but for the remaining period
yield per acre appears to decline steadily (at an average rate of
0.50% per year for the last six reference decades).

Of the eight foodgrain crops, four had upward trends,
including wheat, the second largest grain crop, which rose at
the moderate rate of 0.38% per year. Bajra, fifth ranking
grain crop, had a rate only slightly above zero, and the remaining two crops with positive average trends, maize and ragi,
had small rates of increase and were smallest also in volume of
output.

The other four grain crops had negative or zero average
rates of change in yield per acre. Paramount among these, rice,
comprising about half of foodgrain output, and about four
times greater than wheat in output, declined with sufficient
strength to give aggregate foodgrain yield per acre its downward cast. In fact, despite the somewhat differing trends of
rice and the other grains, the aggregate foodgrain yield per
acre series charted in Figure *7.1* appears almost the same as
the rice series in its relative movements. Only one other crop,
gram, had a rate of decline as steep as that for rice; barley had
a low rate of decline and jowar's rate was zero.

The British India rice yield per acre series is analyzed into
its regional components in Figure *7.2.* Steep decline in Greater
Bengal, which produced at least half of British India rice output, stands out sharply; its ten-reference decade average rate
of change was −0.49% per year. In the remaining parts of
British India the combined average rate of change was about
−0.08% per year (geometric mean between average yield per
acre in the first and second halves of the 56-year period). The
United Provinces trend, seen in the chart, was downward,
though somewhat less steeply than in Greater Bengal. Slightly

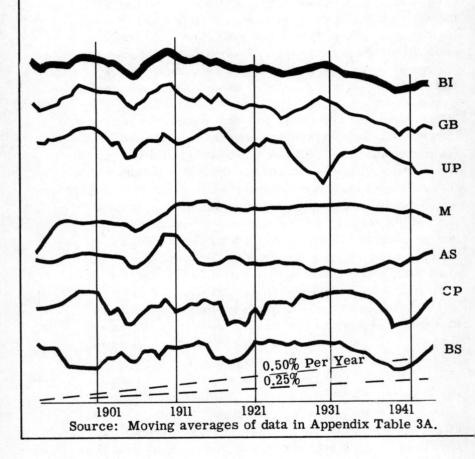

FIGURE 7.2

BRITISH INDIA AND REGIONAL YIELD PER ACRE OF RICE, FIVE YEAR MOVING AVERAGES, SEMILOGARITHMIC SCALE

BI

GB

UP

M

AS

CP

BS

0.50% Per Year

0.25%

1901   1911   1921   1931   1941

Source: Moving averages of data in Appendix Table 3A.

downward trends are apparent in Assam and Central Provinces; in Bombay-Sind the long-period trend appears to show little or no change in yield per acre. Only in Madras was there a noticeable upward trend, but this was being reduced by considerable retardation.

What caused these downward trends? Several elements in the explanation may be suggested, but not much direct evidence can be given. One possible element is the repeated cropping of the same lands for this crop, it being generally assumed that this results in lowering of yield per acre. That this need not necessarily occur for rice is expressed in the following view :[1]

A gradual loss of fertility . . . does not take place in either Burma or Bengal, where rice has been grown on the same land year after year for centuries. Clearly the soil must obtain fresh supplies of nitrogen from somewhere, otherwise the crop would cease to grow. The only likely source is fixation from the atmosphere. . . . It seems probable . . . that actual fixation must take place in the rice fields . . . while the land is under water. The most probable seat of this fixation is in the submerged algal film on the surface of the mud.

This view may be qualified, however, by adding that the initial level of fertility would probably decline and that yield per acre would remain stable after a certain low level was reached. This arguement is considered again in the next chapter.

A second general possibility is that of substitution of sugar-cane (or other cash crops) for rice on good lands, and the shifting of rice to poorer lands. This tendency would not have

[1] Albert Howard, *Crop Production in India: A Critical Survey of Its Problems* (London: 1924), p. 113; cited in V. D. Wickizer and M. K. Bennett, *The Rice Economy of Monsoon Asia* (Stanford: Food Research Institute, 1941), p. 254.

occurred until domestic sugar was brought under protective tariff, consequently it would only help to explain decline starting with the early 1930's. In any case, the overall effect on rice yield per acre would have been limited by the fact that rice was nearly seventy million acres while sugarcane's was at the most about four million.

In eastern Bengal and Assam jute and rice are also substitute crops; rice on better lands there may also have been displaced by jute. Jute area rose to about three million acres over the period, while Greater Bengal rice acreage was about thirty-five million, indicating again that the effect of the displacement would have been quite limited. Jute and rice are also associated in rotation planting in those regions, and this might also have caused lowering of rice yield per acre, since jute is considered a more soil-exhausting crop.[2]

Finally, for the Greater Bengal region, there was a unique circumstance which may have caused decline in rice yield per acre, namely the cessation of flood innundations in western Bengal in the 'moribund' delta area between the Padma, Bhagirathi, and Ganges Rivers (Figure 8.4). Soil fertility in the delta region had been periodically replenished by fresh silts spread by these inundations. Again, however, the limits of this effect are indicated by the relative size of areas involved; net cultivated area of the three main districts affected by this condition, Murshidabad, Nadia, and Jessore, and also including Khulna, is about three million acres compared with about fifty million acres for the region as a whole. The question of innundations is taken up later in the chapter.

Against these tendencies toward lower yield per acre, there were at least two upward, though weak, forces. One was the use of improved rice seed. In 1939 the Imperial Council of

[2] O. H. K. Spate, *India and Pakistan, A General and Regional Geography* (London: Methuen & Co., Ltd., 1954), p. 527.

Agricultural Research stated that "despite the fact that the Council has been financing rice research for the last ten years and new and better yielding varieties have been evolved, the total area under improved rice represents only six percent of the total area under this crop."[3] In 1922/23, however, the proportion of rice land under improved seed was less than one percent.[4]

The other weak though upward influence on rice yield per acre was the slight increase in proportion of rice land irrigated. This rose from 24.8% to 25.9%, averages for the periods 1919/20–23/24 and 1934/35–38/39 based on *Agricultural Statistics* data; comparable data were not available for British India in the years outside of this range.

The wheat yield per acre trend rate was at the opposite extreme among the foodgrains. At the average rate of 0.38% per year it would have increased by about 20% in a half century. The rate of increase in wheat yield per acre was, however, not at all constant during the period, rather being very rapid during the first four reference decades, average 1.25% per year, but nearly zero, 0.02%, in the last four. Figure 7.1 clearly shows this retardation; trend in the reference decade rates was downward at 0.20% per reference decade.

What accounts for the great difference in rice and wheat yield per acre trends? Two positive influences, strong for wheat, were weak for rice. The increased proportion of wheat lands under irrigation, Table 7.2, appears to have been of considerable importance, particularly for the early period. Although irrigation continued to increase there was less gain in proportion of crop irrigated in the later decades. Most of the additional irrigated land was in the Punjab, where the "almost virgin soils" responded generously to irrigation.[5]

[3] Cited in Wickizer and Bennett, *op. cit.*, p. 238.
[4] Imperial Council of Agricultural Research, *Review of Agricultural Operations in India, 1922/23.*
[5] Spate, *op. cit.*, p. 463.

TABLE 7.2

AVERAGE WHEAT ACREAGE SOWN AND IRRIGATED IN BRITISH
INDIA DURING SELECTED PERIODS

Years	Irrigated Acreage (Millions)	Total Acreage Sown (Millions)	Irrigated/ Sown (Percent)
1893/94–97/98	6.5	19.1	33.7
1904/05–08/09	8.4	20.6	40.7
1913/14–17/18	9.6	23.2	41.6
1920/21–24/25	9.5	23.1	40.9
1934/35–38/39	11.5	25.7	44.6

Source : *Agricultural Statistics* and Appendix Table *3A*.
Greater Bengal and Madras are not included in the first two
periods; their share would have been quite small.

A second beneficial influence for wheat yield per acre
(contrasted with rice) was the large increase in proportion of
wheat land under improved seed, from 5% in 1922/23 to 30%
in 1938/39.[6] Wheat yield per acre was generally rising during
that period, as may be seen in Figure *7.1;* it may be noted,
however, that the increases in wheat yield per acre for those
years were small, reflecting both the influence of improved
seed as well as other factors.

The remaining, so called minor, grains were evenly divided
between those with positive and negative average trend rates of
change in yield per acre. As might be expected, there was
relatively little change in either irrigation or use of improved
seed for these crops. Table *7.3* shows that the proportion of
barley land irrigated fell and this may have been a factor of
importance in the decline of barley yield per acre in that
period shown in Figure *7.1.* Bajra and maize showed little

[6] Based on data from Appendix Table *3A* and I.C.A.R., *Review of
Agricultural Operations,* 1922/23 and 1938/39.

change in yield per acre for those years, but jowar showed noticeable decline, apparently attributable to other influences. As to improved seed, this was apparently an insignificant factor for the minor grains. For the combined three millet crops— jowar, bajra, and ragi—area under improved seed was only a half of one percent of area sown as late as 1937/38; for gram 0.6% of area sown was under improved seed.[7]

TABLE 7.3

AREA IRRIGATED/AREA SOWN FOR MINOR FOODGRAIN CROPS IN
BRITISH INDIA
(Percent)

	1920/21	1940/41
Barley	50.2	44.3
Jowar	6.9	6.9
Bajra	9.9	9.4
Maize	19.7	21.9

Source : Computed from data in *Agricultural Statistics;* data for years before 1919/20 not given in this source.

1.2 Nonfoodgrain crops. Trend characteristics of nonfoodgrain yield per acre contrasted markedly with that of the foodgrains, both in the high average reference decade rate, 0.86% per year, and in the acceleration, though only slight, in reference decade rates. At that trend rate, in a half-century, the yield per acre would have risen by over 50%, a notable achievement for a country which was not generally oriented toward technological change. The steady upward growth in productivity, through both the first and last parts of the period, is shown both by the low rate of acceleration and also by the

[7] M. B. Nanavati and J. J. Anjaria, *The Indian Rural Problem* (3rd ed. : Bombay : Indian Society of Agricultural Economics, 1947), p. 44.

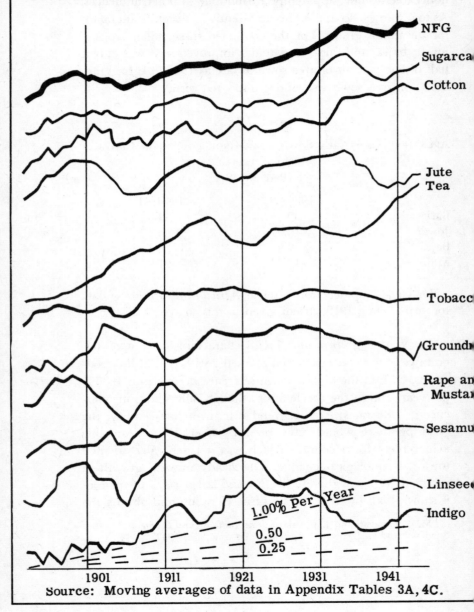

FIGURE 7.3

BRITISH INDIA: YIELD PER ACRE OF NONFOODGRAIN CROPS:
FIVE YEAR MOVING AVERAGES; SEMILOGARITHMIC SCALE

NFG

Sugarca

Cotton

Jute
Tea

Tobacc

Ground

Rape an
Musta

Sesamu

Linsee

Indigo

1.00% Per Year
0.50
0.25

1901   1911   1921   1931   1941

Source: Moving averages of data in Appendix Tables 3A, 4C.

relatively straight rise through the five year moving averages plotted in Figure 7.3.

It must be noted, however, that the aggregate nonfoodgrain yield per acre trend was not typical of most crops in this group, but rather of only three crops—sugarcane, cotton, and tea. These crops ranked high in output, comprising in 1924/25–28/29 for instance, nearly fifty percent of total nonfoodgrain production. Indigo also had a relatively high rate, but this had virtually no effect on the aggregate rate since indigo output was much less than one percent of the total. The other crops—jute, the oilseeds, and tobacco—had much smaller rates of change in yield per acre.

The advances of sugarcane and cotton appear to have been mainly associated with adoption of better types of seed. Improved sugarcane, giving up to triple the yield per acre of older varieties,[8] spread from less than 1% of sugarcane acreage to nearly 70% in 1938/39. Irrigation of the crop increased considerably between the years 1919/20–23/24 and 1934/35–38/39, but the proportion of sugarcane acreage irrigated fell from 68% to 61%, somewhat offsetting the improvement due to better seed. Cotton under improved seed expanded from 13% to 44% of cotton acreage from 1922/23 to 1938/39. The proportion of cotton land irrigated rose from 17% to 29% in the periods 1919/20–23/24 and 1934/35–36/39, giving additional impetus to the growth in yield per acre.

High rates for tea and indigo may not represent improvement in cultivation. The picking of tea leaves might simply have become more intensive as markets grew. Indigo output was declining rapidly as a result of reduced acreage, and it might be expected that lands of marginal fertility would have been progressively relinquished, and that, except for the effect of differences in other costs and transportation, the surviving

[8] Gandhi, *op. cit.,* p. 51.

crop would be concentrated in lands with the highest yield per acre.

Among the crops which had only low rates of increase in yield per acre, jute stands out partly because proportion of jute land under improved seed increased substantially from 13% in 1922/23 to 51% in 1938/39. There was a small upward trend in yield per acre during those years; perhaps the improvement did not affect yield per acre as much as it did some other qualities of the plant. The groundnut crop is also of interest since, despite the tremendous increase in output and exports, almost all the increase was attributable to increased acreage. Only 3% of groundnut acreage was under improved seed as of 1937/38. It could be, of course, that as acreage expanded, progressively poorer soils were used, tending to decrease productivity; this would seem particularly likely in the case of rapid acreage expansion. Data on seed and irrigation are not available for the other oilseed crops and tobacco; the slightly declining acreage trends for these crops do not contribute toward explaining the yield per acre changes.

2. Regional Yield per Acre Trends

2.1 Comparison with British India trends. Of the six regions, two had relatively high (ten-reference decade) average rates of annual increase in all-crop yield per acre, Madras 0.65% and Greater Punjab 0.62%; at these rates yield per acre would have increased by about 35% in a half-century. Two regions had low to moderate rates of increase, Bombay-Sind 0.28% and United Provinces 0.15%; the latter rate, implying a total increase of only 7.5% in the half-century, might be considered small enough to be virtually negligible. In Central Provinces the rate was not much above zero, 0.08% per year. But in Greater Bengal the yield per acre declined at an average rate of 0.34% per year, the equivalent of a 16% total decline in a half century. The negative rate for this top-ranking region (in output) was sufficiently large to offset the positive rates in the other five regions thus giving a British India rate of 0.01%.

For British India as a whole, reference decade rates (for all-crop yield per acre) were higher in the first part of the period compared with the last; retardation in the trend rate of change in reference decade rates also indicated this condition. All but one of the regions, Greater Punjab, conformed to this pattern. The greatest differences between first and last four reference decade average rates, as seen in Table 7.4, were in Madras, Central Provinces, and Greater Bengal. In United Provinces and Bombay-Sind the difference in average rates for first and last parts of the period was small. Only in Greater Punjab was there acceleration in the rate of increase; the average rate for the last four reference decades there was considerably higher than for the earlier period.

TABLE 7.4

BRITISH INDIA AND REGIONAL AGGREGATE YIELD PER ACRE:
AVERAGE TREND RATES OF CHANGE, AND CHANGE IN REFERENCE
DECADE RATES OF CHANGE
(Percent)

Regional Crops	10 RD Av. Per Year	Change in RD Rates, Per RD	First 4 RD Av. Per Year	Last 4 RD Av. Per Year
British India				
All-crops	0.01	−0.09	0.47	−0.02
Foodgrains	−0.18	−0.12	0.29	−0.44
Nonfoodgrains	0.86	0.02	0.81	1.15
Greater Bengal				
All-crops	−0.34	−0.12	0.08	−0.48
Foodgrains	−0.55	−0.11	−0.11	−0.74
Nonfoodgrains	0.59	−0.09	0.74	0.78

United Provinces

All-crops	0.15	–0.05	0.38	0.16
Foodgrains	–0.02	–0.18	0.57	–0.31
Nonfoodgrains	0.24	0.13	–0.34	0.91

Madras

All-crops	0.65	–0.18	1.24	0.19
Foodgrains	0.35	–0.17	0.99	–0.03
Nonfoodgrains	1.25	–0.19	1.58	0.58

Greater Punjab

All-crops	0.62	0.04	0.47	0.90
Foodgrains	0.31	–0.01	0.30	0.47
Nonfoodgrains	1.13	0.24	0.52	1.70

Bombay-Sind

All-crops	0.28	0.04	0.54	0.35
Foodgrains	–0.11	–0.06	0.43	–0.41
Nonfoodgrains	0.92	0.88	0.10	2.08

Central Provinces

All-crops	0.08	–0.32	1.07	–0.91
Foodgrains	0.05	–0.33	1.12	–0.84
Nonfoodgrains	0.77	–0.32	1.60	–0.02

Source : Computed from individual reference decade (RD) rates given in Appendix Tables *5A* and *5B*.

Regional foodgrain rates of change in yield per acre ranged from 0.35% per year to -0.55%. The latter rate for Greater Bengal, corresponding to a 21% total decrease in yield per acre, was the only one lower than the British India average (-0.18% per year). However, two other regions had negative rates, Bombay-Sind (-0.11%) and United Provinces (-0.02%), and in Central Provinces the rate was very low (0.05%). The moderate average rates of increase were in Madras (0.35%) and Greater Punjab (0.31%). Retardation in the rates of change, characteristic of British India as a whole, occurred in all regions except Greater Punjab. Average rates of change for the last four reference decades were negative for all regions except Greater Punjab.

The steeply rising British India nonfoodgrain trend reflects high rates of increase in all regions except United Provinces, where it was only 0.24% per year. In all regions, as in British India, the nonfoodgrain rates were larger than the foodgrain rates. Rates of nearly one percent per year or more occurred in Madras (1.25%), Greater Punjab (1.13%) and Bombay-Sind (0.92%). There was less agreement in the change of rates over time, which was upward for British India as a whole. In three regions—United Provinces, Greater Punjab, and Bombay-Sind—the last four reference decade average rates were much higher than in the first four; the opposite was true in two regions—Madras and Central Provinces, while in Greater Punjab there was little change.

2.2 Leading influences in the individual regions. Greater Punjab. Wheat, which occupied nearly half of foodgrain acreage, had a yield per acre trend pattern similar to that of British India, as may be seen by comparing Figures *7.1* and *7.4;* marked increase in the early part of the period was followed by only a slight rise in the later decades. Yield per acre series of the next ranking crops in acreage—gram, bajra, and maize—as well as the other grains showed no tendency toward change in level of yield per acre. Regional foodgrain yield per acre, Figures *7.4* rose rather steadily but not sharply. Two crops occupied most of nonfoodgrain acreage, cotton and rape-mustard seed. Cotton, with about twice the acreage of rape-mustard, rose rapidly in yield per acre over the period, while rape-mustard, though it showed an upward trend, increased only slightly. The proportion of nonfoodgrain to foodgrain acreage was relatively small in all regions, and it was smaller in Greater Punjab than in British India as a whole,[9]

[9] For all 56 years the ratio of nonfoodgrain to foodgrain acreage was

but the rapid rise in nonfoodgrain yield per acre and the increase in food-grain yield per acre combined to give the most favorable all-crop yield per acre trend of all the regions, one with sustained moderate increase.

FIGURE 7.4

GREATER PUNJAB YIELD PER ACRE OF
ALL-CROPS, FOODGRAINS, AND NONFOODGRAINS,
FIVE YEAR MOVING AVERAGES, SEMILOGARITHMIC
SCALE

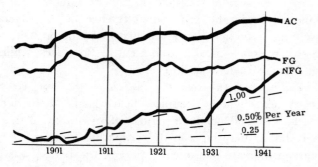

Source: Moving averages of data in Appendix Table 4C.

Madras. In this region all-crop yield per acre rose rapidly until about 1931, when a leveling off in nonfoodgrain yield per acre trend and decline in foodgrain yield per acre trend turned the all-crop trend downward, as seen in Figure 7.5. Up to about 1911 rising rice yield per acre, Figure 7.2 (rice occupied about half of foodgrain acreage), coupled with rising cotton yield per acre (somewhat less than half of nonfoodgrain acreage) gave all-crop yield per acre a strong upward cast. Foodgrain yield per acre then levelled off, in part because of

0.293 for British India, and for the regions: Greater Bengal 0.155, Greater Punjab 0.165, Madras 0.228, United Provinces 0.235, Bombay-Sind 0.264, Central Province 0.416.

declining yield per acre of the next most important grain crops, jowar and bajra. Acceleration in the cotton yield per acre rate of increase kept all-crop yield per acre rising until about 1931. Groundnut, which ultimately occupied as much acreage as cotton, showed no notable change in yield per acre. Sesamum, an important nonfoodgrain crop throughout the period, also showed no trend toward change in yield per acre.

FIGURE 7.5

MADRAS YIELD PER ACRE OF ALL-CROPS
FOODGRAINS, AND NONFOODGRAINS, FIVE
YEAR MOVING AVERAGES, SEMILOGARITHMIC
SCALE

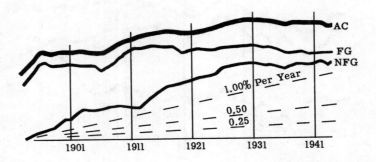

Source: Moving averages of data in Appendix Table 4C.

Bombay-Sind. The millets, jowar and bajra, occupied nearly three-quarters of foodgrain acreage in this region; their yield per acre trends were downward at least for the last half of the period. Rice (Figure 7.2) and wheat, the next ranking grains, showed little or no upward trend. Aggregate foodgrain yield per acre (Figure 7.6) had a slightly downward trend over the period as a whole, more clearly apparent in the second half of the period. Nonfoodgrain yield per acre was dominated by cotton, which occupied about four-fifths of this acreage; trend for cotton was strongly upward, probably much as is shown for aggregate nonfoodgrain yield per acre in Figure 7.6. Increasing nonfoodgrain yield per acre toward the close of the period partially offset the downward trend in foodgrain yield per acre with the result that there was little change in all-crop yield per acre during that time.

FIGURE 7.6

BOMBAY-SIND YIELD PER ACRE OF ALL-CROPS
FOODGRAINS, AND NONFOODGRAINS, FIVE YEAR
MOVING AVERAGES, SEMILOGARITHMIC SCALE

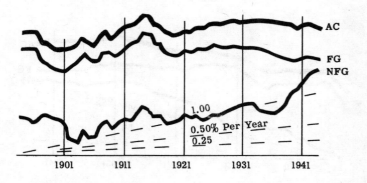

Source: Moving averages of data in Appendix Table 4C.

United Provinces. Rice and wheat, of equal importance, together accounted for about half of foodgrain acreage. Wheat yield per acre showed little tendency to change, but rice (Figure 7.2) trended downward in the second half of the period. In the remaining foodgrain acreage, gram and barley followed in importance; both declined in yield per acre during the second half-period. Aggregate foodgrain yield per acre consequently trended steadily downward, as seen in Figure

7.7, during that part of the period. The small average rate of increase in nonfoodgrain yield per acre reflects the preponderance of oilseeds, about two-thirds of nonfoodgrain acreage. These crops showed little yield per acre change in any of the regions; linseed and rape-mustard trended downward slightly in this region, while sesamum remained about the same. Cotton yield per acre changed little, but sugarcane climbed steeply after about 1931, and this accounts for the sharp rise in the nonfoodgrain yield per acre series, Figure 7.7. This increase was largely offset, in its effect on all-crop yield per acre, by the foodgrain yield per acre decline in the same period.

FIGURE 7.7

UNITED PROVINCES YIELD PER ACRE OF
ALL-CROPS, FOODGRAINS, AND NONFOODGRAINS,
FIVE YEAR MOVING AVERAGES, SEMILOGARITHMIC
SCALE

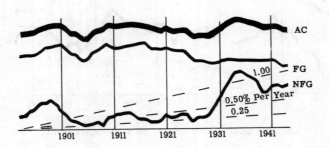

Source: Moving averages of data in Appendix Table 4C.

Central Provinces. The low average rate of increase in yield per acre given by Table 7.3 appears, in Figure 7.8, to have been typical of the middle portion of the period, from about

1901 to 1931. During that time, rice, with nearly a third of foodgrain acreage, changed little in yield per acre (Figure 7.2); the same was true for jowar and wheat, the next ranking grains. Decline in foodgrain yield per acre from 1931 to 1941 appears to have been partly associated with rising nonfoodgrain yield per acre. Cotton, occupying about two-thirds of nonfoodgrain acreage, showed, generally, little tendency toward change in yield per acre. The remaining nonfoodgrain crops, mostly oilseeds, also showed little change; linseed declined slightly during the period.

FIGURE 7.8

CENTRAL PROVINCES YIELD PER ACRE OF ALL-CROPS, FOODGRAINS, AND NONFOODGRAINS, FIVE YEAR MOVING AVERAGES, SEMILOGARITHMIC SCALE

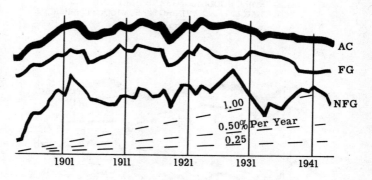

Source: Moving averages of data in Appendix Table 4C.

Greater Bengal. Here, of course, rice was the dominant crop, comprising about seven-eighths of foodgrain acreage and three-quarters of all-crop acreage. The downward sweep of rice yield per acre is very apparent in Figure 7.2; the decline, on closer examination, may be said to have begun about 1911.

The aggregate foodgrain yield per acre series, Figure 7.9, is almost identical with that of rice in this region. Decline also occurred, at least in the second half of the period, for the next ranking grains, gram, maize, and barley.

Nonfoodgrain yield per acre trended steadily upward, judging from Figure 7.9, but the rate of increase was not as rapid as in most regions. Jute, with about a third of nonfoodgrain acreage, showed only slight upward trend (0.14% per year over the whole period), as may be seen from Figure 7.3 (since almost all British India jute was grown in this region). The low rate of increase occurred, despite the spread of improved seed, to about half of jute acreage by about 1938/39. Oilseeds as a group exceeded jute in acreage; rape-mustard, the leading oilseed crop, rose in yield per acre while linseed declined. Sugarcane yield per acre increased, partly because of

FIGURE 7.9

GREATER BENGAL YIELD PER ACRE OF ALL-CROPS, FOODGRAINS, AND NONFOODGRAINS, FIVE YEAR MOVING AVERAGES, SEMILOGARITHMIC SCALE

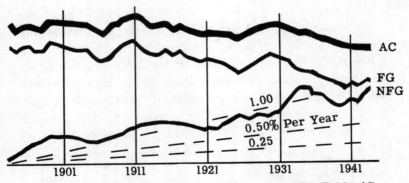

Source: Moving averages of data in Appendix Table 4C.

improved seed, which by 1938/39 had spread to all the sugar-cane acreage. Tea, though relatively small in acreage, increased rapidly in yield per acre.

The importance of rice, and its remarkable decline in yield per acre, raise questions of where and why this was occurring. Figure 7.10, which shows annual yields per acre (not moving averages) and crudely derived trend lines connecting mid-points of the half-periods for each series, plainly shows that the decline is mainly attributable to the Bihar-Orissa portion of Greater Bengal. Decline in Bengal Province was very slight and might not appear if a more refined trend line were derived. For the relatively few years of available data, there appear to be no notable difference between trends of Orissa compared with Bihar, or West Bengal compared with East Bengal. The decline in yield per acre of gram, maize, and barley in the Greater Bengal region is also attributable to conditions in Bihar-Orissa rather than Bengal Province since these crops were relatively insignificant in the latter part of the region.[10]

What then accounts for declining yield per acre in Bihar-Orissa (in the period since its formation as a separate province)? Two elements in a possible explanation merit consideration. First, in the period starting with 1931/32 sugarcane acreage expanded, perhaps, at least in part, by moving into the more fertile rice lands and causing rice to shift to less fertile lands. Rice yield per acre on the remaining rice lands, and lands to which rice had shifted, would then have been less than before the increased importance of sugarcane. Sugarcane acreage rose from somewhat less than 300 thousand acres to over 400 thousand by 1933/34 and a peak of over

[10] In 1940/41, according to *Agricultural Statistics*, acreage (in millions) for Bengal Province was 0.1 for barley, 0.1 maize, and 0.3 for gram; in Bihar-Orissa Province it was 1.3 for barley, 1.4 maize, and 1.5 for gram.

500 thousand acres by 1940/41, subsequently declining to about 400 thousand acres. Rice acreage fell from 14.1 million in 1931/32 to 13.0 million in 1932/33, but rose in the next two years to 13.7 million acres.[11] The million acre rice reduction from 1931/32 to 1932/33 was unusual, but clearly only a small part of it could be attributed to sugarcane expansion.

Apart from the effect of expanding sugarcane acreage on the quality of remaining ricelands, there was also the possible effect of an exchange of crops on rice and sugarcane lands, with the direction of the exchange being detrimental to rice yield per acre and favorable to sugarcane. At the peak acreage for sugarcane, a maximum of 500 thousand acres of high quality rice land might have been replaced with poorer land for rice cultivation. This would only constitute less than 4% of total rice acreage. It does not seem likely that all of the original sugarcane lands were given up in this way; if as much as 200 thousand acres of sugarcane land was formerly under rice, it would represent only 2% of rice acreage. A change affecting only 2% of rice acreage in the Province could not have brought about such a large decrease in rice yield per acre. Even if there were a transfer of fertilizer, equipment, etc., from rice to sugar it is difficult to see how this could have altered rice yield per acre to the extent indicated by Figure 7.10. All that can be claimed, it appears, for the influence of sugarcane's increased importance on rice yield per acre, is that the latter may have declined slightly as a result; but this

[11] Comparison of rice acreage before 1935/36 with later years is affected by the addition of certain rice-growing parts of Madras Province to the new Orissa Province formed in 1935/36. Sugarcane acreage in all of Orissa was only about 30,000 acres, indicating that the additional Madras areas do not much affect comparisons for sugarcane acreage before and after that year.

If all ricelands originally yielded 100 units/acre, and if 2% of ricelands only yielded 50 units/acre, combined rice y/a would have fallen from 100 to 99.

influence of sugarcane was by no means commensurate with the rice yield per acre decline.

The second element in a possible explanation concerns rainfall trends in Bihar-Orissa. Rainfall data for the city of Patna (on the Ganges River, not far from the Bihar-United Provinces border) are given in Figure 7.10. Although there is little trend in rainfall over the period as a whole (-0.18% per year according to a straight line fitted by least squares to the logs of annual rainfall over the fifty-six years), in the period 1911 to 1930 rainfall trended sharply downward, as shown by the movement of five year moving averages for those years. A straight line fitted to average rainfall for 1911–20 and average for 1921–30 trends down at about the same rate as does rice yield per acre for Bihar-Orissa.

Causal relationship between rainfall and rice yield per acre is suggested by the fact that from 1911 to 1930 annual yield per acre changed in the same direction as annual rainfall in 15 of the possible 19 pairs of years under comparison.[12] June-July rainfall (Figure 7.10), might be somewhat more relevant to yield of the main ("winter" harvested) rice crop; for the June-July rainfall series and annual rice yield per acre, the algebraic signs of the differences between the pairs of successive years were in agreement for 17 of the 19 pairs of years. It must be noted, however, that for the following years rainfall and rice yield per acre trends moved in opposite directions.[13]

An adequate explanation for the declining Bihar-Orissa rice yield per acre trend clearly involves more than the two

[12] Of course it is possible that this association was coincidental and that some other factor was mainly responsible for the changes in rice yield per acre.

[13] Decade trend rates for rainfall were: 1911–21 –1.88%, 1916–26 –4.98%, 1921–31 –0.47%; for 1931–41 2.52%, and 1936–44 3.44% change per year.

elements discussed above, but pursuit of this problem would probably require study of district level data, which involves more detail than can be encompassed in this study.

FIGURE 7.10

RAINFALL AT PATNA, BIHAR, AND RICE YIELD PER
ACRE IN SUBDIVISIONS OF THE GREATER BENGAL
REGION, SEMILOGARITHMIC SCALE

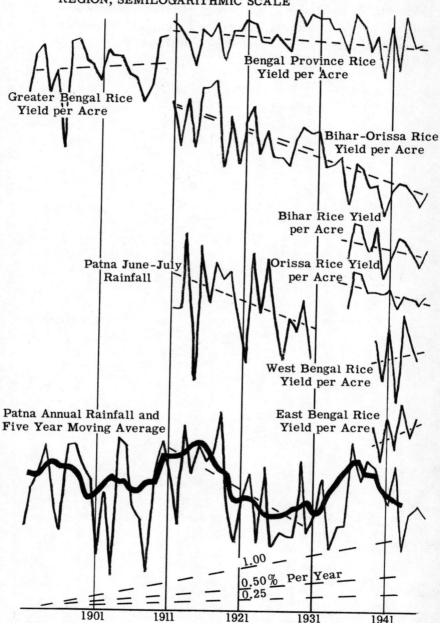

Source: From data in Appendix Tables 3A, 7A.

VIII

Change in Underlying Determinants of Yield per Acre Trends

1. Composition of acreage and output : changing acreage, crop composition of total output. 2. Water supply : rainfall and irrigation. 3. Soil fertility : repeated cropping without change in other conditions; change in the rate of cropping of land; change in the availability and use of fertilizer; inundations, silt, and soil fertility. 4. Technology : improved seed, agricultural education, agricultural equipment. 5. Intensity of cultivation : based on census labor force data, assuming agricultural labor increased at same rate as population, intensity of cultivation in Greater Bengal. 6. Size of landholding and fragmentation.

THE PREVIOUS CHAPTER DESCRIBED THE British India yield per acre trends and analyzed them mainly by showing changes in the individual crops and regions comprising the aggregate. In the present chapter changes in the underlying or fundamental determinants of crop yield per acre, such as water supply and soil fertility, are examined. Some data of this type were used in explaining the trends of individual crops; here the focus will be on all-crop yield per acre trends in British India and the regions. Certain data will be presented for each of the regions, some for Greater Bengal only, and some will refer to British India in general.

1. Composition of Acreage and Output

1.1 Changing acreage. If it is assumed that the most

179

naturally productive lands—those with most favorable soil, climate, and terrain—were used first, then as cultivation expanded into the remaining, submarginal, less productive lands, yield per acre would tend to decline. In all regions except Greater Bengal acreage was expanding (Table 6.2), tending, under the above assumption, to lower average yield per acre except in Greater Bengal where the slight decrease in acreage might have had the opposite effect.

However, lands previously uncultivated might have been rich in soil mineral content but lacking in water or perhaps in need of drainage. In the Punjab, Sind, and other dry lands it seems quite likely that the additional cultivated acreage made posible by irrigation was richer in soil mineral content than previously used lands. In the wet areas it appears likely that the level of fertility for submarginal lands was less than that of existing cultivated land. But even in such areas, it is possible that submarginal land was naturally as fertile as other lands and that the reason why they were previously unused was that improvements were required which were beyond the means of individual cultivators or landholders. This may have applied to the *bhils,* stagnant former water courses in central and western Bengal, some of which were drained and reclaimed for agriculture by government operations.

1.2 Crop composition of total output. Since nonfoodgrain yield per acre is generally higher in value than that of foodgrains, a progressive increase in the proportion of cropland in nonfoodgrains would tend to raise all-crop yield per acre. The extent to which this influenced trends is suggested by Table *8.1,* which gives average percentages of nonfoodgrain to all-crop acreage in the first and second halves of the fifty-six year period.

TABLE 8.1

AVERAGE NONFOODGRAIN/ALL-CROP ACREAGE, BY REGIONS,
1891/92–1918/19 AND 1919/20–46/47
(Percent)

Region	First Half	Second Half
Greater Bengal	14.8	12.8
Madras	14.5	23.3
United Provinces	18.5	19.4
Greater Punjab	12.5	15.3
Bombay-Sind	19.5	22.1
Central Provinces	30.2	28.9
British India	17.7	19.9

Note

Value of non foodgrain y/a in ratio to foodgrain y/a was about as follows : Greater Bengal 2, Madras 1½, United Provinces 2+, Greater Punjab and Bombay-Sind 2, Central Provinces 1, British India less than 2.

Source : Data in Appendix Table *4C*.

Change in yield per acre attributable to this influence would evidently have been small. Small increase in all-crop yield per acre would have tended to occur in United Provinces, Greater Punjab, Bombay-Sind, and for British India as a whole. A slight decrease in yield per acre would have occurred in Greater Bengal. Only in Madras was the change notable, tending toward increase in all-crop yield per acre.

2. Water Supply

Change in the supply of water—rainfall or irrigation—relative to crop acreage generally affects yield per acre. Most of the annual variation in yield per acre is probably due to

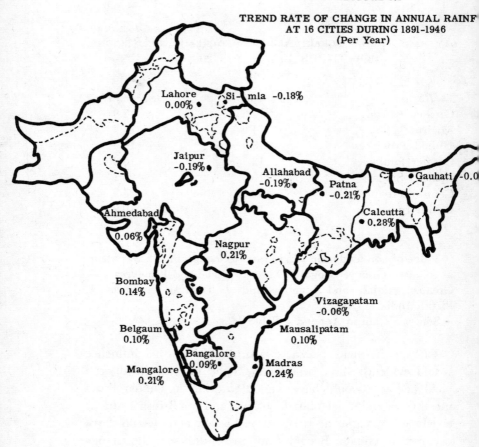

FIGURE 8.1

TREND RATE OF CHANGE IN ANNUAL RAINF
AT 16 CITIES DURING 1891-1946
(Per Year)

fluctuations in rainfall; irrigation tends to reduce these variations. A number of qualifications may be noted, however, with
respect to the influence of these conditions on yield per acre.
For unirrigated areas, rainfall and yield per acre are not always in a positive relationship. Too much rain may lower
yield per acre; seasonal distribution of rainfall is likely to be
more important than total amount in affecting yield per acre
for most years. For irrigated areas, first it should be realized
that the data are usually given in the form of acres irrigated;
availability of water for the same irrigated acreage may vary
with weather conditions. Second, existence of irrigation facilities does not necessarily mean that they will have an uplifting
effect on yield per acre in all years; they may only serve as
insurance against drought, raising yield per acre in what
would otherwise be subnormal years.[1] Third, excessive use of
irrigation water may have injurious effects on soil, and yield
per acre, because of waterlogging or formation of alkali pans
close to the soil surface.[2]

2.1 Rainfall. Over a sufficiently long period, in most regions,
there would be no trends in rainfall. Trend rates of change for
sixteen stations during the fifty-six year period, shown in
Figure *8.1,* and obtained by (least squares) fitting of straight
lines to the logarithms of annual rainfall, were, in fact, found
to be relatively small. It is nonetheless of interest to compare
these with the regional all-crop yield per acre trends.[3]

There does not appear to be much regularity in the statis-

[1] Harold H. Mann, "The Economic Results and Possibilities of Irrigation," *Indian Journal of Agricultural Economics,* XIII, 2 (1958).
[2] O. H. K. Spate, *India and Pakistan* (New York: E. P. Dutton & Co.,
1954), pp. 204–211.
[3] The comparison is slightly affected by the difference in methods used
for obtaining the rainfall and yield per acre trends. Correspondence, or
its absence, between the trends neither proves nor disproves causal connection since "other things" are not likely to have been constant over
such a long period.

tical association between rainfall and yield per acre over the period as a whole. The all-crop yield per acre trend in Madras (0.65%) is of a much higher order of magnitude than the rainfall trends there; in Greater Punjab the almost equally high yield per acre rate of increase (0.62%) is associated with negative or zero rainfall trends. The moderately low yield per acre rate in Bombay-Sind (0.28%) might have resulted from the rainfall trends in that region, but in United Provinces the rainfall and yield per acre (0.15%) trends are in opposite directions. In Central Provinces both yield per acre and rainfall trends were small and in the same direction. In the case of Greater Bengal rainfall trends for the two stations were divergent; the upward trend at Calcutta was opposite to the regional all-crop yield per acre trend (-0.34%), but the negative trend at Patna was in accord with this crop trend.

Rainfall trends over shorter periods of time appear to have some causal influence on yield per acre trends; Figure *7.10* showed a similar trend for the main crop in Bihar-Orissa, rice, and rainfall at Patna during 1911–30, but not, however, for the following period. Decade rainfall trends were computed for three stations–Calcutta and Patna in Greater Bengal, and Allahabad in United Provinces—using the same working decade terminal years as for all-crop yield per acre. Table *8.2* shows a moderate extent of correlation between the rainfall and crop yield per acre trends; trends were in the same direction in six of the ten reference decades at Calcutta, and five of the ten reference decades at Patna and Allahabad.

2.2 Irrigation. Irrigation could have a great effect on yield per acre, as much as 50% increase on the Indo-Gangetic Plain, or even 100% in South India, where rainfall is more variable.[4] Although there was a substantial increase in irrigation during the period, its effect on average yield per acre would depend

[4] Mann, *op. cit.*, pp. 1–2.

TABLE 8.2

REFERENCE DECADE RAINFALL TRENDS AT CALCUTTA, PATNA, AND
ALLAHABAD, AND REGIONAL ALL-CROP YIELD PER ACRE TRENDS
(Percent per Year)

| | Greater Bengal Rainfall | | Yield per | United Provinces Rainfall | Yield per |
	Calcutta	Patna	Acre	Allahabad	Acre
1891/92–1901/02	4.29	–1.12	0.56	–1.88	1.42
1896/97–1906/07	–0.34	–1.28	–0.61	–2.35	–0.64
1901/02–1911/12	–0.87	0.41	0.07	–1.46	0.09
1906/07–1916/17	0.87	2.62	0.29	3.31	0.66
1911/12–1921/22	2.92	–1.88	–0.97	0.35	–0.32
1916/17–1926/27	–1.16	–4.98	–0.81	0.69	–0.32
1921/22–1931/32	3.47	–0.47	0.73	–0.78	–0.56
1926/27–1936/37	–0.58	2.42	–0.30	–1.02	1.63
1931/32–1941/42	0.94	2.52	–1.44	1.84	0.60
1936/37–1946/47	0.43	3.22	–0.90	–1.34	–1.03

Source : Rainfall, calculated from annual data in Smithsonian
Miscellaneous Collections, *World Weather Records,* continued
from 1941 by U.S. Department of Commerce, Weather Bureau;
the annual rainfall data were converted into five year moving
averages and trends were then obtained between the terminal
years for the all-crop yield per acre working decades. Yield per
acre, Appendix Table *5B.*

on the change in proportion of cultivated area under irrigation.
From 1908/09 to 1945/46 irrigated land in British India
increased by 14%, but net area sown increased by 11%; there
was therefore not a great improvement in water supply relative
to area sown. The change would appear somewhat more favorable if measured from 1821/92; unfortunately, however, the
reports of irrigated area in Bengal up to 1907/08 did not
include irrigation from private canals, tanks, and wells.

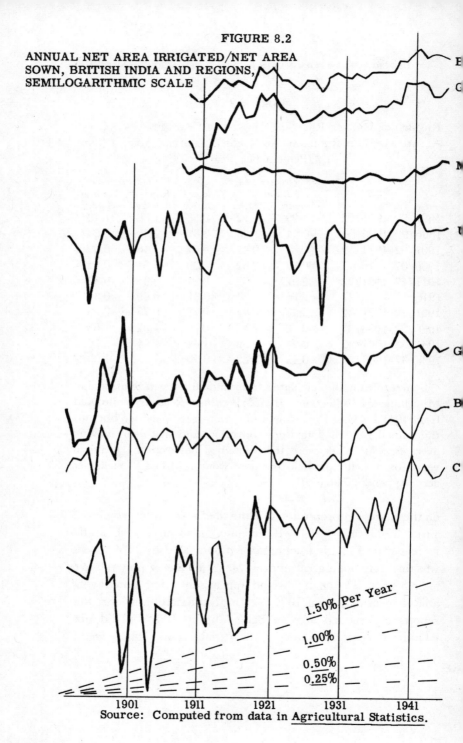

FIGURE 8.2

ANNUAL NET AREA IRRIGATED/NET AREA
SOWN, BRITISH INDIA AND REGIONS,
SEMILOGARITHMIC SCALE

1.50% Per Year

1.00%

0.50%
0.25%

1901   1911   1921   1931   1941
Source: Computed from data in Agricultural Statistics.

Comparison with the earlier years is also affected by the absence of data for the large Madras zamindari areas up to 1906/07; these areas were considerably more irrigated than the previously reported areas of that region.

Table *8.3* reveals that the slight change in proportion of land irrigated, implied by the above data, was characteristic of all but one of the regions.

TABLE 8.3

AVERAGES OF IRRIGATED LAND/CULTIVATED LAND FOR SELECTED
PERIODS, BY REGIONS
(Percent)

Region	First Period	Second Period	Years in Each Period
British India	21.6	23.6	1908/09–21/22, 1922/23–45/46
Greater Bengal	13.3	15.0	*Same*
Madras	28.7	27.9	1907/08–21/22, 1922/23–45/46
United Provinces	28.7	29.4	1891/92–17/18, 1918/19–45/46
Greater Punjab	43.5	55.5	*Same*
Bombay-Sind	15.5	16.4	1891/92–18/19, 1919/20–45/46
Central Provinces	2.9	4.8	1891/92–17/18, 1918/19–45/46

Source : Calculated from annual percentages in Appendix *8A*, which are based on net area irrigated and net area sown data in *Agricultural Statistics*. Data for 1946/47 were not available.

Averages for the earlier and later years of the period changed by only one or two percentage points except in Greater Punjab. In one region, Bombay-Sind, where the averages show a slight increase, there was a long period of decrease, from about 1900 to 1930, seen in Figure *8.2*. In Central Provinces, relative to the proportion of land irrigated in the first part of the period, there was a considerable increase in the average for the last half of the period, but even by then the extent of land involved in irrigation was too small to have much effect on average yield per acre.

The exceptional region was Greater Punjab, where the average percent of land irrigated increased by twelve points between the two halves of the period. Figure *8.2* indicates that the trend was steadily upward in that region.

How much of an effect would this have had on average yield per acre in Greater Punjab? If yield per acre there was 50% higher on irrigated land as compared with unirrigated land, and if at the begining of the half century about 40% of the land was irrigated, then at the indicated trend rate of increase in the proportion of land irrigated (about 0.90% per year), over 60% of the land would have been irrigated by the end of the period. If unirrigated yield per acre is represented by 100 index units, and irrigated by 150 units, then average yield per acre would have been 120 units at the beginning and 130 units at the end of the period. This would correspond to nearly 0.20% per year increase in average yield per acre. Since the average trend rate of increase in yield per acre was actually 0.62% per year, it may be estimated that about a third of the increase in yield per acre in that region was attributable to increased irrigation.

3. Soil Fertility

3.1 Repeated cropping without change in other conditions. Constant use of the same land for the same crops may exhaust the land by "mining" the soil mineral content. Change in other conditions—types of crops grown, the rate of cropping of land, and use of fertilizer—could, of course, offset, or aggravate, the effect of repeated cropping. Rotation of crops is a well-known means of deterring soil-exhaustion, but some rotation systems, like rice-jute (Chapter VII, 1.1), have the opposite effect; the extent and effect of changes in rotation systems on average yield per acre cannot be estimated here. Use of improved, high-yielding, types of seed is likely to drain minerals out of the soil more rapidly than lesser-yielding varieties, as occurred, for example, with the adoption of hybrid corn in the United States Corn Belt. Assuming these and other relevant conditions to have been unchanged (in the next sections changes in these conditions will be considered), what effect is to be expected from repeated cropping of the same land?

The following view, given by the Royal Commission on Agriculture in India, though probably contrary to popular opinion, appears very credible.[5]

Such experimental data as are at our disposal support the view that, when land is cropped year by year, and when the crop is removed and no manure is added, a stabilized condition is reached; natural gains balance the plant food materials removed by crops and by other losses and no appreciable changes are to be expected in the outturn of crops except those due to changing seasons, provided that the same system of cultivation is adhered to. While the paucity of records of crop outturn throughout India over any long period of time makes the matter impossible of exact proof, we are of opinion that the strong presumption is that an overwhelming proportion of the agricultural lands of India long ago reached the condition to which experimental data point. A balance has been established, and no further deterioration is likely to take place under existing conditions of cultivation.

In this view, then, a low but stable yield per acre would have been characteristic of India, except where other conditions were changing.

[5] *Report* (London: H.M. Stationery Office, 1928), p. 76.

3.2 Change in the rate of cropping of land. Doublecropping, raising of a second crop on given land during a single year, is likely to effect yield per acre. If yield per acre is based on net area sown, or area of cultivated land, then an increase in the proportion of land doublecropped would increase yield per acre. If total area sown (or all-crop area), including double-cropped area, is the basis for yield per acre, then an increase in proportion of doublecropped land would probably lower the average yield per acre sown. A second rice crop on the same land in a given year would raise total yield per acre of that land for the year, but on the total rice acreage yield per acre would be less than if only one crop were raised on the land in that year. Repeated cropping of land under the same system of doublecropping would be compatible with a low stable all-crop yield per acre, but an increase in the proportion of land doublecropped would probably cause decreasing yield per acre.

The extent of doublecropping varied regionally, from less than 5% in Bombay-Sind, to about 10% in Central Provinces, 15% in Greater Punjab and Madras, 20% in Greater Bengal, and 25% in United Provinces. Since most of India has altern-ately wet and dry seasons, the second crop is likely to be different from the first, i.e. rice followed by wheat in United Provinces, except where irrigation water is available. Where the crops are different the rate of impoverishment of soil would tend to be less, but this depends on the combination of crops.

Table *8.4* and Figure *8.3* show that there was relatively little change in the proportion of doublecropped land to net area sown. In all regions except United Provinces the propor-tion increased, but only slightly. For British India as a whole the average proportion for the last part of the period was less than one percentage point higher than for the first part. Increase in doublecropping would have thus tended to slightly lower all-crop yield per acre except in United Provinces. The strongest effect would have been experienced in Central Provinces, where the upward trend in doublecropping appears (in Figure *8.3*) to have been continuous over the whole period.

TABLE 8.4

AVERAGE PROPORTION OF DOUBLECROPPED AREA/NET AREA SOWN
FOR 1891/92–1918/19 AND 1919/20–45/46, BY REGIONS
(Percent)

Region	First Period	Second Period
British India	14.7	15.6
Greater Bengal	20.2	21.4
Madras	12.7	14.6
United Provinces	24.7	22.6
Greater Punjab	15.2	16.3
Bombay-Sind	3.5	4.1
Central Provinces	6.3	10.0

Source : Computed from data in Appendix *8B,* based on *Agricultural Statistics.*

Fallowing, temporary idling of cultivated land may also be expected to affect soil fertility. If, out of a given area of generally cultivated land (net area sown plus fallow land), fallow land increases, then soils are "rested" more frequently, allowing greater buildup of nitrogen content and increased organic content from decaying grass roots or other plant materials (depending on the vegetation cover of the fallow land). However, if land was taken out of cultivation when its (anticipated) productivity became submarginal, and if fallow land was returned to cultivation as soon as its (anticipated) productivity was restored to the marginal level, then change in the proportion of land fallowed would merely maintain a given level of yield per acre. It would seem that

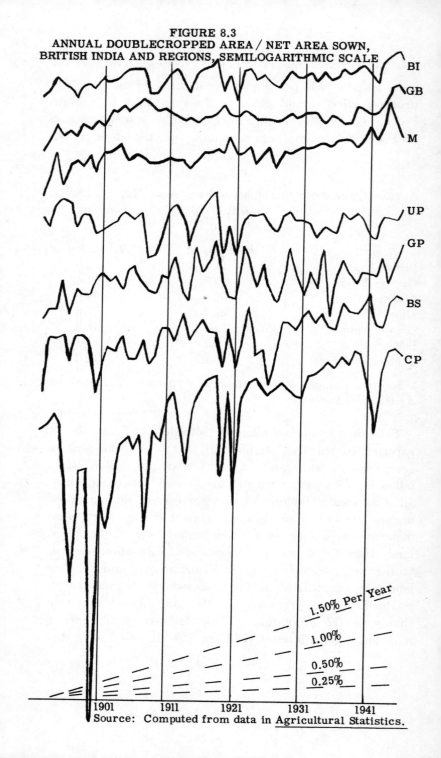

FIGURE 8.3
ANNUAL DOUBLECROPPED AREA / NET AREA SOWN,
BRITISH INDIA AND REGIONS, SEMILOGARITHMIC SCALE

BI

GB

M

UP

GP

BS

CP

1.50% Per Year

1.00%

0.50%

0.25%

1901   1911   1921   1931   1941

Source: Computed from data in Agricultural Statistics.

fallowing would mostly reflect the latter condition, but the motivation for fallowing is not sufficiently well known to clearly estimate its effect on yield per acre.

Change in the proportion of fallow to generally cultivated land is shown in Table 8.5. The British India measure is of questionable validity because the provinces differed in length of period required for land to be defined as fallow, and because there was some change in the relative importance of the combined regions; for a single region the measure is more useful. Two of the regions, Greater Bengal and Madras substantially increased in proportion of land fallowed. The opposite is seen for Greater Punjab and Bombay-Sind, marked decrease there probably being due to extension of irrigation and consequent lessening of the need to hold land fallow in order to accumulate sufficient water for a crop. The changes in United Provinces and Central Provinces were apparently insignificant.

TABLE 8.5

AVERAGE PROPORTION OF FALLOWED TO GENERALLY CULTIVATED LAND, FOR FIRST AND LAST HALVES OF PERIOD, BY REGIONS

Region	First Half	Second Half
British India	21.2	22.4
Greater Bengal	16.0	24.3
Madras	23.9	30.6
United Provinces	9.2	8.4
Greater Punjab	25.9	17.7
Bombay-Sind	46.6	35.3
Central Provinces	16.0	15.8

Note

Periods, 1891/92–1918/19 and 1919/20–45/46, except for Greater Bengal's 1897/98–1920/21, 1921/22–45/46. Data for other years not available.

Source : Appendix 8C, based on data in *Agricultural Statistics*.

3.3 Change in availability and use of fertilizer. Dung is used, among other purposes, for fertilizer, and may have a substantial effect on yield per acre. As early as 1894, the Indian Department of Agriculture reported that yields per acre of rice and wheat were increased several hundred pounds by use of dung (100–130 hundredweights per acre).[6] In some areas, however, where rainfall was insufficient, manure had an adverse effect, drying out the lands and crops.[7]

Experiments were conducted in use of human excrement, "night soil",[8] but this material was ". . . . considered a defilement and even the untouchable workers of the very low castes refused to work in the fields . . . which had been fertilized in this fashion three months previously; only men of the sweeper caste consented to work in these fields."[9]

Dung is also used for other purposes, as a cooking fuel, for which it gives a desirable slow steady heat, and also in mixture for plastering earthen house walls.[10] It may be assumed that these needs would have priority over the use of dung for fertilizer. The rate of increase in human population relative to change in cattle population therefore affects availability of dung for use as fertilizer.

Livestock data are available from quinquennial censuses starting with 1919; in the figures given below only cattle and water buffalo, the larger animals, are included.[11] The propor-

[6] Dr. J. W. Leather, "Notes on Value of Indian Cattle Dung," *Agricultural Ledger,* No. 3, 1894.

[7] From interviews with cultivators reported in the Punjab Board of Inquiry Village Surveys published between 1928 and 1940.

[8] *Agricultural Ledger,* No. 16, 1895.

[9] Translated from Arthur Geddes, *Au Pays de Tagore* : la civilisation rurale du Bengale occidentale et ses facteurs géographiques (Paris : Librarie Arman Colin, 1937), p. 173.

[10] According to the *Food Plan for India* (1945) cited by Spate, *op. cit.,* p. 238, about 40% was said to be used for fuel, 40% for fertiliser, and the remainder wasted.

[11] The censuses were issued by the Department of Commercial Intelli-

tion of cattle to all-crop acreage (average for 1917/18–21/22) for British India was 0.78 head per acre; the figure was unchanged by 1930, but thereafter declined to 0.69 in 1945. In Greater Bengal the proportion rose from 0.89 in 1919 to 0.96 in 1930, but thereafter declined, more steeply than in British India, to 0.69 (the same as for British India). From about 1920 to 1930 the changes in cattle population, human population, and acreage, were such as to leave availability of dung per acre for fertilizer unchanged for British India and slightly more favorable in Greater Bengal. But after that, availability of dung for fertilizer declined considerably.

The benefits from use of chemical fertilizer were generally not known and the amount used was insignificant relative to average yield per acre. Imports, which may be taken as a sufficiently approximate measure of use, were less than two thousand tons average per year during 1898/99–1923/24. There was a great increase in 1924/25 and imports averaged 60 thousand tons in the following years,[12] but even in the latter period imported fertilizer was in a ratio of less than one pound per all-crop acre. Fertilizer was, of course, not spread so thin, but rather was concentrated on growing of certain commercial crops. Even if it were used on only half the sugarcane and cotton acreage, the proportion would have been a mere fifteen pounds per acre. Some upward influence was exerted by use of these imports, but in the aggregate its effect was of virtually negligible significance.

Ironically, exports of fertilizer material, mostly cattle bones and fish meal, were larger than imports in both periods,

gence and Statistics except for the 1945 census, brought out by Ministry of Agriculture.

[12] Based on data from Department of Commercial Intelligence and Statistics, *Annual Statement of Seaborne Trade of British India;* the large jump in 1924/25 suggests the possibility of a change in classifications.

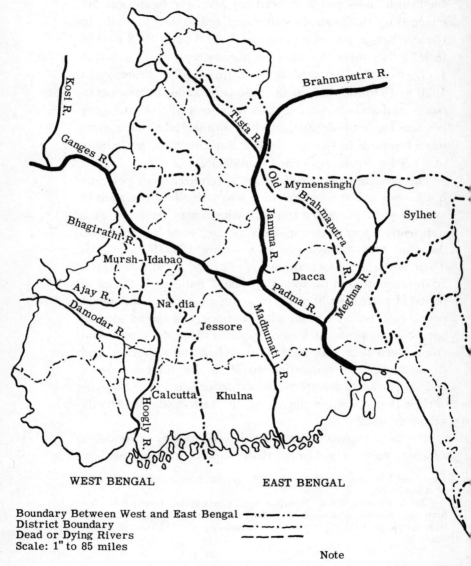

FIGURE 8.4

RIVERS AND ADMINISTRATIVE DIVISIONS OF BENGAL

Boundary Between West and East Bengal —··—··—
District Boundary
Dead or Dying Rivers
Scale: 1" to 85 miles

Note

For other details see S. P. Chatterjee, Bengal in Maps (Calcutta: Orient Longmans Ltd., 1949)

though they were declining. Had these materials not been exported, however, they would not necessarily have been used domestically, in view of costs and the religious bias against using animal material in this manner.

3.4 Inundations, silt, and soil fertility. In addition to the preceding man-influenced changes in conditions affecting soil fertility, there were also, in some parts of India, changes largely brought about by natural forces, namely, those associated with shifting of river courses and areas of inundation. Such changes not only reduced the availability of water in certain areas, but, what was probably more important, where there were no longer floodings, the periodic restoration of soil fertility by fresh layers of flood-distributed silt was also eliminated. There would then be no natural offset to the leaching of soil minerals, a highly active process in hot, humid climates.

One theory accounting for shifts in river courses is that after a delta area becomes sufficiently elevated by gradual silting, rivers become easily diverted, perhaps at a time of unusually heavy flow, into the surrounding, relatively lower, areas.[13] Productivity in the no-longer inundated areas would lessen, but in the aggregate this effect might be offset by increased productivity of other areas receiving the benefit of inundation.[14] It is possible, however, that the increased water and silting in the surrounding areas might be superfluous in its effect on productivity.

In northeastern India there have been notable shifts in river

[13] S. C. Majumdar, *Rivers of the Bengal Delta* (University of Calcutta 1942), pp. 44 ff. See also Arthur Geddes, "The Alluvial Morphology of the Indo-Gangetic Plain," Institute of British Geographers, *Transactions and Papers,* 1960, Publication No. 28.

[14] This is somewhat analagous to W. W. Hunter's observations that in unusually high flooding, ". . . innundations may cause temporary scarcity but the losses of low-lying localities are usually made up by the subsequent abundance on the high grounds." *The Annals of Rural Bengal* (London : Smith, Elder and Co., 1868), p. 50.

courses and attendent changes in inundations. The alluvial cone or fan of the Kosi River in northeastern Bihar (Figure 8.4) ". . . has moved westward in the last 150 years and caused tremendous damage;" the upper Gandak River in north-western Bihar ". . . shifted a mile in course in the 1920's and during the last century has shifted eastward."[15] The Tista River in northern Bengal, a tributary of the Ganges River up to about the end of the 18th century, shifted course to empty into the Brahmaputra River. This in turn, by about 1830, is believed to have caused the main flow of the Brahmaputra to move through the Jamuna River, adversely affecting the flow through the remaining seaward portion of the Brahma-putra River in northeastern Mymensingh District.[16] But the greatest of the changes has been the shifting of the main Ganges flow from the Bhagirathi-Hoogly River to the more eastern-coursing Padma River. This is the change which created the "moribund delta" between the Bhagirathi-Hoogly, Ganges, and Padma Rivers.

The timing of the latter shift suggests, however, that it was not an active influence on soil fertility and yield per acre in the period of this study. Diversion of Ganges waters into the Padma is said to have occurred sometime toward the beginning of the sixteenth century.[17] The Bhagirathi diminished in importance after that, and especially after the beginning of the nineteenth century, when it flooded over the city of Nadia.[18]

[15] Geddes, "Alluvial Morphology," op. cit., p. 262.

[16] Majumdar, op. cit., pp. 51–64.

[17] Majumdar, op. cit., p. 52. Tavernier, the French traveler, wrote in a letter, January 6, 1666, that Bernier was going overland from Rajmahal (on the Ganges in Bihar) to Cossimbazar (on the Bhagirathi in Mur-shidabad District, Bengal) because of a sand block at Suti, northeast of Cossimbazar. The river above Nadia (town) was described as full of shoals in 1683. In 1757 Siraj-ud-daula, the Nawab (or king) of Bengal, is said to have driven immense piles into the river at Suti (presumably to block British navigation). Bengal District Gazeteers : *Murshidabad*, by L. S. S. O'Malley (Calcutta, 1914), pp. 9–11.

[18] Geddes, *Au Pays de Tagore*, pp. 44–51.

Geddes claims, however, that ". . . the general drying-up was accentuated after 1860, largely caused by the construction of dikes and embankments for the railroads and highways."[19] Increase in malaria, decrease in soil fertility, and (slight) decrease in population or slowing down in the rate of growth of population, followed from the cessation of inundations and the stagnant waters left behind by poor drainage.[20] "It is a common belief," he wrote, "confirmed by statistics, that annual output is diminishing. A brahman farmer told us that his fields did not produce half of that which they did twenty years ago; he attributed this to a lessening of piety."[21]

The areas to which Geddes refers, it should be appreciated, are in three or four of the twenty-four districts of Greater Bengal, and comprise only about 5% of its net cultivated area (Chapter VII, 1.1). Moreover, it may be recalled from the

[19] *Au Pays de Tagore*, p. 51. Geddes further notes that ". . . without overlooking their great importance, it is evident that if there had not been the natural beginning of this drying-up, these works would have been delayed for a long time, just as they have waited in eastern Bengal." Translated from the French.

Majumdar, *op. cit.*, p. 51, also stresses the role of flood embankments in preventing the rivers from spilling over into the lands of central and western Bengal.

As late as 1870 and 1886, however, the Bhagirathi is reported to have breached the embankments causing floods. *The Imperial Gazeteer of India* (Oxford, 1908), Vol. XVIII, Murshidabad, pp. 44–53.

[20] Geddes, *Au Pays de Tagore*, pp. 163–164. The same theme is also discussed in other articles by Geddes: "The Population of Bengal, Its Distribution and Changes," *Geographical Journal*, Vol. 89, No. 4, 1937; "The Population of India," *Geographical Review*, Vol. XXXII, 1942; "Half a Century of Population Trends in India, a regional study of net change and variability, 1881–1931," *Geographical Journal*, XCVIII; "Variability in Population Change in India and Regional Variations Therein, 1921–40," Institute of British Geographers, *Transactions and Papers*, 1960, No. 28; International Population Conference, "Variability in Change of Population and its Significance: with examples, India–Pakistan and North America, to 1951," *Proceedings*, Vienna, 1959.

[21] *Au Pays de Tagore*, p. 173. The statistics to which he refers are apparently district-level, and have not been examined for the present study.

previous chapter, that it was the decrease in Bihar-Orissa rice
yield per acre, not that of Bengal Province, in which the
moribund delta is located, which brought about the considerable decrease of all-crop yield per acre in the Greater Bengal
region as a whole.

4. Technology

4.1 Improved seed. Probably the most important of the
technological changes affecting yield per acre was the adoption
of certain types of improved seed (some of which were discussed in the preceding chapter). A regional summary of the
increase in area under improved seed relative to all-crop
acreage is given below, based on data for 1922/23 and 1938/
39. The crops included—rice, wheat, sugarcane, cotton, and
jute—occupied over 90% of the improved seed area.

TABLE 8.6

IMPROVED SEED ACREAGE AS A PERCENTAGE OF ALL-CROP
ACREAGE FOR 1922/23 AND 1938/39, BY REGIONS

Region	1922/23	1938/39
Greater Bengal	0.8	6.2
Madras	1.2	8.5
United Provinces	1.0	5.0
Greater Punjab	5.5	32.9
Bombay-Sind	2.8	15.8
Central Provinces	2.0	8.1
British India	1.9	11.1

Source : Based on data in Appendix Table *4C* and the *Review
of Agricultural Operations,* also the *Review of Agriculture and
Animal Husbandry,* issued by the Imperial Council of Agricultural Research.

From the increase in proportion of crop area under improved seed, it may be surmised that a tendency toward increase in yield per acre due to use of improved seed probably occurred in all regions. But the outstanding advance was in Greater Punjab, where wheat and cotton were the major crops, and also in Bombay-Sind, where these crops were also important.

By how much would yield per acre trend be influenced by change to improved seed? If better seed improved yield per acre by as much as 50% on the average for all crops, then the 1938/39 yield per acre in Greater Punjab would have been about 13% higher than in 1922/23; this would represent a constant growth rate of about 0.75% per year, which is close to the average increase of 0.90% per year in all-crop yield per acre in the last four reference decades. In Bombay-Sind on like assumption, the total increase would have been about 8%, and the annual rate of increase in yield per acre attributable to better seed would have been 0.37%, compared with the 0.35% per year rate of increase in all-crop yield per acre in the last period of time. Finally, in British India as a whole, the increase would have been about 6% over this period of years, or 0.17% per year, compared with the all-crop yield per acre rate of 0.18% per year.

Some evidence of the widespread penetration of this aspect of technological improvement may also be seen at an opposite level of data. A study of twelve Punjab villages, in separate districts of the province, showed that nine of the twelve had at least tried improved seeds, and in four villages such seeds were being employed, particularly for varieties of wheat, American cotton, and sugarcane. Reasons for rejection of improved seed were given as follows:[22]

[22] "Crop Production and Population Trends in Twelve Punjab Villages, 1900–1931," unpublished ms. of the author, 1953; based on the Punjab Board of Inquiry Village Survey.

a sugarcane with double the yield of the local variety was said to have inferior juice and was hard to press; American cotton tried in one village was found to mature too close to the frost season and not yield as much; a brand of wheat tried in one village gave slightly higher yields but it was found that when the ears were cut the grain fell; moreover, the straw yield was poor, and the grinding quality bad; in another case where improved wheat was tried it was found that the cattle would not eat the chaff, thereby causing a feed problem, and it was also found that more labor was required for threshing. In general it was felt that the old seed was more suited to the local soil, and that new seed was too expensive. In one village where improved seed was tested by the Department of Agriculture, only the big land-lords, whose farms were used, knew the results.

Three qualifications may be made concerning the effect of improved seed on yield per acre. First, some improvements do not involve physical yield per acre, but rather quality or other characteristics. Second, there are tendencies for the seed to become mixed with the old strains after successive crops. Third, there is a tendency for seeds which give heavier yields to drain minerals out of the soil more rapidly, so that without additional fertilizer the tendency toward yield improvement from better seed might be offset by that of impoverishment of soil.

4.2 Agricultural education. Another indication of the extent of technological change, though indirect, is the increase in agricultural education.[23] From 1916 to 1946 the number of agricultural colleges increased from five to nine, and their students from 445 to 3110. In the same years the number of lower level agricultural schools increased from one to nine, and their students from fourteen to 891. Of course, this number of graduates or trained persons per year appears infinitesimal

---

[23] Data from education series in the Department of Commercial Intelligence and Statistics, *Statistical Abstract for British India* series.

compared to the number of cultivators and villages. Many of those educated in these schools probably became leaders in their communities or agricultural workers for government.

The effectiveness of this and other types of agricultural education may again be indicated by referring to the Punjab twelve-village study cited above.

A demonstration farm was usually not more than ten miles away from each village, but only three villages reported having had anyone visit them. There was one visitor from each of two villages, and a few visitors from the remaining village. In almost all cases there was a District Agricultural Association but only one big landlord and one cultivator in another village were active members. There were occasional cattle fairs given by the District authorities and there were usually exhibitions and demonstrations at such fairs. Other demonstrations were given in the villages; two such demonstrations given prior to the surveys showed no noticeable effect. In another instance the provincial department of agriculture occupied four acres of land a few miles from one of the villages, but nobody in the village was aware of what was being done there.

4.3 Agricultural equipment. Very little change occurred in the type of equipment used. As of the late 1930's about 32 million plows were being used in India and agricultural department agencies were selling about 7 or 8 thousand per year; for other types of equipment there was even less progress.[24]

Again it may be of interest to observe the village-level response to new types of equipment, according to the twelve-village Punjab study :

Almost every village was said to have experienced no change in agricultural implements used. Villagers were sometimes aware of new type plows being publicized, and in a few villages new plows were being bought. But the unanimous opinion was that the old

[24] Nanavati and Anjaria, *op. cit.,* p. 45.

plows were better for various reasons. The new plows were said to be expensive, to strain the oxen,[25] to be unrepairable locally, to be suited for large fields only, to expose and dry out the undersoil, and to be less effective in uprooting weeds. New plows had been tried in at least five of the villages.

Mechanical seed drillers, which were shown to produce substantially higher yields, were also rejected for the same reasons as given for new plows. New type rotary chaff cutters, however, were adopted in at least two of the villages.

Two villages were changing from leather or earthen buckets for water-drawing to iron buckets. It was found that these eliminated the need for cleaning out broken pots from wells. When iron pots were used on Persian wheels in one village it was found that labor required for tending the wheel was reduced because the improved efficiency made it desirable to lower the operating time.

5. Intensity of Cultivation

Other things remaining the same, it is generally assumed that with increased intensity of cultivation (labor used per acre cultivated), yield per acre also increases, though at a diminishing rate. Increase in the number of agricultural workers does not necessarily mean that the amount of labor, in terms of hours or effort, is changed. The same work could be divided among more workers.

If more labor is actually used it is also possible that output would not increase, that marginal product of labor would be zero. Yield per acre is limited by the number of plants per acre and the vigor with which they grow. Given an initial amount of labor sufficient for the sequence of plowing, seeding,

[25] In this connection it is of interest to see the report by C. P. G. Wade, *Mechanical Cultivation in India, a History of the Large Scale Experiments Carried Out by Burmah-Shell Oil Storage and Distribution Company of India* (Delhi: Imperial Council on Agricultural Research, 1935).

weeding, and harvesting, additional labor is not likely to add to output by performing more of the same kind of work. With India's density of population it would seem that 'sufficient labor' was available at the beginning of the period in most of India.

It is not possible to establish whether or where the marginal product of agricultural labor was zero, but at least it should not be assumed that increased number of agricultural workers means more labor performed or more output produced per acre.

Changes in the intensity of cultivation are examined below from two viewpoints. One is based on census labor force data; unfortunately these are of doubtful use for the present purpose because of changes in census classifications and questionable reliability of the reported data. An alternative viewpoint is based on changes in total population and the assumption that agricultural labor was a constant proportion of population during the period studied.

5.1 Based on census labor force data. Recent studies by the Thorners suggest two ways in which the census labor force data may be used more profitably.[26] One is of general applicability, to use data for males only since the count of females, especially in agriculture, was based on non-uniform and uncertainly applied criteria. To follow this suggestion means eliminating use of the 1891 census, in which dependents were lumped along with workers, and the 1941 census, in which totals for males and females in labor force were not given.

Some question remains even when only male data are considered. In examining the regional data available for decades between 1891 and 1951 the Thorners found a general decline in the proportion of working males (and females) which was

[26] Daniel and Alice Thorner, *Land and Labour in India* (Bombay: Asia Publishing House, 1962), pp. 75–77.

not explicable on ground of change in age structure, urbaniz-
ation, education, or rural unemployment.[27] In Greater Bengal,
for example, males in the work force were 24 million in 1901,
and, despite an increase of 20% in male population by 1931,
only 24.3 million by the latter year. In United Provinces and
Bombay there was virtually no difference in the number of
working males for these two years, though male population
increased by 5% and 20% respectively. In Madras male
workers increased by 12% but male population increased by
22%. For All-India, male workers increased by 7% while
male population increased by 20%.[28]

A second suggestion of the Thorners, applying to the size of
work force in agriculture, is to lump both agricultural labor
and general labor in order to obtain better comparisons between decades. Most general labor was for agricultural purposes, and, again, the criteria for distinguishing between agricultural and general labor apparently were not consistently
applied over the decades. Increases in one of the categories
appear to have been associated with decreases in the other
category.

Agricultural workers per all-crop acre for the decades 1901–
1931 are shown in Table 8.7 for four regions for which data
were available. The decade changes in intensity of cultivation
were for the most part quite small; four were from 5% to 8%,
but the remaining eight were less than 3%. If it is assumed, to

[27] Daniel and Alice Thorner, *The Working Force in India, 1881–1951*
(Census of 1961 Project, Indian Statistical Institute, Bombay Branch)
Text pp. 8–10.
[28] Males of age less than 10 years were 26.5% of male population in
1901 and 28.0% in 1931; males over 50 years were 10.8% of male population in 1901 and 9.5% in 1931. Males over 10 and less than 50 were
62.7% of male population in 1901 and 62.5% in 1931. This slight decrease
is not enough to account for the difference in reported increase in male
work force and male population. Based on data given in 1931 census,
cited in Jathar and Beri, *op. cit.*, 1.43.

TABLE 8.7

MALE AGRICULTURAL WORKERS PER ALL-CROP ACRE, 1901 TO
1931, BY REGIONS

	Greater Bengal	United Provinces	Madras	Central Provinces
1901	.385	.329	.342	.213
1911	.391	.337	.344	.197
1921	.415	.340	.333	.198
1931	.396	.341	.329	.211

Source : Computed from all-crop acreage Appendix Table *4C,*
and agricultural workers and general laborers from Thorners',
Working Force, Tables 28, 58, 79, 106.

approximate the effect of intensification, that the average work
year is 2 thousand hours, then in Greater Bengal from 1911
to 1921 the average acre would have had an increased labor
input of forty-eight hours; in Central Provinces the hours per
acre would have declined by thirty-two from 1901 to 1911.
For the other decade changes an average of about ten hours
per year per acre would have been involved, an amount which
would seem to be negligible.

Comparison of the changes in intensity of cultivation with
changes in all-crop yield per acre in these regions does not
suggest correlation, but, of course, this could have been the
result of changes in other influences, which were not constant
over the period. Six of the decade to decade changes were in
the same direction, and the remaining six changed oppositely.
In three of the largest four changes in Table *8.7,* the yield
per acre changes were in the opposite direction of the change
in intensity of cultivation. None of this evidence seems to suggest that yield per acre was much affected by the changes
taking place in intensity of cultivation.

5.2 Assuming agricultural labor increased at the same rate as population. The British India work force in agriculture was nearly constant in proportion to the total work force (74% to 76%), according to census data assembled by the Thorners for 1881–1931.[29] Census data show that the work force decreased in proportion to population during that period. In this section it is assumed, however, that the work force, or at least the agricultural work force, remained in the same proportion to population over the 1891–1947 period.

Comparison of rates of population growth (Table 5.2) and all-crop acreage (Table 6.2) indicate the change in intensity of cultivation. Where population rates exceed acreage rates, intensity increased; the opposite occurred where population rates were less than acreage rates.

The changes in intensity of cultivation compared with changes in all-crop yield per acre were as follows. On the average for the ten reference decades, intensity and yield per acre moved in the same direction in three regions (Madras, Bombay-Sind, Central Provinces), and in opposite directions in the remaining three regions; in British India as a whole yield per acre remained about the same while intensity increased. On the average for the first four reference decades, intensity and yield per acre moved in opposite directions in five regions and British India, while in Madras there was little change in intensity, but yield per acre rose rapidly. On the average for the last four reference decades, in four regions, both intensity and yield per acre increased, but in Greater Bengal, Central Provinces, and British India as a whole, increasing intensity was associated with decreasing yield per acre.

As in the preceding section, no notable correspondence was

[29] *Land and Labor in India,* pp. 77–81.

found between changes in intensity and yield per acre, though again, this may have resulted from change in other factors.[30]

A contributing factor to the lessened effect of additional labor on output may be noted, however, in the smaller number of plows available for the average worker in the later part of the period (for which data were available). Between 1919 and 1945 the number of plows reported in British India increased by less than 10%, but population (and presumably the agricultural work force) increased by about 30%. In Greater Bengal the changes were similar, a 5% increase in plows and 25% increase in population. In both British India and Greater Bengal, however, the number of plows per acre remained about the same for 1945 as it was in 1919.[31]

5.3 Intensity of cultivation in Greater Bengal. The Greater Bengal region was unusual because intensity of cultivation increased considerably over the whole period while yield per acre declined. Census data concerning both labor force and total population support the view of increasing intensity. The labor force data show a decline in non-agricultural labor force between 1891 and 1931,[32] despite the increase in population;

[30] Described in preceding sections of this chapter. B. F. Johnston and J. W. Mellor, "Agriculture in Economic Development," *American Economic Review*, LI. 4 (September 1961), p. 570, stress the greater importance of improved technology over increase in conventional, i.e. labor, inputs in increasing productivity: "Studies of the growth of agricultural productivity in the United States have underscored the importance of unconventional inputs and suggest that technological change has been about as important as the quantitative increase in conventional inputs in bringing about increased production. Technological innovations were probably even more important in the impressive growth of agricultural productivity in Denmark; the average annual (compound) rate of increase between the 1880's and the decade of the 1930's was about 2%."

[31] Data on plows from quinquennial *Livestock Censuses*, 1919–1945.

[32] Male and female non-agricultural work force (excluding agriculture and general labor), declined from 7.5 to 6.8 million; for males only, the decline was 5.6 to 5.0 million. Thorner, *Work Force of India*, Tables 28, 30.

if this was true, then the agricultural work force must have increased, and since acreage declined slightly, intensity must have increased. The population data lead to a 50% greater ratio of population to all-crop acre in 1891 compared with 1941.

In view of the incongruity of the intensity and yield per acre trends, a check is made below with other data as to whether the non-agricultural labor force might have increased substantially enough during the period to reduce intensity. Greater Bengal population grew from 1891 to 1941 by about 25 million. The work force would have grown by about 8 million, if a third of population were part of it. If three-quarters of the work force were in agriculture, then the agricultural work force would have increased by about 6 million and the remaining 2 million would have been non-agricultural work force.

First, how does this 2 million estimated increase check with what is implied by the urban population growth data?[33] The four cities of Calcutta, Dacca, Jamshedpur, and Patna increased their total population by about 2 million in that period; their work force presumably increased by about 700 thousand. There were 23 other towns in 1941 having populations between 50 and 100 thousand, with a total population of 1.6 million; the increase in their population over 1891 is not conveniently available, but if it was as much as fifty percent, then their work force (non-agricultural) would have increased by about 300 thousand. According to these calculations, towns and cities with population over 50 thousand increased their work force by about one million from 1891 to 1941. It does not seem likely that the non-agricultural work force increase in towns smaller than 50 thousand would have been one

[33] Urban population data from Tables 4 and 5, *Statistical Abstract for British India, 1940–41.*

million. The estimated increase above, of 2 million in non-agricultural labor force, therefore seems generous, but it still leaves a 6 million increase in agricultural labor force.

A second approach for checking the above estimates is to use industry employment figures. Jute manufacturing employment rose from 60 thousand to 300 thousand during 1890–1940; the younger steel industry reached a labor force of about 50 thousand by the latter year.[34] Other industries would have had to increase by 1.65 million employment if the above assumptions held; unfortunately, data for these other forms of employment could not be examined for this study. Trade, transportation, government, cotton textile manufacturing, and food processing probably increased; handicraft and other traditional occupations are likely to have decreased.

None of the data examined above suggest that a large increase in the agricultural work force of Greater Bengal did not occur.

6. Size of Landholding and Fragmentation

Subdivision of landholdings into smaller sizes and scattering of fragments of these holdings into non-contiguous parcels may also influence yield per acre. It is generally agreed that both subdivision and scattering increased during the period. In what direction would this have influenced yield per acre?

Waste of crop area and perhaps labor would tend to reduce yield per acre. More land would probably be used for paths, boundaries, and for the turning of plows at the end of furrows in the smaller plots. The wasted area would probably not be

[34] Data for 1940 from Table *146, Statistical Abstract for British India,* 1940–41; 1890 data from Daniel H. Buchanan, *The Development of Capitalist Enterprise in India* (New York: Macmillan Co., 1934), pp. 138, 281 ff. Data for both industries were for British India, but both industries were then localized in Greater Bengal.

reckoned with in the estimates of crop acreage; crop area would tend to be the same but yield would tend to be less and consequently yield per acre would decline. If labor were scarce, then output might also have been reduced because of wasted time in going from field to field. Smaller output per cultivator might also reduce savings and the opportunity to make improvements.

There are, however, two conditions which may have at least partially offset these effects. First, the cultivators in many instances were not proprietors. If the latter's holding remained the same, net earnings per proprietor need not have been unfavorably affected. Of course, it is also well known that many proprietors had little interest in using their earnings for this purpose, either because of a preference for other types of spending or because of more advantageous return on additional land rather than improvement of previously held land.

Second, assuming that there were an abundance of labor, subdivision of holdings, it is held, may utilize additional labor because smaller plots, especially for rice, facilitate transplanting, pest elimination, weeding, and water control, bringing about increased yield per acre though not increased yield per man. The same view acknowledges that smaller holdings generate less savings, but holds that maximum agricultural output is more important than the financial savings which might otherwise have materialized.[35]

[35] B. H. Farmer, "On Not Controlling Subdivision in Paddy Lands," *Transactions and Papers,* Institute of British Geographers, 1960, pp. 225–235. He criticizes N. Kaldor, J. R. Hicks, and others for their views on this subject given in *Papers by Visiting Economists,* Colombo, Ceylon, 1959.

IX

Summary and Conclusion

1. Methodology and its bearing on measures of trend : choice of price weights, effect of estimates for unreported yields per acre, reliability of the reported rice yields per acre in Bihar-Orissa, typicalness of average trend rates. 2. Productivity, the means of increased output : comparison of acreage and yield per acre changes, the first four reference decades, the last four reference decades, and the ten reference decade, half-century period; significant aspects of the changes in acreage; change in yield per acre; change in the underlying determinants of yield per acre. 3. Output and availability : foodgrains, nonfoodgrains, and all-crops.

1. Methodology and Its Bearing on Measures of Trend

With the completed view of the crop trends it is more feasible to evaluate the effects of decisions concerning methodology on the measurements of trend.

1.1 Choice of price weights. Consideration was given in Chapter IV to the choice of time period from which a price structure would be obtained for the purpose of weighting and combining the output of different crops. Suitable data for the period prior to World War I were not found available. The World War periods and the years of great depression in the early 1930's were ruled out because of abnormal relationship between commercial and non-commercial crops which would be expected for those times. It was found that the structure of prices in the middle Twenties, the period from which the weights were taken, was similar to that for the middle Thirties.

Suppose a different structure of prices, from some other period, was used; how much effect would it have on the output trends? The first full postwar year, 1946/47, had a price structure sufficiciently different from that of the middle years of the Twenties and Thirties to serve for exploring this question. Due in part to government price control, and to conditions in both world and domestic markets, sugarcane and cotton, the crops with high average trend rates of increase in output, had relatively lower prices than was previously customary. Wheat, which also had a high rate of increase in output, had, on the other hand, a higher price relative to other commodities. Groundnut, which also had a high rate of increase in output, was slightly higher in relative price. Rice, which had a declining output trend, had a slightly lower price relative to other commodities. Table *9.1*, for the areas of British India which became part of independent India, shows the change in price for each crop (for which data were available) relative to the change in general price level from 1938/39 to 1946/47.

TABLE 9.1

CHANGE IN AVERAGE BRITISH INDIA CROP PRICE, RELATIVE TO CHANGE IN PRICE LEVEL OF ALL-CROPS, 1938/39 TO 1946/47

Crop	Change in Crop Price Relative to Change in All-Crop Price Level	Crop	Change in Crop Price Relative to Change in All-Crop Price Level
Rice	–3%	Bajra	2%
Jowar	–3%	Groundnut	5%
Linseed	–20%	Maize	11%
Cotton	–25%	Barley	18%
Sugarcane	–37%	Sesamum	21%
Jute	–65%	Gram	22%
		Tobacco	24%
		Rape-Mustard	24%
		Wheat	30%

Source : Computed from Index Numbers of Harvest Prices of Principal Crops in Part A States and Delhi given in Ministry of Agriculture, Directorate of Economics and Statistics, *Indian Agricultural Price Statistics,* June 1950. The price level for these crops in 1946/47 was 333% of 1938/39. Output trend rates for the crops are given in Tables 5.1 and 5.5.

If 1946/47 prices were used as weights, the average rate of increase in aggregate foodgrain output would have been slightly more favorable than with 1924/25–28/29 prices because of the greater importance given to the rapidly rising trend for wheat and the slight decrease in importance of the the negatively sloped rice trend. Prices of foodgrains as a group increased 5% more than the general price level of all-crops and nonfoodgrains as a group consequently had slightly less weight in the all-crop output trend. Reduced importance of nonfoodgrain aggregate would in turn lessen the trend rate of increase in all-crop output. Combining the British India ten-reference decade output rates of change for each crop when weighted by its 1946/47 price gives an average rate of 0.32% per year, as compared with 0.37% when the earlier prices were used as weights.

It is thus seen that, although the aggregate trend rate of increase is affected by the price structure used for weighting the crops, the effect is relatively small. The price structure of 1946/47 was very different from that of 1924/25–28/29 or 1934/35–38/39, but the trend rate for all-crop output was only slightly lowered. In view of this, it seems likely that within the limits of change which occurred in Indian price structures, the choice of period from which weights were taken did not have an important effect on results of this study.

In considering the desirability of alternative price structures another criterion may be raised, namely the relative importance of particular crops to the population. Inasmuch as the price structures reflect marketing of crops, and inasmuch as large portions of some crops were not marketed, especially among the foodgrains (Chapter IV, 1), none of the weighting structures obtained in this way may be considered entirely satisfactory. A price structure taken from the later years of the period would, however, tend to be more representative than one from earlier in the period because the portion of crops marketed in the early part was less than in the later period. In this connection it may also be noted that foreign markets for certain crops may have caused prices of those crops to be disproportionate to their domestic significance (depending on how domestic supply was affected).

1.2 Effect of estimates for unreported yields per acre. One of the important findings of this study is that output increased at a relatively rapid rate during the period of the first four reference decades. For some crops, as was explained in Chapters II and III, yield per acre was unreported during that period and a method was devised for estimating yields per acre of crops in the later period when nearly all were reported. How much error might have resulted from this method of estimating yields per acre, and how much effect might it have had on the output trends?

The six minor foodgrain crops and rice in the less important producing regions (United Provinces, Central Provinces, Bombay-Sind, and Greater Punjab), were chiefly affected by this problem (Table 2.2) Appendix 3A indicates that the reported crops on which estimates were based for the minor foodgrain crops were mainly wheat and sesamum; estimated rice yields per acre were based on sesamum in United Provinces, Central Provinces, and Bombay-Sind, and on wheat in Greater Punjab. Trend in yield per acre of wheat and sesamum during the early part of the period would consequently be carried over into trends for yields per acre of the unreported crops. It was found that wheat's average trend rate of increase in yield per acre was 1.25% per year and sesamum's was 0.58% during that period. In view of this it is not surprising that the minor foodgrains and rice had relatively high rates of increase in yield per acre during that period (Table 7.1).

Is it reasonable to expect that the forces which gave rise to increasing wheat and sesamum yield per acre would also have had a similar effect on the minor foodgrains and in the unreported rice regions? It seems doubtful that the forces raising wheat yield per acre would have had like effect on the minor grains. Much of the rise in wheat yield per acre during the early part of the period was due to the increased proportion of acreage irrigated (Table 7.2), but it is hardly likely that the minor grains would have been subject to such a force, especially in the early part of the period (in the later part of the period for which data were available there appears to have been little change in the proportion of minor foodgrain acreage irrigated, Table 7.3). A small part of the wheat yield per acre increase in the early part of the period was due to use of improved seed; only 5% of the acreage was reported in this category as of 1922/23. For the minor grains, however, even as late as 1937/38 less than one percent was reported under improved seed (Chapter VII, 1.1).

The rising yield per acre reported for sesamum in the early decades was, however, in all likelihood, not caused by either irrigation or improved seed, but rather by favorable rainfall trends for that period. A part of the increase for wheat yield per acre may have also been due to this cause. Minor grains and other crops would presumably have also benefitted from the favorable weather trends. But a portion of the yield per acre increase estimated for the unreported grains was due to a partly unwarranted element in the statistical relationship derived between wheat and these grains.

Rising output shown for the minor foodgrains in the early part of the period reflects increasing acreage (Table 6.1), as well as increasing yield per acre. The average rate of increase in minor foodgrain output during the first four reference decades may be approximated as 1.25% per year (combined crop rates weighted by their average outputs). Acreage for these crops increased at an average rate of about 0.65% per year (combined crop rates weighted by their average acreage), and the rate of increase for yield per acre was about 0.60% (combined crop rates weighted by their outputs). Since sesamum yield per acre increased at a rate of 0.58% during the same period, the 0.60% per year increase for minor grains does not appear unusual. But if, say, half of the minor foodgrain yield per acre rate of increase was due to unwarranted statistical relationship with wheat, then it might be said that 0.30/1.25 or about a quarter of the percentage rate of increase in minor foodgrain output could be attributed to this cause, and three-quarters to acreage or yield per acre factors making for increase.

In the aggregate of foodgrain output the minor foodgrains constituted about a quarter of the total. If these crops had a weight of about a quarter in determining the trend rate of increase for aggregate foodgrain output (0.61% for the first four reference decades), and if a quarter of the trend rate of increase in minor foodgrain output is attributable to exaggeration caused by the statistical association with wheat, then the latter would have been responsible for only a sixteenth of trend rate of increase in aggregate foodgrain output.

To sum up on this problem, it appears that the use of wheat yields per acre in estimating the yields per acre for some other grain crops is likely to have given an upward bias to the yield per acre trends for the latter crops. As a result the percentage rate of increase in minor foodgrain output may have been exaggerated by about a quarter. In the aggregate foodgrain output rate of increase, however, the effect of this exaggeration would have been relatively small, only about a sixteenth of the percentage rate.

1.3 Reliability of reported rice yields per acre in Bihar-Orissa. Attention was drawn, in Chapters VII and VIII, to the steep decline of rice yield per acre in Greater Bengal. From the comparison of Bengal and Bihar-Orissa rice yields per acre in Figure 7.2, it was seen that the regional decline was attributable to Bihar-Orissa Province in the period after 1911/12, when the latter was separated from the original Bengal Province. Although declining rice yield per acre also occurred in United Provinces during that period, the decline there was not as steep as in Bihar-Orissa, as may be inferred from Figure 7.2 and Table 7.4. In the absence of evidence (during the course of this study) which would explain the Bihar-Orissa decline, there appears to be some justification for questioning the reliability of this portion of the data. These grounds are strengthened, though not conclusively, by an examination of the changes in standard yield per acre in Bengal and Bihar-Orissa, shown in Table 9.2.

In the original province the standard was relatively high, 1234 pounds, but remained unchanged during the years up to the division into Bengal and Bihar-Orissa. As early as 1892 it was believed, by the head of the local Agricultural Department, that the standard for the main, winter, rice crop, based on the weight of cuttings from what were believed to be typical plots, was nearer to 1110 pounds, but his impressions were not strong enough to justify a change in the standard.[1]

---

[1] *Agricultural Statistics,* 20th issue, p. xxv.

TABLE 9.2

QUINQUENNIAL STANDARD YIELD PER ACRE AND AVERAGE OF
CONDITION REPORTS FOR RICE IN BENGAL AND BIHAR-ORISSA

	Bengal		Bihar-Orissa	
	S	C	S	C
1891/92–1896/97	1234	71.8	Part of Bengal	
1897/98–1901/02	1234	83.2		
1902/03–1906/07	1234	79.1		
1907/08–1911/12	1234	79.3		
1912/13–1916/17	983	94.1	1234	84.2
1917/18–1921/22	1036	86.9	1234	92.0
1922/23–1926/27	1029	83.6	987	87.2
1927/28–1931/32	1022	88.8	987	90.4
1932/33–1936/37	1111	74.1	987	71.6
1937/38–1941/42	1030	72.2	823	78.6
Annual Trend Rate	–0.47	–0.01	–0.80	0.10

Notes and Sources

a. (S), standard for winter rice (main variety) in pounds, as
reported in *Estimates;* (C), condition, percentage of standard,
yield per acre reported in *Estimates* divided by standard; trend
rate, in percentage change per year, obtained by fitting a simple
exponential equation to above data.

b. Bihar and Orissa became separate provinces in 1935. (S)
above in last quinquennium is for Bihar only; in Orissa it was
800 pounds.

c. Estimating standards were generally set at the district level
and the provincial average was not directly used for estimating,
except in the early years, according to *Agricultural Statistics,*
34th issue, for 1917/18, p. 280.

Since the condition reports, or percentages of actual yields
compared with standard, were considerably below 100% for
those years, the high standard did not necessarily mean high

reported yields per acre. Starting with 1912/13 the standard was reduced in Bengal; condition reports rose, somewhat off-setting the reduction in standard. But in Bihar-Orissa the 1234 pound standard remained for another decade, and condition reports also rose. Subsequently the standard was reduced by nearly a third, and condition reports were also somewhat reduced.

If the reported rice yields per acre for the last ten years of the period may be taken as a comparison of rice yield per acre in the two portions of the Greater Bengal region, then Bihar-Orissa yield per acre was about 25% less than that in Bengal. By the close of the period the standard yields per acre for Bengal and the remaining part of the region were in approximately the same relationship as the average yields per acre. But in the first decade of separate existence, the Bihar-Orissa standard was about a third higher than that in Bengal.

The possibility appears, therefore, that when Bihar-Orissa became a separate province, the former 1234 pound standard was erroneously continued, and was not offset by a downward movement in condition reports. In the next decades the stand-ard was reduced to bring it closer to reality, but it was not until the Thirties that average condition reports declined noticeably. It appears that progressive reduction in the Bihar-Orissa rice yield per acre standards, which were not offset by opposite movements in condition reports, largely account for the decline of yield per acre in that province.

How much effect would such a downward bias in Bihar-Orissa rice yield per acre have had on the crop trends for Greater Bengal and British India? One way of exploring this question is to assume that there was no trend toward change in rice yield per acre in that region (starting with 1912/13, when the two provinces were separate). The contrast in output trend rates when recomputed on the basis of this assumption, and as previously given (in Chapter V), is shown in Table *9.3*.[2]

TABLE 9.3

GREATER BENGAL AND BRITISH INDIA OUTPUT AND YIELD PER ACRE TRENDS AS ORIGINALLY GIVEN AND AS MODIFIED BY THE ASSUMPTION OF CONSTANT LEVEL OF GREATER BENGAL RICE YIELD PER ACRE FROM 1912/13 TO 1946/47

(Percent per Year)

| | Greater Bengal | | | | British India | | | |
| | Av. Last Four RD | | Av. All Ten RD | | Av. Last Four RD | | Av. All Ten RD | |
	Orig.	Modified	Orig.	Modified	Orig.	Modified	Orig.	Modified
FG Y/A	–0.74	0.08	–0.55	–0.10	–0.44	–0.15	–0.18	0.04
AC Y/A	–0.48	0.21	–0.34	0.07	–0.02	0.18	0.01	0.27
FG Y	–0.61	0.39	–0.73	–0.15	0.03	0.30	0.11	0.30
AC Y	–0.23	0.40	–0.45	0.00	0.35	0.56	0.37	0.55

Note: "Original" rates are given in Chapters V and VII. The method used for deriving trend rates for the recomputed annual series of output and yield per acre was the same as that used for obtaining trends from the original series. FG and AC Y/A stand for foodgrain and all-crop yield per acre; FG and AC Y stand for foodgrain and all-crop output.

[2] The annual series were recomputed in the following manner: (1) annual rice yields per acre reported for the period up to 1911/12 in Greater Bengal were reduced by 22% to make the average for that period equal to the average for 1937/38–41/42, 749 pounds; (2) a parabolic trend was fitted to reported rice yields (as given in Appendix Table *3A*) for 1912/13–46/47. The relative deviation of each year's reported yield per acre from the trend value for that year was obtained. The yield per acre for each year in the annual series was established as 749 plus or minus this relative deviation; this series thus contained annual fluctuation but no trend (given in Appendix Table *9A*). (3) Greater Bengal rice output was recomputed by multiplying annual acreage by the yield per acre series established in the manner described above. (4) The Greater Bengal and British India aggregate foodgrain and all-crop series for output and yield per acre were recomputed by taking out the original Greater Bengal rice output and using in its place the recomputed output series (Appendix Tables *9B* and *9C* give the recomputed annual series for the aggregates.)

The difference in trend rates between the original and modified series is especially noticeable for the last four reference decades in Greater Bengal, about three-quarters of a percentage point more favorable than the original trend rate of change. For the region's ten-reference decade average rate the difference is about a half of percentage point. For British India the modified series give trends which are about a quarter of a percentage point more favorable than given by the original series. Since the above modified rates are probably the most favorable which might be expected from a correction due to the element of unreliability in the Bihar-Orissa rice yield per acre series,[3] the original and modified trend rates may be taken as the limits within which the actual trends fell.

How significant is the change up to the more favorable limit of trend rates? The modified trend rates for output, though more favorable, remain less than the population growth rates of about one percent per year in the last four reference decades. For Greater Bengal the originally negative output trend rates for the last four reference decades are replaced with more credible, rising, trends, even though per capita output would still have been falling. For British India the virtually changeless level of foodgrain output in the last part of the period is replaced with a trend which was rising, though relatively slowly. The British India all-crop yield per acre trend is no longer seen as almost at constant level, but rather it pitched upward at a rate which appears beyond the range of that which might have been caused by rainfall alone. The difference in results for British India calls attention to the import-

[3] If instead of removing the trend from the whole Greater Bengal rice yield per acre series after 1912/13, the Bengal Province component was left unchanged and only the Bihar-Orissa Province portion was revised, then the modified rates would be somewhat less favorable than those given above.

ance of viewing the aggregate in terms of its regional components.

1.4 The typicalness of average trend rates. Attention was called in the preceding chapters to the fact that rates of change for many of the series were higher in the first part of the period than in the last, and that an average of these rates consequently may not be typical of any part of the period. The British India nonfoodgrain output rate of increase, for instance, was 1.31% over the entire period, compared with 1.66% and 1.08% for the first and last four reference decades; Madras all-crop output, similarly, was 0.98% for the half-century compared with 1.71% and 0.42% in the first and last four reference decades. In some cases where the ten-reference decade rate average was very similar to the rate for the last four reference decades (as it was for British India all-crop output, foodgrain output, and all-crop yield per acre), it was because the first four reference decades were offset by the middle two. If the ten reference decade average rates are viewed in combination with the rates of retardation (or, more rarely, acceleration) in reference decade rates, then the danger of misinterpreting the significance of the average rates may be avoided.[4]

The groupings of reference decades into first and last four reference decades, rather than first and last five (or halves of the period), was chosen to minimize the combining of very dissimilar rates. In both the middle two reference decades (1911/12–21/22 and 1916/17–26/27) rates for British India all-crop and foodgrain output and yield per acre as well as the British India aggregate acreage rates were negative. The characteristic of negative rates in the middle two reference

---

[4] Individual reference decade rates for crops and regions are given in Appendix Tables 5A and 5B; average rates were given in tables of Chapters V–VII.

decades was typical of Greater Bengal and United Provinces. In the other regions, however, negative rates were generally found for the first of the two middle decades but not for both; for these regions a different grouping of reference decades would have been more suitable, but this would have made interregional comparisons more complicated.

The dissimilarity of reference decade rates within the four or ten reference decade groups suggested the question of whether the averaging of such rates might have given rather different results than a single trend fitted to the entire time span for the group of reference decades. This might seem particularly possible where only four reference decades were averaged.

A number of series were tested to see the extent to which a trend rate obtained by fitting a straight line to logarithms of quinquennial averages would differ from the average of reference decade rates for those years. For British India all-crop output the ten-reference decade rate was 0.37% compared with 0.40% from the alternative measure of trend suggested above; for the first four reference decades both measures gave a rate of 0.84%. On the other hand, a grouping of the last six reference decades, including the negative rates of the two middle decades, gave a rate of only 0.06% compared with 0.29% from a straight line logarithmic trend.

Several comparisons were made for series in which the last four reference decades contained rates which were quite dissimilar. For British India foodgrain acreage the individual rates were 0.06%, 0.21%, 0.18%, and 1.10% in the last reference decade; the average rate was 0.39% compared with 0.34% obtained by the alternative method. British India nonfoodgrain output rates in those decades were 2.31%, 1.40%, 1.25%, and −0.66% in the last reference decade; the average of these rates, 1.08%, was similar to the alternative rate of

1.16%. Similar results were obtained by averaging the British India all-crop yield per acre rates (0.28%, 0.39%, –0.34%, and –0.42%) and by using the alternative method, –0.02% and –0.06% respectively. In one case, British India foodgrain output, the individual rates (–0.17%, 0.06%, –0.51%, and 0.75%) averaged to 0.03% whereas the rate of the straight line fitted to logarithms of the quinquennial averages was –0.20%. It appears for the most part that even where rates within the group were dissimilar, the method of averaging rates did not give results much different from those of the alternative method.

2. Productivity, the Means of Increased Output

2.1 Comparison of acreage and yield per acre changes. The following section characterizes and contrasts the changes in acreage and yield per acre by crops and regions in the first part of the period, in the last part, and in the period as a whole. For each time period the analysis of change will follow the same sequence—first the pattern of change for the British India aggregate of crops will be given, then the extent of conformity of the individual crops and regions to the British India pattern will be described. Each aggregate will be considered in turn : foodgrains, nonfoodgrains, and then all-crops. Rates on which analysis is based are given in Tables *6.1, 6.4, 6.5, 7.1,* and *7.4.*

2.11 The first four reference decades. The pattern for the British India foodgrain aggregate was upward trends, approximately equal in rate, for both acreage and yield per acre. Of the eight *crops*, five had distinctively larger yield per acre than acreage rates (two of the latter, jowar and ragi, were negative) and the remaining three crops—bajra, gram, and barley—had the opposite condition. Since rice and wheat were among the five crops, the period might be characterized, from the viewpoint of foodgrain crops, as one in which yield per acre increase was of somewhat greater importance than acreage expansion. In three of six *regions*—Madras, Bombay-Sind, and Central Provinces—yield per acre also rose more rapidly than acreage; in two other regions the reverse was true, and in Greater Bengal both trend rates were about equally negative.

The British India nonfoodgrain aggregate also had upward trends, of approximately equal rates, for both acreage and yield per acre; the percentage rates were more than twice as large as the foodgrain rates. All ten *crops* had upward yield per acre trends, and seven of these were more favorable than the corresponding acreage trends (rates for four of which, including sugarcane, were negative). However, the three crops which had larger acreage than yield per acre trend rates— coton, jute, and groundnut—were among the most important in value of output. Three *regions* had larger acreage than yield per acre trend rates—Greater Punjab, Bombay-Sind, and United Provinces (where the yield per acre rate was negative) —and two, Madras and Central Provinces, had approximately equal rates; Greater Bengal yield per acre trended upward while its acreage decreased.

For all-crops as a group at the British India level, acreage expanded somewhat more rapidly than yield per acre. Nonetheless, all eighteen *crops* had upward yield per acre trends, twelve of which, including rice and wheat, were more favorable than their acreage rates (six of which, including sugarcane, were negative). Four of the six *regions* also had more favorable yield per acre than acreage trends—Madras, Bombay-Sind, Central Provinces, and Greater Bengal (where the acreage rate was negative). Evidently the rapid rates of acreage increase in the Greater Punjab and United Provinces, and in the cotton, jute, and groundnut crops, more than offset the favorable yield per acre rates in the other comparisons.

2.12 The last four reference decades. It was seen above that in the first period, acreage and yield per acre shared in expanding output of both foodgrain and nonfoodgrain aggregates. In the last period, however, trends for acreage and yield per acre of the aggregates were not in the same direction and were, moreover, different for the foodgrains compared with the nonfoodgrains.

Britsh India aggregate foodgrain acreage continued upward as in the first period, but this tendency toward increased output was offset by an equally strong downward trend in yield per acre. Acreage trends were upward for five *crops* (excluding gram, barley, and ragi) while yield per acre trend rates were all negative or negligibly upward (as for wheat and maize), The *regional* trends conformed almost perfectly to this pattern —acreage trends were upward except in Madras where there was little change in level, and yield per acre trends were downward or negligible except in Greater Punjab where it exceeded the acreage rate.

The British India nonfoodgrain aggregate, on the other hand, continued its upward movement in yield per acre but levelled off in acreage. There was little conformity of the individual crops to this pattern, however. Six of the ten *crops* had downward yield per acre trends, but the others, especially sugarcane, cotton, and tea, which counted heavily in output, had continued upward trends. Downward acreage trends also occurred for six crops, but this was offset by the upward trends of sugarcane, tea, groundnut, and tobacco. *Regional* yield per acre trends were upward except in Central Provinces where there was little change in level; two regions showed little change in acreage level, and the upward acreage trends in

Madras, United Provinces, and Greater Punjab were apparently offset by steep decline in Central Provinces.

For the British India all-crop aggregate, upward foodgrain acreage more than offset the negligible change in nonfoodgrain acreage, and the downward yield per acre trend for foodgrains, though it represented a much larger share of output, was offset by the upward trend of nonfoodgrains. Of the eighteen *crops,* a total of twelve had downward yield per acre trends, and nine had downward acreage trends; for seven crops (among which was jute) trends were downward for both acreage and yield per acre. All the *regional* acreage trends were upward, but declining yield per acre trends in Greater Punjab and Central Provinces offset rising trends for the other regions.

To sum up, the difference between the first and last period behavior for the all-crop aggregate was that in the first period, both acreage and yield per acre rose, but in the last period acreage continued to rise while there was little change in level of yield per acre.

2.13 The ten-reference decade, half-century, period. Foodgrains, in aggregate, at the British India level, had an upward slightly accelerating acreage trend and a downward yield per acre trend with increasing decade rates of decrease. Only three of the foodgrain *crops* exhibited a similar pattern, but one of these was rice, which, of course, had much weight in the aggregate. Acceleration in the decade acreage rates for rice also explains the similar condition for the aggregate; for otherwise, with the exception of a slight acceleration in jowar decade rates for acreage, all other trends showed deceleration. The four remaining important crops had upward trends for both acreage and yield per acre, but rates for the former exceeded those for the latter. Only one *region,* Bombay-Sind, displayed the same pattern as the British India aggregate. In three regions the trend for acreage was more favorable than for yield per acre, either because the latter though upward was less rapid (Greater Punjab), or because it was, in average, close to zero (United Provinces and Central Provinces). In two regions the average acreage trend rate was about zero, but yield per acre in one of these regions, Greater Bengal, trended downward while in the other, Madras, it was upward. All regional trend rates of change in reference decade rates were negative except for acreage in Greater Bengal, Bombay-Sind, and Central Provinces.

Nonfoodgrains, in aggregate, for British India, had upward trends for both acreage and yield per acre, but the percentage rate for the latter was twice as large as for acreage; acreage rates, moreover, were decelerating while yield per acre showed more steady rate of increase over the decades. Three important *crops* had a similar pattern—sugarcane, cotton, and tea—and most of the remainder at least had more favorable yield per acre than acreage trends, either because the yield per acre rates were positive and acreage negative, as it was for four crops, or because yield per acre declined less rapidly than acreage, as was the case for one crop. Jute was the only crop which had about equal rates for both yield per acre and acreage. Groundnut was the only crop which had a much larger rate for acreage than yield per acre. Rates of change in reference decade rates were generally negative, but there was acceleration for four acreage trends, notably for sugarcane, and four of the rates for yield per acre were close to zero. Among the *regions,* two had trend patterns similar to the British India aggregate, United Provinces and Central Provinces, and this pattern was reinforced by Greater Bengal's negative acreage and positive yield per acre rates; the other three regions had relatively large but equal rates for both acreage and yield per acre. Yield per acre trends were accelerating in United Provinces, Greater Punjab, and especially Bombay-Sind.

In summary, for the aggregate of all-crops, at the British India level, the acreage trend rate was positive, though decade rates were decelerating, and the yield per acre rate was about zero in average, though also decelerating in decade rates. This pattern reflects the upward acreage trends for both foodgrains and nonfoodgrains, and the offsetting trend rates for yield per acre, negative for foodgrains and positive for nonfoodgrains. In four regions the trend rates for acreage were larger than for yield per acre, though the latter also trended upward. In Madras the yield per acre was also rising, even more rapidly than acreage. But in Greater Bengal the steep downward rate for yield per acre was enough to offset the upward yield per acre trends elsewhere; there was relatively little change in acreage in this region.

2.2 *Significant aspects of the changes in acreage :* first, concerning all-crop acreage. Upward movement in acreage contributed most of the increase in output at the British India level both in first and last parts of the period. The expansion in acreage was drawn in about equal measure from additional doublecropping of land and from additional land brought under cultivation (Table 6.1); however, in two regions, United Provinces and Madras, a part of the increase was accompanied by decrease in acreage of crops other than those included in this study. Regional increases in net area of land under cultivation (Table 6.3), were associated with decreases in fallow land (especially in Bombay-Sind, and also in United Provinces), decreases in forest (notably in Greater Punjab and Central Provinces), decreases in "cultivable waste" (mostly in Greater Punjab), and in land previously classified as "not available for cultivation" (particularly in Madras and Bombay-Sind).

The rate of increase in all-crop acreage slowed down, however, and with it, output for British India as a whole and four of the regions. Of the other two regions, there was no change in the rate of acreage increase in Bombay-Sind, and in Greater Bengal acreage turned upward after initial decline (Table 6.2). The confines of limited land and applicable technology evidently provided increasing but not insurmountable resistance to expansion in most parts of British India. Returns to labor and capital employed on the additional lands were apparently sufficient to justify their use even if they were lower than on previously cultivated land.

A second observation concerns the pattern of regional all-crop acreage trends. Four of the regions had half-century average rates which conformed very closely to the British India rate, but it is interesting that the remaining two regions, Greater Bengal and Greater Punjab, were at extreme opposites in their acreage trends. An important reason for this difference is that Greater Punjab apparently had the largest proportion of unused cultivable land at the outset of the period and Greater Bengal the smallest (Chapter VI, 2.2). Underlying this condition is the influence of climate : largely because Greater Punjab was a dry land, Figure 6.2, much of its vast expanse was uncultivated until construction of large-scale irrigation works, but Greater Bengal, being wet, was densely populated at a much earlier stage of history and consequently had less potential for expansion.

Greater Bengal and Greater Punjab were also extreme opposites in the change of their all-crop acreage rates over time. Of the six regions the largest decrease in rate of acreage expansion occurred in Greater Punjab. This appears to be associated with the fact that the region's irrigated acreage doubled in the first half of the period, but increased by only about a third in the last half. In Greater Bengal, on the other hand, because of decreasing acreage in the early years, and resumed expansion, especially in the last decade when Burma's rice was cut off, the rate of acreage expansion increased.

A third significant aspect of acreage change concerns the relationship between foodgrain and nonfoodgrain trends. Expanded cultivation of the nonfoodgrains did not curtail foodgrain acreage. At the British India level there is not a single reference decade in which upward nonfoodgrain trends were accompanied by downward movement in foodgrains. In three reference decades, including, very noticeably, the last, foodgrain acreage rose while nonfoodgrain acreage fell, and in six other instances, when both aggregates were expanding, the nonfoodgrain rate exceeded that of foodgrains (in 1911/12–21/22 both declined at about the same rate). Among the regions also, neither the ten reference decade nor first and last period average rates disclosed any instances of upward nonfoodgrain acreage accompanied by downward foodgrains.

2.3 Change in yield per acre. Outstanding among the statistical findings concerning yield per acre for the half- century period as a whole (Tables *7.1* and *7.4*), is the near-zero average percent rate of change in British India for all-crops. This average reflects three sets of opposing tendencies in yield per acre. First, moderately decreasing all-crop yield per acre (mainly for rice) in Greater Bengal offset upward trends, varying from slow to rapid, in the other five regions. Second, slowly decreasing foodgrain yield per acre (especially for rice) offset rapidly rising nonfoodgrain yield per acre (mainly sugarcane, cotton, and tea) for British India as a whole. Third, increasing British India all-crop yield per acre up to about 1911/12 was offset by slightly decreasing yield per acre in the succeeding period (Figure *7.1*).

In the period of the last four reference decades, the pattern of rates was similar in that the average percent rate of change in yield per acre was also nearly zero. Two regions, Greater

Bengal and Central Provinces, had steep rates of decline in all-crop yield per acre; these were offset by upward trends elsewhere, especially in Greater Punjab where the increase was at an average rate of nearly one percent per year. Downward trend in foodgrain yield per acre was offset by rapidly rising nonfoodgrain yield per acre for British India as a whole, as it was, too, over the ten reference decade period. Three regions exhibited this same pattern of foodgrain versus nonfoodgrain yield per acre trends, and the other three regions were somewhat similar to it, differing in that in Madras the foodgrain rate was virtually zero, in Central Provinces the nonfoodgrain rate was nearly zero, and, notably, in Greater Punjab the foodgrain rate was moderately upward though smaller than for nonfoodgrains.

Yield per acre trends in the earlier period differed from this general pattern in that both foodgrain and nonfoodgrain yield per acre trends were generally upward, though, consistent with the pattern described above, in most regions nonfoodgrain yield per acre rates were considerably larger than those for foodgrains. The all-crop yield per acre trend rates were consequently more rapid than in the later period except in Madras.

To summarize, in most parts of British India all-crop yield per acre trends were rising during the entire period, though, in the later part of the period, only rapidly enough to offset declining trends in Greater Bengal and Central Provinces. Nonfoodgrain trends were almost all upward while foodgrain trends were either more slowly rising or downward.

2.4 Change in the underlying determinants of yield per acre. The underlying determinants which cause yield per acre trends may be grouped into three categories: natural forces, changes in which are not primarily due to man's influence; unplanned consequences of changes in agriculture which were not explicitly aimed at raising yield per acre; and conscious efforts to improve yield per acre.

First, the most pervasive natural influence making for change in yield per acre is weather. No effort was made to examine the influence of variations in temperature and wind on yield per acre trends; these appear to be generally less critical for the region as a whole than rainfall. The effect of annual rainfall variations on yield per acre trends was minimized by two methodological devices of the study : fitting the decade trends to five year moving annual averages and the averaging of decade trend rates. Inasmuch as rainfall does not fluctuate in exactly five year cycles,[5] and inasmuch as an average of only four reference decades may not be sufficient for eliminating upward and downward movements due to rainfall fluctuations, this natural force was of some importance in influencing yield per acre trends.

The rainfall influence on yield per acre depends on timing and amount. Some effort was made to recognize the effect of timing by correlating June-July rainfall with yield per acre in Bombay-Sind, Greater Bengal, and United Provinces, but results were inconclusive. Trends in annual rainfall over the entire fifty-six year period ranged from 0.28% to -0.21% per year for sixteen stations (Figure 8.1), but, again, there was not much association between yield per acre and rainfall trends over the period as a whole, or even over individual reference decades (Table 8.2). However, a downward rainfall trend at one station, Patna in Bihar, over a twenty year period (Figure 7.10), may help explain the downward yield per acre trend in rice for that area. The influence of rainfall was probably not completely eliminated from the measures of crop trends ob-

[5] For the 17 stations for which data were obtained for this study, the average trough-to-trough cycle length ranged from 3.6 to 4.6 years, averaging to 4.1 years. Figure 7.10 shows an annual and a five year moving average for one rainfall series.

tained for this study, especially for the shorter periods, but there appeared to be no feasible method for further reducing its effects on the measures of crop trends.

Another natural force affecting yield per acre trends is shift in river courses. The only such phenomenon investigated for this study (Chapter VIII, 3.4), was that in the Bhagirathi-Hoogly, Ganges, Padma River "moribund" delta area of Bengal. It appears, though not without some question, that the cutting-off of flood silts from this area, and the consequent decline in soil fertility, pre-dated the period of this study. In any case, the area constituted a relatively small part of Greater Bengal, and it may be, moreover, that loss in the affected area was more or less offset by gain in distribution of flood silts to other, eastern parts of the region.

Finally, note may be made of the epidemics which struck wide areas of British India in 1918 and Greater Bengal in 1943/44. Sickness and death left fields neglected and crops unharvested in many areas. The 1918 catastrophe pulled down trends for 1911/12–21/22, but did not have an equally uplifting effect on the trends for 1916/17–26/27.

A second group of underlying determinants of yield per acre consisted of the unplanned consequences of changes in agriculture not consciously aimed at altering yield per acre. This includes changes in acreage, frequency of cropping, number of livestock, and size of population. With respect to changes in acreage, it may first be noted that increasing acreage, which occurred in all regions except Greater Bengal in the first part of the period, would tend to decrease yields per acre where the additional land was lower in average productivity than the previously cultivated land or where the additional crop area resulted from double cropping. But in Greater Punjab and Sind, where soil had not been subjected to leaching, and where land had not been under cultivation, additional lands may well have been higher in soil fertility, and consequently more productive, than previously cultivated land, after irrigation had been extended into the dry areas.

Changes in the division of acreage between foodgrains and nonfoodgrains also altered average yield per acre since average nonfoodgrain (value of) yield per acre was nearly double that of foodgrains. In four regions, and in British India as a whole, the proportion of land under nonfoodgrain crops increased, though the increase was small except in Madras (Table *8.1*). In this connection it appears that an important influence on foodgrain compared with nonfoodgrain yield per acre trends was the increasing practice of taking more productive lands out of non-marketed crops, mostly foodgrains, and replacing them with cash crops, mostly nonfoodgrains, the former becoming more concentrated on poorer lands; unfortunately, little evidence could be offered on this (Chapter VII, 1.1 on jute and rice, and Chapter VII, 2.2 on sugarcane and rice in Greater Bengal).

Frequency of cropping does not, according to the view adopted by this study, necessarily mean declining yield per acre. After a low enough level of yield per acre is reached, a continuation of the same frequency has no further effect in changing yield per acre (Chapter VIII, 3.1); this condition is believed to have been characteristic of India. If, however, the frequency of crops per year should rise, it appears reasonable to expect that average yield per acre on all the crop acres sown would decline. Where the proportion of doublecropped land increased, this tendency would be present; however, there was relatively small increase in the proportion except in one region, Central Provinces (Table *8.4*). Fallowing may also change the frequency of cropping, decreased proportion of land in fallow tending to reduce average yield per acre. The fallow land proportion increased slightly for British India as a whole, reflecting large increases in Greater Bengal and Madras and decreases in Greater Punjab and Bombay-Sind (Table 8.5).

Change in the proportion of livestock to acreage could affect yield per acre by altering the availability of dung for fertilizer and work animals needed for plowing. Date available for the second half of the period show a decrease in cattle per all-crop acre for British India as a whole, thus tending to decrease yield per acre (Chapter VIII, 3.3).

Change in population affects yield per acre in part by altering the availability of cattle dung for fertilizer, inasmuch as dung has household uses; between 1919 and 1945 cattle decreased slightly in number, though not during the whole period, while population increased by about 25%, thus decreasing the availablity for fertilizer. Population increase, by adding to agricultural labor, also affects the intensity of cultivation; in four regions population increased more rapidly over the half-century than acreage, while in the other two, and in British India as a whole, there was not much difference in the two rates. In regions where the inter-decade changes in agricultural workers per acre appeared greatest, the effect on additional labor time per acre seemed relatively small (Chapter VIII, 5). Moreover, it could well be that the proportion of labor to land had already reached a level where the marginal product of further labor was zero. For these reasons, or others, there was little correlation between the changes in intensity of cultivation and yield per acre.

There were, finally, certain means directed at raising the yield per acre. Weakest of these, in the period studied, was the use of synthetic fertilizer, At its peak the volume of imported chemical fertilizer averaged to less than a pound per acre per year. It was estimated that if all the imported fertilizer had been used on half the acreage of sugarcane and cotton, it would still have given only fifteen pounds annually. Imports increased substantially and were a force, though very weak, toward higher yield per acre, probably concentrated on the crops mentioned.

Irrigation does not entirely belong under the heading of efforts directed primarily at raising yield per acre; much of it, especially in the western areas, was aimed at making it possible to extend acreage. An increase in the proportion of land irrigated would tend, however, to raise average yield per acre. For British India the increase in this proportion was small, the large increase in Greater Punjab having been offset by slight change in other regions (Table 8.3).

Improved seed appears to have given the most widespread tendency toward higher yield per acre. Data for the 1922/23–38/39 period showed substantial change in proportion of land under improved seed for all regions, especially Greater Punjab and Bombay-Sind (Table 8.6). If improved seed raised yield per acre by as much as 50% then this factor may account for most of the increase in average yield per acre during that period. In some cases, however, the improvement in seed may not have been directed at raising physical yield per acre but rather at quality.

In summary, it is difficult to evaluate the effect on yield per acre of the natural forces and of the consequences of changes in agriculture not directed at raising yield per acre. Among the latter, it would seem that although constant cropping of the same land would not have much affected the low level of yield per acre, the increase in proportion of land double-cropped and the decreased availability of dung for fertilizer may have outweighed whatever upward influence was imparted by increased intensity of cultivation and increased proportion of land in fallow. The upward influence of efforts directed at raising yield per acre appears to have been sufficient to offset the net downward effect of other influences.

It may be noted, finally, that although acreage was the predominant means of output expansion, and although the overall average rate of change in yield per acre was nearly zero, considerable gains in yield per acre were achieved for certain commercial crops with favorable markets, especially sugarcane and cotton, and in the regions in which such crops shared an important part of output. The British India zero rate of change in yield per acre was not a sign of stagnation, but of balance between forward-moving elements in yield per acre change and elements making for retrogression. Were it not for the former the yield per acre trend would probably have been downward.

3. Output and Availability

3.1 Foodgrains. The significance of the output findings with respect to domestic consumption should be qualified by the effects of trade, as well as deductions for waste and seed. It was assumed in this study that the proportion of output deducted for the latter remained constant over the period; while this does not appear unreasonable for seed, it seems likely that the proportion of output wasted would have declined somewhat,[6] making trends in net availability of grains slightly more favorable than is given in this study. For all grains an allowance of 12.5% is customarily made to obtain net availability.[7] If lessening of waste reduced the allowance by 25%, then over

---

[6] See comments by S. Patel, *op. cit.,* p. 243.

[7] Economic and Statistical Advisor, Ministry of Agriculture, India, *Indian Food Statistics,* August 1949, p. iv. For the individual crops (in Undivided India) the allowances were: rice 6.7%, wheat 15.6%, gram 18.7%, jowar 12.4%, maize 16.0% bajra 12.9%, barley 22.7%, ragi 10.7%, small millets 22.5%.

the fifty-six years of this study net availability would have increased at an approximate rate of 0.05 percentage points per year more than the rates given in Chapter V. If the same reduction in waste occurred entirely during the last half of the period, then rates of increase in availability of grains for that part of the period would have been understated by as much as 0.10 percentage points per year.

Change in the extent and direction of the net balance of grain trade flows had little effect in altering the output trends to allow for availability. The trend in availability of grains (aggregated on the basis of tonnage) after allowing for sea trade with foreign countries and Burma was only 0.08 percentage points per year more favorable than the output trend for the period as a whole (Table 5.4). In the early part of the period the net outflow of grain diminished, and in the later part there was an increasing net inflow. Availability of grains in Greater Bengal, on a similar basis, was seen to decline 0.11 percentage points per year less rapidly than the decline in output.

For the last four reference decades, however, when the divergence of foodgrain output and population growth rates was greatest, the availability trend rate was less unfavorable by only 0.03 percentage points per year for British India, and only 0.06 points for Greater Bengal. Considering the smallness of these magnitudes, it appears that the output trends may serve as measures of the trends in domestic consumption.

British India foodgrain output increased at an average rate of only 0.11%; this rate was not typical, however, of the individual foodgrain crops or of the regions, but bears the heavy influence of steeply declining rice output, 0.76% per year, in Greater Bengal. Rice output in British India, reflecting this, also declined though at a less rapid rate, 0.09%. One other crop, ragi, also had a negative rate, and two crops, jowar and barley, had rates of nearly zero (Table *5.1*). Except for Greater Bengal (-0.73% per year), the other regional food-grain rates were larger than the British India average; the combined rate for these five regions was 0.47% per year.

For the entire period, the British India average population growth rate, 0.67%, far exceeded the foodgrain output rate; in Greater Bengal, where the population growth rate was about the same as for British India, the divergence between these trends was even greater. But in two regions, United Provinces and Greater Punjab, the foodgrain output rate was not unfavorable compared with population growth, and in the other three regions the difference between foodgrain and population rates was much less than in British India as a whole. The combined five region rates, excluding Greater Bengal, were even closer, 0.47% and 0.64% for foodgrain and population respectively. In general, it might be said that although the foodgrain and population trend rates diverged very unfavorably in Greater Bengal, in other regions of British India there was much less difference in the rates (Table *5.2*).

It is particularly important, however, to observe the changed relationship of foodgrain and population rates during the course of the period, since the individual reference decade rates were decelerating for foodgrains and accelerating for population. Thus, although both trends pointed upward in the first four reference decades the British India foodgrain rate of expansion exceeded that of population, and this was true of all five regions except Greater Bengal. But in the last four reference decades the foodgrain rate was either negative (four regions), or positive but less than the population rate.

It was found, furthermore, that in the period starting with the decline, or slowing-down, of the foodgrain trend in each region (1911/12 for British India), and extending to 1941, the average rate of decline in per capita foodgrain output was about one percent, or slightly more, per year (Table 5.3). In Greater Bengal the period of decline was about thirty years and the reduction in per capita output was 38%. Even in Greater Punjab there was a twenty year period of decline in per capita foodgrain output, totaling to 18%.

Declines of this magnitude are probably noticeable in the lifetime of an adult person. Moreover, since many families were probably able to maintain their previous levels of consumption, those who were not able to do so must have suffered a decline of more than one percent per year. Cultivator families with rights to the produce of the land, and upper income families would be in the former category, while agricultural laborers, non-cultivating village workers, and low income urban families would have been in the last category. For instance, if the average rate of decline in per capita grain output were one percent per year, and if a third of the families were able to maintain their initial levels of consumption, then the remaining families would have suffered a reduction, on the average of 1.5% per year. In Madras, where the rate of decline in per capita foodgrain output was 1.40% per year, if a third of the families maintained their consumption levels, then the remaining families would have experienced a fall of over 2% per year in their grain consumption.

3.2 Nonfoodgrains. The rapid average growth rate in non-foodgrain output, 1.31% per year for British India, contrasts brightly with the low rate for foodgrains. There was a considerable slowing-down in the decade rates of growth, but even in the last four reference decades the average rate was over one percent per year. These rates are high, not only in comparison with the foodgrain rates but also with population growth. By 1911/12 per capita nonfoodgrain output had risen to 28% over 1893/94, and by 1941/42, despite the deceleration in crop output and the sharp acceleration in population growth, per capita output had climbed another 14% beyond the 1911/12 level.

Despite the much greater significance of trade relative to availability of nonfoodgrains, the trend in net amounts available after allowing for trade was almost the same as the output trend, only 0.11 percentage points per year higher than the latter (Table 5.7). The absolute amounts available were nearly a third less than output, but in the later part of the period the generally more rapid growth of output compared with trade resulted in a slightly larger portion of output (and imports) left available for domestic consumption.

On examination of the trend rates in output and availability of individual crops, three important crops—sugarcane, cotton, and tobacco—were found to have had slower-rising availability than output trends; for the last two crops, this was because exports increased more rapidly than output, and for sugarcane it was because of the dimunition in imports. Five crops were in the opposite relationship, availability trend rates larger than those for output; for the three oilseeds—sesamum, rape-mustard, and linseed—exports declined much more rapidly than output, while for groundnut and tea exports expanded less rapidly than output. The increase in tea consumption, relative to the very low initial level appears to have been very large.

In the aggregate per capita availability of nonfoodgrains increased since the output trend rate exceeded that of population and the changes in trade allowed total availability to increase slightly more rapidly than total output. Among the individual crops there was increasing per capita availability for sugarcane, tea, groundnut, and linseed. Though total availability rose for the remaining crops, their per capita measure nonetheless declined. For two of the latter crops—sesamum and rape-mustard—it appears that increasing per capita use of groundnut (for oil) supplanted the use of some of the more traditional sources of vegetable oil. In Madras and Bombay-Sind, and in the lesser-producing region of Central Provinces, where groundnut output rose sharply, sesamum output dropped noticeably, suggesting that the former was substituted in use for the latter; moreover, since availability of groundnut appears to have far exceeded normal oil use in the main two producing regions, shipment of groundnut to other regions apparently accounts for some of their decrease in sesamum and rape-mustard output, particularly in Greater Bengal. The decline in per capita availability of tobacco seems surprising since tobacco can be grown in many parts of India, and since its users would presumably be strongly habituated to it. The decline in per capita availability of cotton was relatively small, about ten percent in forty years.

That foreign trade was an important influence on output trends of nonfoodgrain crops is suggested by the association between the trade and output trends indicated above. The four crops with high average rates of increase in output (Table 5.5), were favorably affected by trade—tea and groundnut over the whole period, cotton mostly in the first half of the period, and sugarcane by protection against imports in the later part of the period. Four crops unfavorably affected by trade—sesamum, rape and mustard, and linseed (oilseed), and indigo (displaced by synthetic dye)—had output trend rates which were either low positive or steeply negative. A very large part of the jute crop was exported in either raw or manufactured form; its fairly low rate of increase in output reflects the conditions for exports. Tobacco exports appear to have risen considerably but output showed almost no upward trend, perhaps, at least in part, because of scarcity of soils suitable for growing export grades of leaf.

It may be observed that there was no instance of a crop

which had an unfavorable stimulus from foreign trade and which, nonetheless, achieved a relatively rapid rate of growth in output (relative to population). Among the foodgrains, however, wheat, exports of which fell considerably, continued to increase in output at a moderately rapid rate, though not as rapidly as during the period when its foreign markets were expanding. Only one crop, bajra, appears to have achieved a relatively high expansion rate despite its unimportance in trade. Other than these exceptions, it may be generalized that crops with high growth rates for output were favorably stimulated by foreign trade, and crops with low growth rates were either unfavorably affected by trade or not involved in trade.

It has been seen that although the aggregate nonfoodgrain rate of output increase was high, there was considerable diversity of trends among the individual crops ranging from steeply negative to steeply positive. Among the regions there was more similarity to the British India rate in that only one region, Greater Bengal, had an average rate much less than one percent (Table 5.6). Each of the other regions benefitted from the relatively important share of rapid-rising nonfoodgrain crops in the nonfoodgrain aggregate for that region: cotton and sugarcane in Greater Punjab; groundnut, sugarcane, and cotton in Madras; cotton, groundnut, and sugarcane in Bombay-Sind; cotton in Central Provinces; and sugarcane in United Provinces. In Greater Bengal the slow-rising jute crop dominated and tea expansion was not sufficient to offset the decline of oilseeds and indigo.

High regional rates of expansion in nonfoodgrain output (relative to population growth) characterized both early and later parts of the period. The main reason, from a regional viewpoint, for decline in the average British India nonfoodgrain rate from first to last four reference decades was the change in Central Provinces. From the distinction of having the highest nonfoodgrain expansion rate in the first part of the period, the region reversed to become the only one with a (steeply) negative rate in the last part of the period, reflecting the changing favor for its cotton crop and the absence of other rapid-rising crops with weight in the nonfoodgrain total.

3.3 All-crop output. A meaningful summary of the all-crop output trends, (Table *5.8*), must recognize that Greater Bengal, atypical of the other regions, had the heaviest weight in the British India all-crop aggregate, and that, also, the first and last parts of the period had very different trends; consequently the average rates for the entire period may be misleading.

During the first part of the period, up to about 1911/12, despite the negative output trend in Greater Bengal, output rose rapidly, outstripping the rate of population growth in British India and also in the combined five other regions. For these five regions output grew at 1.41% compared with 0.34% per year for population. In the last part of the period the ranking of the trends was reversed, the British India output rate having been only 0.35% while population was growing at 1.12% per year. The Central Provinces output trend was, like Greater Bengal, negative. In Bombay-Sind the output rate was slightly larger than earlier in the period, though, as was true for all regions, it was less than the regional population growth rate. In the other three regions the average output rates were less than the earlier period rates.

The turning points in per capita all-crop output (Figure *5.6*), were about 1921/22 for United Provinces, Central Provinces, and Greater Punjab, and about 1931/32 for Bombay-Sind and Madras; Greater Bengal's per capita measure declined from the outset of the period. After the downturn occurred, and up to 1941/42, per capita output declined (Table *5.9*), most rapidly in Central Provinces and Madras, at nearly two percent per year, and least rapidly in United Provinces and Greater Punjab, where the rate was about two-thirds of one percent; in Bombay-Sind and greater Punjab the rates were somewhat less than one percent per year. For British India the decline in per capita output was 0.72% per year after 1911/12.

It thus appears that output trends were generally less favorable in the later part of the period and that when population growth approached the more rapid rates which characterize the modern period, existing institutions were unable to prevent a serious deterioration in the per capita output and availability of agricultural materials. Ironically, considering that a large part of agriculture was not commercial, and despite the presumably low absolute levels of grain consumption, the crops which increased most rapidly, especially in the later decades, were the market-oriented nonfoodgrains.

Appendix Tables

ALL-INDIA AND BRITISH INDIA ANNUAL INDEXES OF ALL-CROP AND
FOODGRAIN CROP OUTPUT ACCORDING TO 1951 STUDY

	All-India		Br. India			All-India		Br. India	
	AC	FG	AC	FG		AC	FG	AC	FG
1893/94	97	79	99	80					
	100	83	102	84					
	91	73	94	75					
1896/97	74	58	73	55	1921/22	106	82	105	82
	99	81	102	82		110	83	108	83
	103	84	106	86		100	74	100	72
	87	72	89	73		101	74	99	71
	94	76	93	73		100	73	99	70
1901/02	90	71	91	71	1926/27	100	73	101	71
	102	82	103	82		97	69	98	67
	100	80	99	78		103	73	102	71
	96	77	98	77		106	76	104	73
	93	74	93	72		105	76	105	73
1906/07	99	76	100	75	1931/32	104	77	104	75
	84	65	85	64		106	75	104	71
	90	70	88	69		105	73	103	70
	109	87	106	86		103	73	102	70
	109	87	110	87		102	69	100	66
1911/12	105	83	103	82	1936/37	113	76	112	73
	102	79	102	77		108	74	107	70
	93	69	92	67		99	68	94	64
	100	77	100	73		105	72	104	69
	107	82	106	81		103	68	115	74
1916/17	113	87	113	86	1941/42	100	71	99	67
	111	86	112	85		108	76	104	70
	80	60	80	58		112	78	113	77
	109	84	110	81		107	77	107	74
	88	65	88	65		100	70	102	69

Notes

Crops were aggregated by weighting with average 1924/25–28/29
village level prices for British India. Base for the All-India indexes is the
average output of all-crops in All-India during 1924/25–28/29; base for
British India was similarly computed on British India output. AC and FG
represent all-crops and foodgrain crops respectively.

Source: For All-India, Blyn, *op. cit.*, Appendix XVII; for British
India, computed from crop output tables in Appendix XIV of the 1951
study.

APPENDIX 1B

TOTAL REPORTED AREA AND AREA SOWN OF BRITISH INDIA REGIONS AND
PROVINCES, 1937/38

(Thousand Acres)

	Total Reported Area	Total Area Sown
Greater Bengal	*114,154*	*59,976*
Bengal	49,258	29,719
Bihar	44,314	23,810
Orissa	20,582	6,447
United Provinces	*67,848*	*44,771*
Madras	*79,808*	*36,919*
Greater Punjab	*69,945*	*34,539*
Punjab	61,001	31,752
N.W.F.P.	8,576	2,519
Delhi	368	268
Bombay-Sind	*78,900*	*35,395*
Bombay	48,721	29,683
Sind	30,179	5,712
Central Provinces	*63,004*	*27,285*
Assam	35,484	7,081
Ajmer-Merwara	1,771	393
Coorg	1,012	146
British India	511,926	246,505
Baluchistan	34,852	No Data

Source : *Agricultural Statistics.*

APPENDIX 3A

ANNUAL CROP OUTPUT, ACREAGE, AND YIELD PER ACRE FOR BRITISH INDIA AND LEADING REGIONS ACCORDING TO ADJUSTED SERIES*
(Tons and acres in 000's; y/a—lbs.)

1. Rice

British India

Yield	Acres	Y/A	Yield	Acres	Y/A	Yield	Acres	Y/A
1891			*1911*			*1931*		
22093	65073	759	28611	66055	970	27721	68511	905
24868	64625	862	26486	67942	874	25348	66906	847
28167	66168	954	25573	66171	867	24891	67270	829
30067	67218	1004	24277	67042	813	24842	66706	833
27142	66969	905	29371	68097	968	22337	67533	739
1896			*1916*			*1936*		
18322	64171	638	30286	70021	970	26709	68721	871
30219	67145	1008	30996	69843	995	25728	69194	831
31434	68898	954	20332	66882	679	22924	69916	735
26647	65115	916	27938	67870	921	24202	70040	775
26052	63096	927	23308	67492	773	20769	68745	676
1901			*1921*			*1941*		
23840	63195	842	27859	68514	912	24033	69588	773
29241	66887	977	28515	69116	923	22985	70581	730
26335	62272	939	23568	65622	806	28968	76031	856
25860	65321	889	25291	67086	844	26578	78840	757
24233	67167	806	25254	67966	833	25137	75514	744
1906			*1926*			*1946*		
25484	65479	871	24110	65874	820	26132	77139	759
21190	65888	721	22687	64152	793			
22531	62499	806	26515	68345	869			
31457	68175	1035	25802	66503	869			
32087	68346	1053	26472	67301	883			

Greater Bengal

1891			1896			1901		
14290	39552	806	8981	36177	556	13610	35095	869
16700	37325	1030	19971	39550	1122	17949	37554	1071
18711	37887	1104	20292	39605	1147	15833	34932	1015
20843	38640	788	17898	39491	1015	17361	38355	1015
15826	37448	948	15575	36014	968	15186	37308	912

* Given in crop years, i.e., 1891 stands for 1891/92.

1. Rice—Continued

Yield	Acres	Y/A	Yield	Acres	Y/A	Yield	Acres	Y/A
1906			*1921*			*1936*		
14655	36808	892	15677	37052	947	14177	35129	904
12200	36147	756	16330	37135	985	13172	34904	845
12722	33812	843	12407	34342	809	11136	34914	714
19829	38494	1154	13734	35497	857	12173	35047	778
20021	38567	1163	13107	35419	829	8839	33139	597
1911			*1926*			*1941*		
17541	37800	1039	12143	33804	805	12973	35773	812
14325	36835	871	10871	32158	757	10546	35402	667
15532	36069	965	15272	35755	957	15538	39779	875
12358	36580	756	14213	34454	924	13992	42307	741
17047	37171	1027	14821	34509	962	12875	39416	732
1916			*1931*			*1946*		
16836	37378	1009	15231	36220	942	13482	40319	749
17639	36766	1074	13565	34851	872			
11672	36406	718	12974	34901	832			
15231	36198	943	12961	34474	842			
13065	35822	817	10509	34238	687			

Madras

1891			*1911*			*1931*		
2495	8080	693	4629	10289	1007	5385	11538	1045
2314	8971	749	5284	10944	1081	5406	11534	1050
3085	9394	735	4986	10678	1045	5314	11704	1017
2971	9196	724	5058	10876	1041	4981	11056	1009
4695	9633	1091	5415	11230	1081	5106	11294	1013
1896			*1916*			*1936*		
4026	9268	973	6022	11533	1170	5283	11431	1035
3992	9709	922	5512	11655	1059	5334	11698	1021
4593	10032	1022	4203	10469	899	4504	11322	891
3288	9000	818	5370	11646	1033	4876	11379	960
4083	9227	991	4987	11096	1007	5552	12233	1017
1901			*1921*			*1941*		
4287	9601	1001	5230	11280	1039	5283	11399	1038
4786	10827	990	5233	11286	1039	5002	11947	938
4854	10875	998	4531	10518	965	5294	12297	964
3379	8851	853	4908	10870	1011	5433	12478	975
3822	9245	925	5322	11323	1053	4602	11641	885
1906			*1926*			*1946*		
4207	9722	969	4742	10842	980	5324	12508	953
4331	10614	914	5083	10930	1042			
3639	10305	791	5197	11019	1056			
4606	10359	996	5255	11262	1045			
5227	10781	1086	5376	11678	1031			

1. Rice—Continued

United Provinces

Yield	Acres	Y/A	Yield	Acres	Y/A	Yield	Acres	Y/A
1891			*1911*			*1931*		
2001	7139	628	1797	5274	763	1989	6555	680
2232	7646	654	1998	6811	657	1327	6140	484
2533	7902	718	1286	6173	487	1736	5980	650
2457	7998	688	2032	6199	734	1937	6437	674
2631	8207	718	2309	6431	804	1949	6626	659
1896			*1916*			*1936*		
1816	6647	612	2671	7138	838	1919	6641	647
2134	6532	732	2646	7417	799	2024	7032	645
2143	6705	716	1446	6729	481	2070	7794	595
1893	5492	772	2260	6573	770	2427	7765	700
2526	7173	789	1554	6841	509	1807	7292	555
1901			*1921*			*1941*		
2261	7133	710	2308	6847	755	1572	6554	537
2371	6980	761	2104	6982	675	1839	7033	586
1857	6038	689	1959	6981	629	1874	7108	591
1796	7084	568	2275	7072	721	1540	7163	481
1636	6078	603	2159	7417	652	1837	7045	584
1906			*1926*			*1946*		
2680	7726	777	2341	7437	705	1774	7363	540
1545	6966	497	2183	7266	673			
1915	5892	728	1104	7024	352			
1978	6120	724	1523	6814	501			
1956	6034	726	1704	6722	568			

Assam

Yield	Acres	Y/A	Yield	Acres	Y/A	Yield	Acres	Y/A
1891			*1906*			*1921*		
959	2892	743	1114	3431	727	1344	4335	694
1174	3215	818	1128	4063	622	1511	4438	763
1190	3165	842	1409	4346	726	1495	4596	729
1133	3443	737	1951	4483	975	1507	4499	750
1216	3445	791	1827	4406	929	1588	4402	808
1896			*1911*			*1926*		
1116	3790	660	1973	4458	991	1536	4498	765
1463	3864	848	1946	4486	972	1308	4173	702
1491	3899	857	1339	4327	693	1677	4963	757
1326	3654	813	1459	4541	720	1346	4230	713
1207	3391	797	1320	4438	666	1366	4491	658
1901			*1916*			*1931*		
1228	3602	764	1497	4513	743	1589	4588	757
1483	3998	831	1935	4629	936	1677	4651	771
1437	3960	813	1293	4406	657	1421	4698	655
1439	3964	813	1543	4256	812	1481	4770	683
1282	3803	755	1547	4427	783	1610	5285	681

1. Rice — Continued

Yield 1936	Acres	Y/A	Yield 1941	Acres	Y/A	Yield 1946	Acres	Y/A
1904	5433	785	1803	5460	740	2061	5620	821
1745	5056	773	1866	5756	726			
1742	5352	729	2353	5879	896			
1742	5352	729	1914	5759	744			
1805	5426	745	2176	6041	807			

Central Provinces

1891			1911			1931		
1051	4314	546	1498	4821	696	1772	5527	718
1142	4451	575	1290	4999	578	1660	5595	665
1300	4510	646	825	4985	371	1657	5637	658
1252	4574	613	1600	4919	729	1757	5631	699
1455	5046	646	1692	5051	749	1545	5900	586
1896			**1916**			**1936**		
1236	5244	528	1496	5141	652	1880	5997	702
1200	4060	662	1629	5170	706	1666	6077	614
1484	5161	644	744	5306	314	1811	6107	664
1498	4752	706	1654	5071	731	1539	6211	555
1300	4018	725	739	5125	323	1183	6183	429
1901			**1921**			**1941**		
1302	4579	637	1578	5071	697	977	6067	361
1422	4589	694	1471	5144	641	1908	5967	716
992	3621	614	1565	5170	678	1914	6195	692
866	4047	479	1174	5171	509	1807	6345	638
973	4206	518	1443	5198	622	1722	6395	603
1906			**1926**			**1946**		
1361	4287	711	1648	5280	699	1488	6447	517
823	4598	401	1562	5410	647			
1333	4543	657	1466	5445	603			
1410	4837	653	1787	5480	730			
1383	4728	655	1404	5541	568			

Bombay-Sind

Yield 1891	Acres	Y/A	Yield 1896	Acres	Y/A	Yield 1901	Acres	Y/A
1039	2299	1013	915	2399	854	882	2400	823
1060	2308	1029	1150	2549	1011	974	2228	979
1043	2418	966	1128	2623	963	1067	2446	977
1096	2437	1008	449	2149	468	781	2339	748
1036	2367	980	1070	2391	1003	1109	2525	984

1. Rice—Continued

Yield	Acres	Y/A	Yield	Acres	Y/A	Yield	Acres	Y/A
1906			*1921*			*1936*		
1166	2669	979	1386	3000	1036	1155	3012	859
870	2694	724	1492	3095	1080	1367	3268	937
1220	2755	992	1264	3021	937	1286	3271	881
1346	2960	1019	1396	3088	1013	1111	3190	780
1358	2993	1016	1269	3122	908	1229	3390	812
1911			*1926*			*1941*		
946	2770	765	1354	3006	1009	1077	3294	732
1331	2947	1012	1329	3151	945	1345	3252	926
1290	3013	959	1459	3132	1043	1512	3394	998
1439	3009	1071	1283	3171	906	1390	3399	916
1286	2904	992	1410	3261	969	1428	3513	910
1916			*1931*			*1946*		
1356	3130	971	1427	3159	1012	1479	3418	969
1254	3080	912	1355	3136	968			
677	2712	559	1363	3140	999			
1482	3043	1091	1331	3177	938			
1058	3140	824	1228	3097	888			

Notes

Greater Bengal. See Appendix 9ᴀ for a modified version of this series.
Madras. Estimates acreage and output up to 1906/07 raised by 40%,
as explained in Chapter III, 2. 1.

United Provinces. Y/a up to 1910/11 obtained from relationship with
sesamum y/a. Agreement in signs of first differences (asfd) for the two
series starting with 1911/12, 23 out of 36 possible. Relative mean deviation (rmd) of y/a predicted with regression equation for 1911/12–25/26
11.3%.

Other regions. Assam: adjustments involving Bengal 1905/06–10/11
and 1941/42–46/47 described in Chapter III, 1.3. Y/a up to 1904/05
obtained from relationship with Bengal rice y/a, asfd 21/35, rmd 1911/
12–28/29 9.6%. Acreage up to 1897/98 raised to 2.4 times acreage
reported in *Agricultural Statistics* to adjust for increase in reporting
area, most of which appears to have been rice land, judging from jump
in acreage starting with 1898/99. Central Provinces: y/a up to 1912/13
gotten from relationship with U.P. rice y/a, asfd 21/33, rmd 1915/16–
25/26 10.1%. Bombay-Sind: y/a up to 1911/12 based on relationship
with sesamum y/a, asfd 29/34, rmd 1912/13–33/34 3.4%.

APPENDIX TABLE 3A

2. Wheat

British India

Yield	Acres	Y/A	Yield	Acres	Y/A	Yield	Acres	Y/A
1891			*1911*			*1931*		
5049	21006	538	8460	24940	760	7263	25124	648
6690	22680	661	8163	23866	766	7580	24813	684
6377	23836	599	7147	22622	708	7472	27393	611
5995	22833	588	8496	25324	752	7708	25459	678
4601	19114	539	7342	23762	692	7531	24930	677
1896			*1916*			*1936*		
4796	16682	644	8401	24930	755	7863	25040	703
6414	20160	668	8276	26310	705	8612	26483	728
6062	20848	651	6469	19017	762	7988	26780	668
5151	16957	680	6610	23396	824	8929	26123	766
6595	20797	710	5669	20329	625	8095	26464	685
1901			*1921*			*1941*		
5626	20422	617	8345	21889	841	8249	26094	707
7165	20250	793	8126	24264	750	9060	26017	780
8566	23598	813	7958	24178	737	7850	25854	680
6756	23599	641	7175	24702	651	8576	27142	708
5891	22510	586	7141	23861	670	7408	26866	618
1906			*1926*			*1946*		
7508	24486	687	7361	24033	686	6869	26637	578
5303	18338	648	6330	24438	580			
6654	21102	706	7267	24812	656			
8480	22653	839	8932	24633	812			
8679	24300	800	7610	24610	693			

Greater Punjab

1891			1901			1911		
1420	6224	511	2006	8023	560	3641	10924	749
2236	7123	703	2549	7818	730	3019	9693	697
2560	8265	694	3377	8760	864	3086	9522	730
2395	8052	666	3123	8594	814	3600	11133	726
1754	6893	570	3790	9597	885	2434	9890	551
1896			*1906*			*1916*		
1872	6584	637	3572	10246	781	2881	10565	611
2359	8013	659	2438	8349	656	3334	11121	673
1978	7729	573	3069	9427	732	2840	8582	743
1823	6366	641	3492	9704	809	3254	9877	850
2941	8766	496	3645	9911	808	2190	8503	578

2. Wheat—Continued

Yield	Acres	Y/A	Yield	Acres	Y/A	Yield	Acres	Y/A
1921			*1931*			*1941*		
3964	9777	912	3019	10136	667	4141	11112	835
3547	10807	769	3067	9652	712	4467	11633	860
3745	10778	782	3061	10860	831	3702	11002	754
2801	10730	598	3293	10075	710	4272	11608	824
3224	10628	695	3323	10367	718	3618	11740	690
1926			*1936*			*1946*		
3256	10427	718	3705	10517	789	3494	10906	792
2524	10069	579	3994	11029	811			
3309	11076	654	3484	10547	740			
4039	11041	806	4034	10539	857			
3348	10215	734	3603	11020	733			

United Provinces

Yield	Acres	Y/A	Yield	Acres	Y/A	Yield	Acres	Y/A
1891			*1911*			*1931*		
2035	6502	701	3032	7578	896	2610	7748	755
2354	6307	836	2938	7382	891	2713	7667	793
1853	6675	622	2221	6406	777	2537	8453	672
1470	6334	520	3042	7301	933	2523	7549	749
1591	5177	688	2700	6599	916	2498	7053	793
1896			*1916*			*1936*		
1851	4932	841	3061	6764	1014	2468	7484	739
2250	5985	842	2889	7248	890	2780	7810	797
2277	6349	803	2304	5444	948	2694	8520	708
2410	6203	870	2996	7037	954	3167	8109	875
2385	6790	787	2362	6557	807	2826	7935	796
1901			*1921*			*1941*		
2402	6462	833	2685	6873	875	2571	7873	731
2972	6910	963	2574	6984	826	2685	7546	797
3230	7789	929	2640	7182	823	2526	7672	738
1897	7706	551	2419	7368	735	2646	7892	751
2429	6479	841	2287	6884	744	2305	8056	641
1906			*1926*			*1946*		
2164	7044	688	2492	6714	831	2349	8020	656
1675	4406	851	2361	7467	708			
2124	5695	835	2480	7112	781			
2975	6491	1027	3309	7182	1032			
2919	7342	890	2686	7612	790			

2. Wheat—Continued

Bombay-Sind

Yield	Acres	Y/A	Yield	Acres	Y/A	Yield	Acres	Y/A
1891			*1911*			*1931*		
452	2157	457	294	1352	484	444	2314	430
691	2462	624	586	1718	753	602	2627	513
641	2459	677	533	1910	608	631	3232	437
776	2890	642	715	2236	893	559	2809	446
426	2097	453	636	2273	616	607	2810	484
1896			*1916*			*1936*		
317	1422	488	680	2271	655	606	2585	525
613	1982	694	748	2701	607	674	2987	505
629	2200	645	259	1108	510	702	3039	517
135	1159	246	509	1981	573	637	2953	483
313	1402	493	268	1452	413	643	2956	487
1901			*1921*			*1941*		
213	1599	316	434	1933	500	613	2756	498
440	1554	641	416	2028	526	751	2795	602
589	2104	618	261	1563	406	778	3051	571
494	2240	389	378	1958	474	658	3389	435
380	1548	534	285	1501	445	641	2955	486
1906			*1926*			*1946*		
435	1907	503	318	1802	470	352	3357	235
369	1732	473	395	1875	560			
413	1823	505	406	2058	441			
468	1830	570	430	2050	499			
516	1951	595	441	2285	432			

Central Provinces

Yield	Acres	Y/A	Yield	Acres	Y/A	Yield	Acres	Y/A
1891			*1906*			*1921*		
896	4972	419	904	3714	545	676	2448	619
928	5182	401	489	2715	405	1028	3008	766
746	4914	340	699	2773	565	814	3277	556
653	4282	342	958	3064	700	1069	3307	724
471	3461	305	973	3586	608	881	3524	560
1896			*1911*			*1926*		
356	2351	339	874	3611	542	773	3734	464
585	2562	511	1025	3610	636	591	3664	361
510	2942	388	664	3269	455	515	3184	362
202	1651	274	749	3265	514	588	2983	442
471	2299	459	943	3504	603	635	3098	459
1901			*1916*			*1931*		
605	2900	467	1125	3847	655	673	3513	429
701	2502	628	763	3884	440	655	3451	425
821	3374	545	677	2781	545	715	3441	465
832	3497	533	637	3199	586	763	3626	471
834	3444	542	352	2568	307	641	3389	424

2. Wheat—Continued

Yield 1936	Acres	Y/A	Yield 1941	Acres	Y/A	Yield 1946	Acres	Y/A
600	3140	428	390	2851	306	112	2883	87
673	3358	449	511	2544	450			
672	3382	445	370	2688	308			
614	3184	432	503	2797	403			
572	3229	397	436	2679	365			

Notes

Punjab. Estimates notes that from 1907/08 Indian States were included with reports from the province. There is some question as to whether preceding years included States. *Agricultural Statistics* for the province only shows an average of 6% less acreage than *Estimates.* Acreage from the former source used from 1907/08 on.

Central Provinces. Indian States were included from at least 1898/99, according to *Estimates,* but acreage is the same both in the latter and *Agricultural Statistics* until 1906/07. Acreage from the latter was used from 1907/08–21/22.

Other regions. Ajmer-Merwara and Madras output were calculated from their *Agricultural Statistics* acreage and the yield per acre in the rest of India and included in the British India total.

APPENDIX TABLE 3A

3. *Jowar*

British India

Yield	Acres	Y/A	Yield	Acres	Y/A	Yield	Acres	Y/A
1891			*1911*			*1931*		
3312	20471	358	3634	17871	480	4433	20923	475
3993	21744	411	4641	20331	513	4627	20804	498
3922	19677	446	4305	20649	468	4555	20801	491
4035	21052	429	5479	20560	596	4605	21214	486
4409	21808	453	6361	22385	636	4459	20947	477
1896			*1916*			*1936*		
3792	20205	420	5034	21205	532	4610	23469	440
5547	24070	516	4416	20475	483	4039	20699	437
5393	21992	549	3351	20031	375	4147	20829	446
2989	21691	308	5561	21865	570	4612	21670	466
4363	22008	444	3630	21962	370	4607	21244	485
1901			*1921*			*1941*		
4474	21784	460	5500	23340	540	4155	21972	424
5682	23031	553	4981	21933	521	4235	21867	434
4640	20817	499	4285	20348	482	4636	22179	468
4474	23003	435	4755	21652	499	4293	21926	438
4289	20810	462	4159	19840	474	3688	22071	375
1906			*1926*			*1946*		
4489	20820	483	4238	20190	479	3488	22130	353
3586	21052	381	4888	20651	538			
4666	23645	442	4693	20016	532			
5026	21008	536	5050	22940	498			
4555	20750	492	5024	22338	504			

Bombay-Sind

1891			*1901*			*1911*		
1437	8757	367	826	7311	254	1015	6267	363
1720	7682	501	1852	8045	515	1614	7452	485
1915	7879	544	1501	6760	497	1577	7295	484
1778	7728	516	1264	9028	313	1904	7140	597
1231	7597	364	1390	7241	429	2226	8098	616
1896			*1906*			*1916*		
1080	6172	392	1129	6272	404	2009	8060	558
2164	8687	558	1197	7036	380	1788	8707	460
1862	8057	518	1508	8327	406	1083	7656	317
790	8941	198	1410	6908	458	1994	8408	531
1168	6599	396	1528	7184	478	1210	8810	307

3. Jowar—Continued

Yield	Acres	Y/A	Yield	Acres	Y/A	Yield	Acres	Y/A
1921			*1931*			*1941*		
1737	8615	434	1665	7894	442	1433	9127	409
1691	8720	352	1730	8212	472	1207	7888	348
1243	7902	451	1634	8279	450	1461	8013	255
1835	9197	422	1767	8391	367	1331	8561	294
1566	8315	524	1765	8281	346	1047	9191	300
1926			*1936*			*1946*		
1473	8036	506	1696	10043	389	1194	9105	261
1831	7822	418	1316	8512	351			
1756	7772	466	1421	8179	394			
1752	9387	472	1328	8474	352			
1912	9193	472	1523	8649	343			

Madras

Yield	Acres	Y/A	Yield	Acres	Y/A	Yield	Acres	Y/A
1891			*1911*			*1931*		
1000	5551	408	1369	5166	591	1314	4831	609
1108	5637	440	1216	5220	522	1291	4534	638
1053	5460	431	1396	5790	539	1283	4412	651
971	5103	425	1490	5102	654	1276	5143	566
1540	5372	640	1662	5525	673	1370	5102	601
1896			*1916*			*1936*		
1448	5653	571	1442	4761	670	1316	5170	569
1309	5390	541	1395	4890	639	1106	4641	534
1548	5768	600	1342	5069	593	1276	4957	577
1122	5229	480	1509	5498	615	1398	5095	615
1484	5710	582	1420	5222	609	1338	4711	639
1901			*1921*			*1941*		
1608	6099	588	1524	5573	612	1223	4941	554
1447	5565	581	1438	5255	613	1105	4851	507
1309	4987	586	1271	4647	613	1157	5025	516
1283	5717	501	1405	4944	631	1209	4683	579
1376	5666	543	1292	4546	637	912	4188	489
1906			*1926*			*1946*		
1401	5518	569	1211	4692	578	890	4565	436
1269	5279	537	1339	4830	621			
1143	5480	464	1363	4615	656			
1319	5054	585	1483	5174	642			
1487	5205	637	1275	4761	600			

3. Jowar — Continued

Central Provinces

Yield	Acres	Y/A	Yield	Acres	Y/A	Yield	Acres	Y/A
1891			*1911*			*1931*		
537	3490	345	986	4048	546	783	4290	409
506	3557	319	980	3991	550	944	4251	496
512	3391	338	918	3919	525	1025	4320	531
545	3733	326	1274	4299	664	962	4334	497
978	3961	553	1645	4955	743	845	4227	448
1896			*1916*			*1936*		
668	4099	365	881	4188	471	1015	4658	488
1174	5036	521	747	3820	438	1061	4248	559
1254	4368	644	654	4652	315	929	4331	480
448	4665	215	1243	4365	638	1162	4791	543
838	5050	371	501	4492	250	1085	4533	536
1901			*1921*			*1941*		
1353	4850	625	1444	4984	649	976	4739	461
1556	5421	644	1211	4526	599	1125	5307	475
977	4613	475	1000	4078	550	1330	5648	527
1427	4561	703	957	4162	515	1068	5200	460
881	4521	436	763	3840	445	1017	5046	451
1906			*1926*			*1946*		
995	4436	501	888	4159	478	825	5009	369
728	4644	352	994	4273	521			
1051	4963	475	1109	4169	596			
1447	4885	664	1036	4293	541			
696	4267	365	1181	4716	561			

United Provinces

Yield	Acres	Y/A	Yield	Acres	Y/A	Yield	Acres	Y/A
1891			*1906*			*1921*		
104	606	388	697	2721	575	647	2684	540
112	585	429	187	2393	176	486	2270	540
124	528	533	720	2950	547	598	2479	480
448	2075	484	624	2579	542	411	2047	540
454	1907	533	600	2468	545	400	1990	450
1896			*1911*			*1926*		
365	2264	362	355	1633	487	524	2301	450
593	2402	554	598	2169	618	567	2446	510
570	2426	528	227	2063	246	334	2264	510
530	2086	570	630	2413	585	643	2469	330
674	2584	585	665	2546	585	538	2509	583
1901			*1916*			*1931*		
562	2434	518	523	2402	488	526	2619	480
626	2503	560	372	1982	420	497	2381	450
567	2543	501	198	1852	239	493	2632	467
298	2294	292	562	2330	540	450	2241	420
380	2449	347	351	2313	340	449	2237	450

3. Jowar—Continued

Yield 1936	Acres	Y/A	Yield 1941	Acres	Y/A	Yield 1946	Acres	Y/A
426	2122	450	388	2129	468	423	2261	419
436	2232	437	641	2590	554			
421	2245	420	536	2380	504			
531	2307	516	506	2267	500			
518	2224	522	564	2546	496			

Notes

Bombay-Sind. Y/a to 1910/11 based on relationship with wheat y/a; agreement in signs of first differences for the two series, 20 out of 34 possible; relative mean deviation of predicted y/a from actual y/a 11.3% for 1911/12–21/22.

Madras. Acreage raised by 19.5% up to 1906/07 to account for zamindari lands, based on proportion of zamindari acreage to other, ryotwari, acreage, and jowar grown in each district according to data available for later years. Y/a to 1911/12 based on rice y/a, asfd 26/34, rmd 5.8% for 1912/13–22/23. Discontinuity in y/a trend before and after 1915/16 adjusted by raising earlier years, as indicated in Chapter III, 2.2.

Other regions. Central Provinces: y/a up to 1910/11 based on cotton y/a, asfd 25/35, rmd 9.6% for 1911/12–25/26. United Provinces: y/a up to 1910/11 estimated from relationship with sesamum y/a, asfd 17/35, rmd 12.9% for 1911/12–1922/23.

APPENDIX TABLE 3A

4. Gram

British India

Yield	Acres	Y/A	Yield	Acres	Y/A	Yield	Acres	Y/A
1891			*1911*			*1931*		
2167	9313	521	4486	13807	728	3693	15668	528
2680	10371	579	3400	11745	648	3341	13744	545
2444	10450	524	1965	8916	493	3662	16312	503
3041	13531	503	3895	13834	631	3352	13462	558
2868	11861	542	3460	13189	588	3546	14534	547
1896			*1916*			*1936*		
2183	8275	591	4273	15347	624	3820	15528	551
2746	10169	605	4446	16277	610	3240	13663	531
2586	9904	585	1917	7319	584	2729	11685	521
2077	7534	617	3685	12559	656	3093	11689	591
2650	10921	543	2361	9143	578	3185	12700	560
1901			*1921*			*1941*		
2651	9633	616	4332	14623	668	3015	12741	529
3126	10446	670	5172	16395	711	4006	14979	597
3404	11562	659	4441	14397	693	3306	14800	499
2645	10844	546	4165	16473	569	3768	15962	528
3125	10964	638	3846	14300	607	3648	16955	481
1906			*1926*			*1946*		
3423	13362	574	3940	14583	611	3461	13989	554
1690	6738	562	3174	13920	519			
2923	11198	585	2580	13608	431			
3899	13114	666	2973	11426	590			
3955	13876	638	3311	13393	554			

United Provinces

1891			*1901*			*1911*		
969	3636	597	1693	5670	669	2493	6873	812
1140	3805	671	1803	5457	740	1817	5507	739
874	3533	554	1747	5429	721	551	3037	406
1451	6515	499	1203	5221	516	1773	5343	743
1686	6402	590	1577	5241	674	2025	6083	745
1896			*1906*			*1916*		
1236	4107	674	1480	5620	590	2268	6469	785
1420	4721	674	728	2400	679	1882	6387	660
1512	5187	653	1174	3926	670	773	2727	635
1398	4544	689	1727	4992	775	1644	4947	740
1443	5019	644	1826	5843	700	1180	3961	667

4. Gram—Continued

Yield	Acres	Y/A	Yield	Acres	Y/A	Yield	Acres	Y/A
1921			*1931*			*1941*		
2114	6058	793	1560	5686	614	1417	5289	600
2543	7121	800	1398	5399	580	1911	6080	704
2307	6356	813	1276	5300	539	1472	6358	519
1987	6817	653	1525	5510	620	1658	6118	607
2070	6641	698	1718	5680	677	1496	6140	546
1926			*1936*			*1946*		
1772	6012	659	1917	6445	666	1508	5691	593
1501	5931	567	1643	5757	639			
1065	5424	440	1481	5530	600			
1247	4208	664	1678	5399	696			
1402	5102	615	1560	5106	677			

Greater Punjab

Yield	Acres	Y/A	Yield	Acres	Y/A	Yield	Acres	Y/A
1891			*1911*			*1931*		
446	2709	369	1173	4301	524	1114	5886	425
715	3339	480	773	3643	477	930	4232	496
672	3171	475	615	3056	451	1451	6925	462
610	2980	459	1348	5521	549	838	3911	**484**
293	1627	403	472	3856	276	1003	5027	450
1896			*1916*			*1936*		
241	1223	442	902	5443	372	1018	5237	437
514	2533	455	1566	6345	555	682	3976	386
269	1488	405	498	2276	495	390	2408	364
131	659	444	1055	4416	538	524	2549	461
552	3428	361	380	2393	357	713	3631	442
1901			*1921*			*1941*		
228	1284	398	1208	5528	491	670	3636	414
473	2139	496	1541	5744	602	1137	4104	626
758	2966	573	1168	4497	583	864	4337	449
620	2557	544	1205	6032	488	1022	5290	434
800	3061	586	807	4011	453	1234	6480	428
1906			*1926*			*1946*		
1126	4808	525	1233	4947	588	1009	3794	600
379	1917	443	896	4413	459			
985	4442	497	747	4429	383			
1210	5007	542	793	3421	525			
1139	4720	541	928	4364	478			

Greater Bengal

Yield	Acres	Y/A	Yield	Acres	Y/A	Yield	Acres	Y/A
1891			*1896*			*1901*		
428	1252	766	394	1141	775	369	1020	811
460	1318	783	396	1093	812	383	1078	796
480	1397	770	394	1074	822	431	1205	802
541	1566	774	362	1014	800	388	1087	799
522	1513	773	337	964	784	357	1035	773

4. Gram—Continued

Yield	Acres	Y/A	Yield	Acres	Y/A	Yield	Acres	Y/A
1906			*1921*			*1936*		
390	1115	784	681	1623	940	525	1616	719
281	824	765	704	1682	937	532	1645	715
304	914	746	570	1557	820	524	1689	679
387	1072	810	543	1563	778	554	1764	690
421	1117	844	561	1547	812	555	1763	692
1911			*1926*			*1941*		
508	1229	907	595	1547	862	624	1776	786
413	1099	842	448	1419	707	617	1874	709
512	1277	898	484	1431	758	577	1889	669
401	1387	648	579	1621	800	631	2066	691
571	1579	733	580	1633	796	518	1974	579
1916			*1931*			*1946*		
656	1581	929	559	1645	761	553	1919	633
592	1656	801	557	1676	744			
401	1287	757	544	1659	734			
640	1662	863	565	1662	760			
600	1569	857	430	1531	629			

Central Provinces

Yield	Acres	Y/A	Yield	Acres	Y/A	Yield	Acres	Y/A
1891			*1911*			*1931*		
200	914	491	244	818	668	250	1327	422
200	953	470	280	808	776	250	1365	410
239	1341	399	190	829	513	202	1240	365
251	1399	401	247	852	649	254	1238	460
216	1350	358	238	783	681	231	1217	407
1896			*1916*			*1936*		
192	1078	398	266	894	666	209	1154	405
266	997	599	216	845	573	223	1191	419
231	1140	455	187	649	645	185	1107	374
105	736	321	209	748	626	196	1012	434
222	925	538	129	647	446	197	1152	383
1901			*1921*			*1941*		
269	1007	548	193	637	678	157	1117	315
331	1009	736	220	770	640	181	1068	380
323	1132	639	282	1188	531	181	1251	324
300	1076	625	274	1120	548	257	1354	425
288	1015	636	285	1277	500	228	1307	390
1906			*1926*			*1946*		
305	1070	639	225	1140	442	192	1365	315
194	915	475	178	1104	351			
335	1132	663	153	1308	262			
428	1169	821	219	1214	404			
421	1332	713	226	1332	380			

Notes

United Provinces. Y/a to 1910/11 based on relationship with wheat y/a; agreement of signs of first differences of two series, 26 out of possible 35. Relative mean deviation of predicted yields per acre from actual, 10.0% for 1911/12–29/30.

Other regions. Greater Punjab: y/a to 1910/11 based on wheat y/a, asfd 25/35, rmd 11.4% for 1911/12–29/30. Greater Bengal: y/a to 1910/11 based on rape and mustard y/a, asfd 27/35, rmd 9.9% for 1911/12–29/30. Central Provinces: y/a to 1910/11 based on wheat y/a, asfd 26/35, 7.4% for 1911/12–21/22.

Appendix Table 3a

5. Bajra

British India

Yield	Acres	Y/A	Yield	Acres	Y/A	Yield	Acres	Y/A
1891			*1911*			*1931*		
1521	11060	307	2088	12774	366	2235	13928	358
2119	13560	350	2596	15749	369	2253	14026	361
1717	10996	350	2234	14808	338	2091	13129	356
1815	11944	340	2821	16255	388	2087	13093	356
1786	11210	356	2713	14337	422	2264	13058	388
1896			*1916*			*1936*		
1675	10531	357	2923	15225	432	1911	11449	374
2216	13494	368	2154	12729	381	1904	12495	340
2255	11895	458	1414	11205	284	1842	12776	323
1357	8858	343	2232	14552	435	2020	13360	338
2340	15663	336	1969	11986	367	2389	14083	381
1901			*1921*			*1941*		
2230	13814	358	2640	15888	372	2248	14183	354
2421	14279	379	2420	13919	390	2674	16774	356
2440	14751	370	2199	13674	361	2603	15471	376
1825	10876	373	2218	11964	414	2369	14974	354
1968	12163	363	1982	12257	363	2181	13824	354
1906			*1926*			*1946*		
2779	15713	396	2455	11789	398	2052	13467	340
2190	15036	326	2415	14062	385			
2539	15923	357	2136	12953	370			
2901	16218	400	1998	13285	336			
2576	15297	378	2354	13697	385			

Madras

1891			1901			1911		
609	3085	442	1017	3823	596	869	3384	575
819	3577	513	943	3765	561	744	3606	463
801	3531	508	937	3754	559	719	3273	493
757	3446	492	876	3221	609	940	3482	605
735	3348	492	874	3711	528	1009	3673	617
1896			*1906*			*1916*		
754	2992	565	988	3994	554	925	3411	607
831	3337	558	866	3526	550	906	3309	614
942	3466	609	894	3608	555	701	3030	517
729	3035	538	939	3770	558	850	3265	582
715	3666	437	991	3924	566	814	3012	605

5. Bajra—Continued

Yield	Acres	Y/A	Yield	Acres	Y/A	Yield	Acres	Y/A
1921			*1931*			*1941*		
825	3197	578	780	2877	607	641	2488	576
816	3078	594	784	2817	623	607	2654	511
632	2645	535	691	2559	605	639	2681	533
833	3047	612	627	2697	520	606	2438	556
819	3074	596	716	2712	591	493	2313	475
1926			*1936*			*1946*		
783	3080	569	710	2760	573	518	2362	488
836	3276	571	664	2516	578			
829	3067	605	644	2712	531			
761	2888	591	704	2791	562			
775	2913	596	714	2553	623			

Bombay-Sind

Yield	Acres	Y/A	Yield	Acres	Y/A	Yield	Acres	Y/A
1891			*1911*			*1931*		
569	5534	230	446	5078	197	569	5229	244
783	6310	278	813	6299	289	624	5113	273
558	4845	258	836	6016	311	574	4631	278
575	5215	247	802	6209	289	583	4819	271
617	5027	275	822	5530	332	537	4658	307
1896			*1916*			*1936*		
511	4669	245	906	5666	358	379	3391	251
693	5583	278	445	4161	240	598	4872	276
710	4959	321	256	3294	175	611	5006	273
146	3110	105	818	5461	336	533	4739	251
769	6625	260	497	3764	296	579	4798	271
1901			*1921*			*1941*		
613	6331	217	756	6113	278	591	4594	287
789	6140	288	613	4944	278	888	6168	323
709	5777	275	619	5363	258	832	5951	314
353	3612	219	609	4105	332	604	5588	242
606	5222	260	543	4651	262	540	4767	253
1906			*1926*			*1946*		
974	6691	326	791	5736	309	562	5047	249
634	6041	235	760	5725	298			
668	5989	250	707	5024	316			
995	6577	339	504	4376	258			
737	5934	278	659	5078	291			

United Provinces

Yield	Acres	Y/A	Yield	Acres	Y/A	Yield	Acres	Y/A
1891			*1896*			*1901*		
110	606	405	257	1449	398	382	1960	437
108	585	415	358	1798	446	412	2014	458
110	561	441	334	1703	440	480	2486	433
254	1328	428	384	1856	463	339	1993	381
273	1387	441	432	2063	469	382	2165	395

5. Bajra—Continued

Yield	Acres	Y/A	Yield	Acres	Y/A	Yield	Acres	Y/A
1906			*1921*			*1936*		
451	2177	464	556	2662	468	372	2046	408
389	2492	350	461	2347	439	323	2096	345
527	2652	445	458	2333	439	308	2057	336
515	2602	443	330	1789	412	464	2388	435
506	2551	444	271	1574	385	451	2435	414
1911			*1926*			*1941*		
601	2880	468	445	1909	522	481	2953	365
611	2618	522	401	1921	468	658	3040	484
269	2188	276	266	1973	300	566	2705	468
612	2770	495	366	2128	383	547	2841	432
620	2806	495	398	2024	439	551	2856	432
1916			*1931*			*1946*		
469	2548	412	343	2150	356	469	2605	403
407	2209	412	429	2185	439			
293	2986	220	379	2141	396			
629	2695	522	451	2159	466			
395	2385	372	457	2292	446			

Greater Punjab

Yield	Acres	Y/A	Yield	Acres	Y/A	Yield	Acres	Y/A
1891			*1911*			*1931*		
166	1510	246	114	1231	207	490	3458	318
284	2629	242	358	2941	273	354	3675	215
183	1762	233	346	3074	251	401	3602	249
183	1739	236	400	3030	296	380	3237	262
108	1242	196	172	2033	188	411	3222	287
1896			*1916*			*1936*		
118	1188	223	570	3354	381	396	3023	293
274	2540	242	349	2829	280	264	2758	215
111	1557	160	114	1676	152	240	2804	193
62	657	211	468	2905	370	274	3222	190
373	3030	275	223	2602	190	596	4063	334
1901			*1921*			*1941*		
154	1472	236	423	3650	260	485	3926	278
220	2138	230	474	3325	320	759	4664	363
276	2527	245	429	3081	311	507	3876	293
208	1864	252	388	2787	311	565	4858	260
76	901	190	300	2760	244	557	3656	340
1906			*1926*			*1946*		
323	2672	272	384	2859	300	346	3216	253
260	2804	208	357	2919	273			
389	3405	255	270	2663	228			
374	3017	278	312	3682	190			
285	2644	242	458	3445	298			

Notes

Madras. Y/a up to 1911/12 estimated from relationship with sesamum y/a; agreement in signs of first differences for the two series, 24 out of 34 possible. Relative mean deviation of predicted yields per acre from actual for 1916/17–32/33 is 2.8%. Discontinuity in yield per acre trend before and after 1915/16 adjusted as indicated in III 2.2. Acreage up to 1906/07 raised by 23.6% of *Agricultural Statistics* acreage to account for zamindari lands, based on proportion of zamindari acreage to other, ryotwari, acreage, and bajra grown in each district, according to data available for later years.

Other regions. Bombay-Sind: y/a up to 1911/12 based on cotton y/a, asfd 23/35, rmd 8.7% for 1911/12–23/24. United Provinces: y/a up to 1911/12 estimated from relationship with sesamum y/a, asfd 27/34, rmd 11.4% for 1911/12–26/27. Greater Punjab: y/a up to 1911/12 related to sugarcane y/a, asfd 23/34, rmd 17.3% for 1912/13–22/23.

APPENDIX TABLE 3A

6. Barley

British India

Yield 1891	Acres	Y/A	Yield 1911	Acres	Y/A	Yield 1931	Acres	Y/A
1495	3475	963	3435	8377	918	2389	6384	838
1709	4659	822	3010	7306	923	2352	6322	833
1597	4654	737	2690	7157	842	2422	6615	816
2221	7189	692	3170	7834	907	2512	6493	866
2051	5818	791	3177	7944	896	2326	6087	855
1896			1916			1936		
2475	6341	874	3345	7900	946	2312	6446	803
3151	8061	876	3361	8427	886	2086	6225	750
2735	7073	867	2787	6395	974	1953	6113	678
2680	6611	907	3216	7419	967	1982	6014	738
2748	7592	811	2510	6203	906	2261	6244	812
1901			1921			1941		
2480	6217	894	3129	7303	959	1989	6509	684
2823	6549	965	3118	7350	950	2226	6793	730
3196	7480	956	2938	7166	923	2149	6683	688
2476	7494	739	2645	6898	858	2311	6622	781
2548	7326	780	2585	6573	875	2086	6732	694
1906			1926			1946		
2759	7700	802	2555	6311	905	2322	6723	773
2958	7629	878	2095	6772	693			
3139	8002	878	2521	7483	756			
3550	8104	981	2294	7001	739			
3298	7840	943	2393	6609	811			

United Provinces

1891			1901			1911		
818	2166	846	1763	4092	965	2379	5214	1022
800	1850	968	1973	4089	1081	2108	4643	1017
713	2059	776	2178	4647	1051	1679	4376	859
1454	4763	684	1406	4423	712	2048	4576	1003
1436	3852	835	1422	4127	772	2259	5020	1008
1896			1906			1916		
1739	4008	972	1660	4454	835	2350	5000	1053
2103	4843	973	2002	4572	981	2286	5092	1006
1860	4442	938	2225	5150	968	1859	3831	1092
1860	4175	998	2536	5202	1092	2116	4378	1083
1762	4272	924	2290	5048	1016	1772	3869	1026

6. Barley—Continued

Yield	Acres	Y/A	Yield	Acres	Y/A	Yield	Acres	Y/A
1921			*1931*			*1941*		
2052	4304	1068	1607	4050	889	1210	4016	675
2091	4286	1092	1534	3844	894	1394	4130	756
1919	4226	1017	1710	4272	897	1317	4202	702
1751	4278	917	1676	4080	920	1561	4039	866
1733	4058	956	1677	3784	993	1455	4361	747
1926			*1936*			*1946*		
1699	3929	969	1558	4060	859	1663	4436	840
1306	4282	683	1301	3755	776			
1608	4383	822	1182	3901	679			
1371	4269	719	1216	3735	729			
1575	4223	836	1488	3772	883			

Greater Bengal

Yield	Acres	Y/A	Yield	Acres	Y/A	Yield	Acres	Y/A
1891			*1911*			*1931*		
358	1000	803	546	1435	854	541	1443	840
374	1017	824	524	1356	866	587	1612	816
378	1048	809	547	1399	876	484	1392	779
371	1023	813	508	1382	824	600	1563	860
372	1028	812	511	1408	813	394	1365	646
1896			*1916*			*1936*		
384	1056	814	580	1362	954	463	1367	759
531	1384	860	514	1407	818	492	1396	789
574	1471	874	464	1331	781	451	1395	724
546	1448	846	562	1446	871	436	1303	750
541	1470	825	551	1418	870	475	1400	760
1901			*1921*			*1941*		
513	1339	859	638	1456	982	479	1387	773
546	1457	841	524	1489	788	461	1405	735
574	1516	848	528	1373	861	452	1418	716
570	1514	845	553	1410	879	451	1421	710
577	1592	812	534	1429	849	397	1371	649
1906			*1926*			*1946*		
547	1485	826	530	1359	874	408	1331	687
447	1250	802	478	1359	789			
410	1183	778	516	1376	840			
504	1318	858	544	1434	850			
556	1386	900	561	1438	868			

Greater Punjab

Yield	Acres	Y/A	Yield	Acres	Y/A	Yield	Acres	Y/A
1891			*1896*			*1901*		
301	1235	547	337	1221	619	194	759	575
499	1706	656	493	1753	631	285	950	672
484	1668	651	284	1094	582	419	1255	748
373	1318	635	256	925	621	482	1502	720
228	881	580	430	1792	538	526	1551	760

6. *Barley*

Yield	Acres	Y/A	Yield	Acres	Y/A	Yield	Acres	Y/A
1906			*1921*			*1936*		
527	1685	701	421	1484	638	277	967	638
490	1745	630	483	1512	713	282	1023	614
474	1579	673	476	1474	723	205	759	605
483	1510	717	322	1149	621	316	921	770
424	1328	716	303	1056	639	288	1026	614
1911			*1926*			*1941*		
484	1698	639	311	972	704	291	1067	608
353	1280	620	293	1071	605	356	1201	634
443	1307	760	385	1670	509	360	987	824
588	1793	734	361	1237	674	284	1093	566
376	1426	584	242	881	601	225	948	517
1916			*1931*			*1946*		
391	1463	600	228	836	609	240	900	578
535	1813	659	218	818	593			
445	1171	860	216	897	506			
514	1519	773	224	799	632			
176	868	450	240	883	606			

United Provinces. Y/a up to 1912/13 based on relationship with wheat y/a, agreement in signs of first differences for the two regions, 24 out of 33 possible. Relative mean deviation of predicted yields per acre from actual is 6.3% for 1913/14–28/29.

Other regions. Greater Bengal: Y/a up to 1914/15 related to rape and mustard y/a, asfd 23/31, rmd 4.9% for 1915/16–29/30. Greater Punjab: y/a up to 1910/11 based on wheat y/a, asfd 26/35, rmd 8.4% for 1911/12–29/30. Ajmer-Merwara included with Punjab; its maximum output was only twenty thousand tons.

Appendix Table 3a

7. Maize

British India

Yield	Acres	Y/A	Yield	Acres	Y/A	Yield	Acres	Y/A
1891			*1911*			*1931*		
1631	4991	732	2023	5403	838	2229	5871	850
1936	5354	811	2307	6056	853	2110	6023	785
1741	5141	759	2275	5978	853	1869	5817	719
1657	4947	750	2238	5988	838	2132	5924	806
1699	5275	721	2596	6514	892	2118	5936	799
1896			*1916*			*1936*		
1755	5707	690	2492	6354	878	1836	5731	719
2383	6336	842	2523	6288	898	2009	5623	800
2175	6087	800	1865	5888	710	1770	5711	694
1635	5148	712	2558	6462	887	2118	5754	824
2024	5803	782	2052	5993	767	2095	5718	821
1901			*1921*			*1941*		
2067	6141	755	2418	6081	767	1912	5611	763
2231	6253	800	1868	5729	720	2356	6464	816
2239	6048	829	2153	5658	838	2274	6439	792
1986	5877	757	1650	5121	712	2244	6406	780
1990	5712	780	1837	5240	772	2214	6462	767
1906			*1926*			*1946*		
2289	6089	842	1882	5325	779	1925	6338	680
1285	6153	468	2218	5726	853			
2612	6575	889	1962	5787	749			
2422	6313	860	2409	6330	840			
2386	6163	867	2362	6230	849			

United Provinces

Yield	Acres	Y/A	Yield	Acres	Y/A	Yield	Acres	Y/A
1891			*1901*			*1911*		
508	1420	802	843	2150	878	703	1791	879
562	1520	826	888	2147	926	920	2205	934
575	1451	887	852	2195	868	721	2136	756
531	1392	858	700	2100	746	1050	2376	990
580	1469	887	754	2171	778	1154	2612	990
1896			*1906*			*1916*		
629	1795	787	910	2165	942	953	2426	880
812	2025	899	665	2202	678	1026	2321	990
758	1923	884	1017	2544	895	508	1882	605
669	1606	937	986	2475	892	1014	2430	935
798	1880	953	870	2179	894	629	2094	673

7. Maize—Continued

Yield 1921	Acres	Y/A	Yield 1931	Acres	Y/A	Yield 1941	Acres	Y/A
815	2075	879	833	2116	882	594	1920	692
598	1873	715	751	2137	787	946	2424	874
766	1835	929	695	2023	769	932	2495	837
533	1550	770	796	2121	840	956	2424	883
554	1612	770	808	2120	846	965	2536	852
1926			*1936*			*1946*		
660	1679	880	534	1965	609	753	2364	713
770	1862	926	730	1948	839			
689	2004	770	607	2054	662			
914	2327	880	836	2098	892			
933	2375	880	811	2111	860			

Greater Punjab

Yield 1891	Acres	Y/A	Yield 1911	Acres	Y/A	Yield 1931	Acres	Y/A
582	1269	1029	550	1365	902	592	1455	911
629	1332	1059	602	1517	887	542	1486	817
542	1312	925	729	1513	1079	477	1524	702
436	1156	846	486	1466	743	626	1613	869
505	1343	843	702	1615	972	570	1566	816
1896			*1916*			*1936*		
514	1373	839	681	1721	885	606	1538	884
722	1625	996	569	1682	756	627	1576	891
587	1581	832	605	1601	757	598	1598	839
339	1240	612	619	1606	861	635	1610	885
480	1486	724	509	1481	768	660	1617	914
1901			*1921*			*1941*		
497	1592	701	598	1577	872	665	1658	899
553	1686	735	611	1575	758	668	1784	838
622	1550	899	596	1490	895	702	1807	870
557	1443	865	555	1353	918	740	1843	900
432	1238	783	502	1368	838	715	1832	880
1906			*1926*			*1946*		
536	1586	757	517	1414	820	728	1832	877
338	1574	481	652	1570	930			
893	1666	1201	560	1513	822			
563	1398	903	618	1626	851			
623	1644	850	637	1568	910			

Greater Bengal

Yield 1891	Acres	Y/A	Yield 1896	Acres	Y/A	Yield 1901	Acres	Y/A
434	2000	486	430	2059	468	565	1948	651
593	2133	624	630	2212	640	562	1957	644
487	2032	539	606	2111	644	543	1853	658
551	2041	606	472	1802	588	538	1886	638
450	2053	490	578	2014	643	597	1847	724

7. Maize—Continued

Yield	Acres	Y/A	Yield	Acres	Y/A	Yield	Acres	Y/A
1906			*1921*			*1936*		
586	1824	719	757	1890	897	508	1723	660
583	1856	705	373	1717	487	471	1636	645
471	1847	572	532	1762	651	375	1596	526
612	1918	716	285	1653	386	466	1556	671
660	1844	802	524	1734	377	423	1498	633
1911			*1926*			*1941*		
574	1756	733	466	1695	616	485	1556	698
560	1796	713	541	1726	702	589	1775	743
565	1806	701	448	1719	584	484	1646	659
422	1587	596	627	1811	775	444	1660	599
508	1752	650	552	1724	717	423	1628	582
1916			*1931*			*1946*		
549	1669	737	552	1778	695	337	1679	450
637	1756	810	587	1901	649			
521	1871	621	473	1774	597			
651	1864	782	491	1729	636			
663	1848	803	529	1775	667			

Notes

United Provinces. Y/a up to 1910/11 based on relationship with sesamum y/a; agreement in signs of first differences for two series is 24 out of possible 35. Relative mean deviation of predicted yields per acre from actual is 10.1% for 1911/12–24/25.

Other regions. Greater Punjab: y/a to 1910/11 related to sesamum y/a, asfd 20/35, rmd is 7.7% for 1911/12–21/22. Greater Bengal: y/a to 1911/12 based on sugarcane y/a, asfd 19/34, rmd 11.2% for 1912/13–24/25. Bengal acreage for 1891/92 approximated at slightly less than 1893/94.

APPENDIX TABLE 3A

8. Ragi

British India

Yield 1891	Acres	Y/A	Yield 1911	Acres	Y/A	Yield 1931	Acres	Y/A
1298	4711	618	1539	4296	802	1431	3870	829
1402	4464	703	1415	4456	712	1435	3826	840
1357	4220	721	1252	4371	641	1367	3732	820
1426	4518	706	1572	4251	829	1236	3737	741
1389	4459	699	1631	4338	842	1286	3534	815
1896			*1916*			*1936*		
1521	4547	750	1558	4072	858	1357	3584	849
1582	4599	771	1614	4265	847	1273	3464	822
1677	4510	831	1292	4004	724	1206	3472	777
1394	4153	753	1541	4222	818	1235	3403	813
1303	4419	661	1601	4238	847	1322	3502	844
1901			*1921*			*1941*		
1713	4678	820	1551	4211	824	1276	3512	813
1614	4537	797	1555	4262	818	1234	3571	775
1510	4226	800	1457	4220	773	1249	3416	820
1567	4202	836	1335	3980	750	1179	3284	804
1453	4264	764	1388	3881	802	963	3207	672
1906			*1926*			*1946*		
1585	4438	800	1380	3854	802	1048	3189	737
1534	4539	757	1403	3851	815			
1543	4464	775	1451	3903	833			
1583	4545	780	1457	3999	815			
1553	4289	811	1462	3972	824			

Madras

1891			1901			1911		
815	2511	727	1228	2807	980	1034	2448	946
879	2334	844	1131	2745	923	884	2600	762
903	2419	836	1066	2597	920	901	2490	811
915	2534	809	1158	2589	1002	1080	2432	995
888	2458	809	1000	2578	869	1146	2529	1015
1896			*1906*			*1916*		
1065	2567	929	1077	2648	911	1070	2398	999
1028	2509	918	1047	2592	905	1124	2492	1010
1140	2549	1002	1075	2638	913	905	2386	850
999	2530	885	1018	2484	918	1057	2473	957
800	2491	719	1035	2490	931	1132	2548	995

8. Ragi—Continued

Yield 1921	Acres	Y/A	Yield 1931	Acres	Y/A	Yield 1941	Acres	Y/A
1058	2493	951	982	2201	999	896	2025	991
1127	2583	977	992	2168	1025	809	2046	886
1018	2592	880	943	2124	995	843	2000	944
1097	2441	1007	823	2157	855	801	1945	922
1020	2331	980	866	1995	972	621	1911	728
1926			*1936*			*1946*		
950	2273	936	929	2054	1012	717	1733	927
965	2302	939	835	1878	997			
1001	2254	995	778	1892	921			
985	2270	972	832	1909	976			
948	2166	980	920	2010	1025			

Greater Bengal

Yield 1891	Acres	Y/A	Yield 1911	Acres	Y/A	Yield 1931	Acres	Y/A
191	790	542	308	1025	673	218	748	653
217	790	615	282	954	663	204	727	629
204	803	570	136	967	316	177	660	601
261	964	606	241	899	601	177	637	622
245	1010	545	248	881	629	169	594	638
1896			*1916*			*1936*		
243	1021	533	239	795	675	196	647	678
298	1069	624	270	875	692	192	655	656
299	1071	626	236	861	614	174	653	596
252	947	596	261	852	685	188	609	692
287	1029	626	254	826	690	171	574	668
1901			*1921*			*1941*		
281	1001	630	260	843	692	176	601	654
278	996	626	200	826	543	168	587	641
262	927	633	228	812	630	153	565	607
259	933	623	155	713	489	154	573	600
282	945	668	171	788	485	123	481	571
1906			*1926*			*1946*		
273	919	666	209	766	611	130	566	515
283	964	658	211	720	657			
214	818	588	198	747	594			
316	1067	664	245	789	695			
263	851	692	242	816	665			

Bombay-Sind

Yield 1891	Acres	Y/A	Yield 1896	Acres	Y/A	Yield 1901	Acres	Y/A
189	681	623	160	564	637	142	521	613
190	641	665	167	563	665	144	478	674
179	640	628	179	573	701	144	487	662
181	635	638	100	433	517	122	446	614
187	635	662	148	511	650	134	461	650

8. Ragi—Continued

Yield	Acres	Y/A	Yield	Acres	Y/A	Yield	Acres	Y/A
1906			*1921*			*1936*		
161	513	706	186	628	665	185	602	688
180	643	628	188	635	665	200	646	693
184	645	641	174	604	648	201	646	697
185	672	617	201	635	711	150	595	565
197	665	665	166	572	651	179	640	626
1911			*1926*			*1941*		
155	583	596	189	613	692	154	599	576
189	637	665	191	627	682	195	623	701
190	660	693	212	681	697	196	571	769
197	655	674	196	677	648	167	540	693
177	648	611	204	669	676	166	524	709
1916			*1931*			*1946*		
207	634	733	182	643	636	151	523	647
182	645	632	195	662	661			
130	524	557	201	677	665			
163	594	615	190	648	659			
181	598	680	204	664	690			

Notes

British India. Provincial data were not available from *Estimates* for 1935/36–37/38. Output reported for British India was prorated among the regions according to the acreage, available from *Agricultural Statistics,* and the yield per acre, computed as indicated below, for each region.

Madras. Y/a up to 1937/38 based on relationship with bajra y/a, agreement in signs of first differences for these two series, 6 out 7 possible. Relative mean deviation of predicted yields per acre from actual is 5.3% for 1938/39–46/47.

Other Regions. Great Bengal: Y/a up to 1937/38 based on maize y/a, asfd 5/7, rmd of 4.0% for 1938/39–46/47. Bombay-Sind: Y/a up to 1937/38 related to bajra y/a, asfd, 5/7, rmd 6.7% for 1938/39–46/47.

APPENDIX TABLE 3A

9. Sugarcane*

British India

Yield	Acres	Y/A	Yield	Acres	Y/A	Yield	Acres	Y/A
1891			*1911*			*1931*		
2634	3141	1879	2653	2390	2486	3790	2852	2977
2753	2830	2180	2758	2542	2430	4450	3179	3136
2613	2939	1534	2395	2509	2139	4669	3165	3304
2918	2807	2330	2753	2280	2704	4884	3316	3299
2884	2969	2175	2731	2354	2598	5605	3829	3279
1896			*1916*			*1936*		
2204	2692	1835	2898	2380	2728	6134	4223	3254
3051	2790	2451	3307	2775	2668	5099	3700	3087
2902	2724	2385	2366	2824	1875	3148	2988	2360
2408	2763	1953	2843	2620	2430	4334	3469	2799
2838	2587	2457	2424	2474	2193	5434	4402	2767
1901			*1921*			*1941*		
2503	2543	2204	2526	2326	2433	4040	3338	2710
2431	2422	2249	2912	2657	2455	4768	3435	3109
2385	2327	2296	3230	2845	2543	5456	4035	3028
2603	2427	2404	2453	2465	2229	5063	3943	2876
2237	2262	2215	2907	2619	2486	5027	3614	3116
1906			*1926*			*1946*		
2685	2491	2415	3173	2856	2489	5316	3927	3031
2304	2707	1906	3082	2869	2406			
2101	2249	2092	2599	2497	2332			
2350	2176	2419	2607	2402	2431			
2486	2174	2563	3068	2684	2560			

United Provinces

1891			*1901*			*1911*		
1002	1363	1646	1100	1233	1998	1412	1345	2352
982	1209	1820	1021	1155	1980	1452	1431	2274
1334	1322	2260	1007	1093	2063	1079	1380	1752
1134	1233	2055	1315	1217	2421	1486	1192	2793
1402	1389	2260	1034	1234	1877	1404	1261	2493
1896			*1906*			*1916*		
829	1214	1534	1425	1392	2294	1439	1202	2681
1309	1248	2352	1039	1488	1564	1604	1489	2413
1342	1232	2439	955	1123	1904	987	1544	1432
969	1264	1718	1066	1040	2296	1453	1414	2302
1326	1216	2442	1186	1049	2533	1027	1285	1789

* Raw Sugar (Gur).

9. Sugarcane—Continued

Yield 1921	Acres	Y/A	Yield 1931	Acres	Y/A	Yield 1941	Acres	Y/A
1119	1151	2174	2207	1577	3135	1847	1755	2356
1342	1349	2228	2577	1773	3256	2570	1865	3087
1634	1544	2371	2532	1713	3311	2855	2240	2856
1056	1292	1831	2719	1814	3358	2411	2166	2493
1412	1419	2229	3275	2212	3316	2223	1818	2740
1926			*1936*			*1946*		
1680	1613	2333	3765	2465	3421	2410	2051	2632
1522	1585	2151	3144	2181	3229			
1210	1344	2017	1432	1628	1970			
1301	1349	2160	2129	1876	2542			
1581	1489	2378	2845	2518	2531			

Greater Bengal

Yield 1891	Acres	Y/A	Yield 1911	Acres	Y/A	Yield 1931	Acres	Y/A
884	1159	1710	560	486	2580	580	515	2522
1050	1071	2196	556	488	2551	767	535	3210
874	1031	1899	534	481	2486	1080	665	3638
922	967	2135	527	499	2365	1165	721	3618
728	945	1726	516	493	2345	1226	790	3476
1896			*1916*			*1936*		
617	840	1647	517	482	2401	1139	829	3075
979	973	2253	530	470	2527	903	667	3031
871	861	2267	496	494	2249	845	691	2751
817	884	2070	574	493	2607	1023	775	2957
811	802	2265	554	505	2457	1088	857	2843
1901			*1921*			*1941*		
676	661	2292	576	527	2448	878	715	2751
682	674	2267	502	507	2218	860	723	2663
654	632	2318	536	509	2359	926	780	2659
635	633	2247	462	495	2090	848	690	2751
576	574	2551	563	509	2477	926	724	2865
1906			*1926*			*1946*		
553	554	2533	518	490	2368	852	698	2735
549	563	2482	545	498	2451			
407	509	2014	529	483	2453			
468	472	2522	524	477	2460			
532	480	2825	555	483	2574			

Greater Punjab

Yield 1891	Acres	Y/A	Yield 1896	Acres	Y/A	Yield 1901	Acres	Y/A
263	363	1623	262	398	1474	296	427	1552
222	314	1586	246	348	1586	255	377	1514
224	328	1530	184	395	1045	288	399	615
235	340	1549	228	368	1389	266	359	1657
222	386	1288	299	369	1814	114	204	1250

9. Sugarcane—Continued

Yield	Acres	Y/A	Yield	Acres	Y/A	Yield	Acres	Y/A
1906			*1921*			*1936*		
251	313	1794	332	414	1796	550	631	1953
267	437	1366	477	545	1960	366	586	1400
301	401	1682	479	534	2009	287	406	1584
372	456	1826	386	442	1955	396	489	1812
306	432	1586	368	446	1848	578	648	1998
1911			*1926*			*1941*		
196	322	1362	416	508	1834	508	545	2088
313	404	1734	451	548	1841	523	526	2226
344	443	1738	352	454	1736	676	645	2348
331	398	1864	270	361	1673	806	701	2574
308	378	1823	362	478	1696	867	672	2889
1916			*1931*			*1946*		
380	444	1915	425	522	1823	887	732	2715
469	534	1967	492	615	1792			
329	511	1440	419	518	1812			
369	516	1602	375	513	1637			
357	493	1622	428	536	1788			

Madras

Yield	Acres	Y/A	Yield	Acres	Y/A	Yield	Acres	Y/A
1891			*1911*			*1931*		
267	113	5285	265	108	5488	324	116	6257
238	99	5397	238	99	5376	339	121	6276
265	113	5261	212	84	5654	349	122	6408
275	120	5194	188	74	5681	351	125	6290
318	114	6250	251	95	5921	370	134	6182
1896			*1916*			*1936*		
291	113	5778	267	114	5246	363	135	5981
291	113	5782	363	127	6403	512	113	6182
267	104	5754	314	123	5718	299	111	6026
268	118	5092	264	93	6359	437	152	6451
275	112	5513	273	103	5937	514	177	6496
1901			*1921*			*1941*		
294	102	6462	315	119	5929	339	124	6115
251	92	6114	358	131	6122	356	137	5824
227	88	5773	320	121	5924	465	170	6138
243	96	5670	313	110	6374	491	172	6384
310	122	5701	315	113	6244	454	175	5936
1906			*1926*			*1946*		
270	104	5816	305	114	5993	619	217	6384
221	87	5678	283	106	5980			
224	90	5567	245	89	6166			
221	88	5636	275	98	6286			
233	95	5481	321	115	6253			

9. Sugarcane—Continued

Bombay-Sind

Yield	Acres	Y/A	Yield	Acres	Y/A	Yield	Acres	Y/A
1891			*1911*			*1931*		
159	78	4575	166	70	5312	184	69	6071
198	71	6246	138	58	5343	187	75	6003
263	87	6776	165	63	5856	201	73	6208
252	88	6426	168	60	6260	201	79	5555
150	74	4534	198	69	6444	193	88	5694
1896			*1916*			*1936*		
150	69	4885	239	80	6696	221	89	5587
177	57	6947	279	96	6501	220	78	5300
176	61	6456	185	89	4656	173	83	4668
80	73	2462	130	53	5517	204	108	4229
88	40	4935	162	63	5764	268	126	4764
1901			*1921*			*1941*		
76	54	3163	132	57	5188	314	122	5766
163	57	6416	171	64	5985	374	113	7412
163	59	6186	197	73	6045	374	121	6924
103	59	3894	171	62	6178	415	126	7376
141	59	5345	185	68	6094	425	130	7323
1906			*1926*			*1946*		
119	53	5035	184	68	6061	422	131	7215
167	64	5836	203	68	6687			
167	67	5577	186	65	6410			
172	63	6117	175	66	5939			
174	61	6401	184	65	6341			

Notes

Yield given in raw sugar, gur.

United Provinces. Minor districts up to 1912/13 and seed allowance up to 1916/17 added to *Estimates,* per Chapter III 1.1 and 1.2. Y/a up to 1897/98 based on relationship with sesamum y/a; agreement in signs of first differences of the two series is 34 out of possible 48. Relative mean deviation of predicted yields per acre from actual is 19.8% for 1898/99–1910/11.

Greater Bengal. Y/a up to 1897/98 based on sesamum y/a, asfd 32/48, rmd 10.7% for 1898/99–1909/10. Greater Bengal and Assam combined report in *Estimates* for 1905/06–10/11 separated on basis of provincial acreage in *Agricultural Statistics* and relationship of yields per acre of the two regions during 1911/12–20/21.

Madras. Zamindari areas added to *Estimates* up to 1910/11 as described in Chapter III, 3.1. Y/a trend discontinuity before and after 1915/16 adjusted as indicated in Chapter III, 2.1. Y/a up to 1900/01 projected backward from straight line trend for 1901/02–46/47 with annual deviations from trend scaled from percentage annual deviations of rice y/a from its trend.

Bombay-Sind. Y/a to 1906/07 based on wheat y/a, asfd 23/39, rmd 7.9% for 1907/08–19/20. Bombay Province separated from combined Province-States report in *Estimates* for 1907/08–21/22 according to *Agricultural Statistics* acreage and relationship of Province and States y/a from 1922/23 to 1935/36.

APPENDIX TABLE 3A

10. Cotton

British India

Yield	Acres	Y/A	Yield	Acres	Y/A	Yield	Acres	Y/A
1891			*1911*			*1931*		
1278	8908	57	2494	14401	69	2425	14256	68
1554	8934	65	3109	13912	89	2911	12790	91
1723	10476	66	3506	15576	89	3336	14103	94
1504	9940	61	3510	14964	94	3114	14026	89
1870	9849	76	2663	11346	94	3758	12244	121
1896			*1916*			*1936*		
1986	9689	82	2797	13530	82	4186	14862	113
1748	9159	76	2500	15230	68	3714	15357	97
2103	9370	90	2646	14061	75	3259	13893	94
864	8481	41	3953	14877	106	3381	13346	101
2204	9873	89	2426	13744	72	4140	14083	117
1901			*1921*			*1941*		
2116	9475	89	2780	11344	98	4180	14763	112
2481	9353	106	2954	13304	89	3179	11837	107
2280	12073	76	3255	15080	86	3439	12436	110
2724	13058	84	3738	19430	77	2592	9497	109
2315	13079	71	3732	17720	84	2520	9280	109
1906			*1926*			*1946*		
3220	13938	92	2959	15240	72	2420	9257	105
2219	13749	65	3431	14479	95			
2475	12795	77	3755	16188	93			
3265	13017	100	3598	15802	91			
2686	14125	76	3326	13824	96			

Bombay-Sind

Yield	Acres	Y/A	Yield	Acres	Y/A	Yield	Acres	Y/A
1891			*1901*			*1911*		
409	2622	62	413	2929	57	595	4443	54
559	2769	81	646	3048	85	957	4198	91
580	3187	73	752	3779	80	1016	4455	91
486	2811	69	523	3606	58	1062	4657	91
564	2833	80	736	3980	74	715	3355	85
1896			*1906*			*1916*		
436	2537	69	1047	4171	100	1059	4488	94
475	2329	81	662	4139	64	858	4743	73
679	2737	98	621	3550	70	553	4287	51
70	2141	13	1087	4083	105	1114	4337	103
438	2369	74	946	4660	81	620	3806	65

10. Cotton—Continued

Yield	Acres	Y/A	Yield	Acres	Y/A	Yield	Acres	Y/A
1921			*1931*			*1941*		
744	2977	99	758	4321	67	1238	4976	100
887	3977	89	896	4223	83	957	3534	108
917	4889	75	875	4225	83	1128	3902	116
1030	5317	77	825	4280	77	689	2215	124
1046	5474	76	1120	4931	91	562	1991	112
1926			*1936*			*1946*		
748	4590	65	1151	4632	99	605	2195	110
979	4876	80	1088	4833	90			
1049	5191	81	1018	4555	89			
789	4804	66	988	4576	86			
765	3831	74	1280	4816	106			

Greater Punjab

Yield	Acres	Y/A	Yield	Acres	Y/A	Yield	Acres	Y/A
1891			*1911*			*1931*		
109	500	87	234	1519	61	544	2182	100
116	548	85	353	1499	95	559	1908	117
183	890	82	558	1885	119	931	2474	151
214	1030	83	455	1748	105	952	2366	161
183	1054	69	183	853	86	1238	2824	176
1896			*1916*			*1936*		
197	994	79	313	1093	115	1461	2932	200
211	993	85	284	1681	68	1145	3159	145
98	701	56	458	1457	127	1107	2924	152
123	735	67	634	2122	110	1020	2658	154
217	1065	81	541	1984	96	1218	2687	182
1901			*1921*			*1941*		
184	886	83	277	1166	112	1230	2816	176
206	1069	76	362	1290	130	1069	2336	182
234	1083	86	576	1776	137	1048	2618	160
322	1351	96	804	2369	117	940	2435	154
78	745	38	798	2740	82	955	2342	163
1906			*1926*			*1946*		
330	1322	101	524	2558	112	938	2229	168
327	1366	96	517	1854	84			
342	1502	83	529	2528	127			
358	1309	110	705	2229	123			
284	1283	88	671	2181	100			

Central Provinces

Yield	Acres	Y/A	Yield	Acres	Y/A	Yield	Acres	Y/A
1891			*1896*			*1901*		
404	3033	53	427	3058	56	880	3671	96
353	2870	49	559	2819	80	971	3902	99
377	2913	52	782	3145	99	760	4144	73
339	2717	50	222	2696	33	1229	4553	108
562	2636	85	1000	3526	57	818	4849	67

10. Cotton—Continued

Yield	Acres	Y/A	Yield	Acres	Y/A	Yield	Acres	Y/A
1906			*1921*			*1936*		
881	4678	77	1127	4414	102	851	3952	86
595	4432	54	1040	4857	86	713	4047	70
766	4176	73	1020	4933	83	536	3653	59
1070	4167	102	1000	5247	76	721	3270	88
629	4487	56	980	5385	73	901	3572	101
1911			*1926*			*1941*		
913	4648	78	977	4864	80	988	3805	104
910	4493	81	1235	4796	103	539	3273	65
961	4754	81	1334	5078	105	624	3203	78
1097	4708	93	1252	5175	97	466	2803	66
1106	4061	109	1136	4750	96	535	2956	72
1916			*1931*			*1946*		
691	4402	63	442	4620	38	462	2967	62
591	4582	52	820	4000	82			
807	4135	78	758	4270	71			
1289	4600	112	617	4201	59			
514	4477	46	616	4068	61			

Madras

Yield	Acres	Y/A	Yield	Acres	Y/A	Yield	Acres	Y/A
1891			*1911*			*1931*		
143	1543	37	437	2676	66	421	2204	76
181	1046	44	394	2389	68	407	1949	84
209	2139	39	428	2697	63	450	2156	83
184	1889	39	338	2087	65	474	2304	82
212	2015	42	343	2060	66	533	2664	80
1896			*1916*			*1936*		
182	1731	42	347	2168	64	494	2487	79
211	1873	45	500	2700	74	502	2546	79
226	1641	55	580	3133	74	369	1929	77
176	1716	41	402	2339	69	452	2196	82
204	1704	48	354	2121	67	530	2413	88
1901			*1921*			*1941*		
226	1677	54	339	1783	76	562	2541	88
289	1962	59	429	2323	74	475	2210	86
305	2066	59	480	2628	73	482	2187	88
229	2178	42	563	2865	79	381	1670	91
253	1982	51	565	2888	78	361	1611	90
1906			*1926*			*1946*		
275	2113	52	386	2204	70	334	1555	85
334	2190	61	444	2100	85			
288	1989	58	524	2465	85			
330	2029	65	509	2476	82			
412	2323	71	378	2041	74			

10. Cotton—Continued

United Provinces

Yield	Acres	Y/A	Yield	Acres	Y/A	Yield	Acres	Y/A
1891			*1911*			*1931*		
164	1012	65	248	901	109	205	739	111
162	838	77	421	1119	148	169	516	131
297	1069	111	477	1548	122	265	805	132
198	1215	65	483	1532	125	192	705	109
280	1061	105	260	821	126	194	588	132
1896			*1916*			*1936*		
261	1150	90	307	1174	104	174	692	101
225	920	98	196	1305	60	196	581	133
261	933	112	172	850	81	179	652	110
228	997	91	436	1271	138	147	484	121
294	1046	112	334	1141	116	146	394	148
1901			*1921*			*1941*		
369	1154	128	241	808	118	105	429	98
328	1239	106	177	646	110	92	311	118
184	841	87	210	638	132	112	372	120
366	1190	122	275	1035	106	62	202	133
392	1362	115	275	990	111	58	196	118
1906			*1926*			*1946*		
635	1463	172	257	796	129	44	168	105
263	1430	73	196	630	124			
424	1377	122	252	701	144			
381	1224	124	286	916	125			
346	1333	103	319	822	155			

Notes

Yield given in 000's bales of 400 lbs. of ginned cotton; Y/A in lbs.

Bombay-Sind, Greater Punjab. States eliminated from combined Provinces—States *Estimates* reports up to 1921/22, per Chapter III, 1.3.

Central Provinces. Acreage and output, to 1896/97 raised above *Estimates* to include zamindari land of Raipur, Bilaspur, and Drug districts. These districts were almost wholly zamindari; their cotton acreage reported in *Agricultural Statistics* was added to the acreage in *Estimates.*

Madras. Zamindari lands added up to 1910/11, as explained in Chapter III, 2.1. *Estimates* acreage up to 1906/07 raised by 24.1%. States eliminated from *Estimates* to 1921/22, per Chapter III, 1.3. Y/a trend discontinuity up to and after 1915/16 adjusted by raising early years, per Chapter III, 2.2.

United Provinces. States eliminated from combined *Estimates* report for Province-States for 1904/05–21/22, per Chapter III, 1.3.

APPENDIX TABLE 3A

11. Jute

British India

Yield	Acres	Y/A	Yield	Acres	Y/A	Yield	Acres	Y/A
1891			7913	2924	1083	9831	3109	1265
2957	1396	846	*1911*			10258	3381	1214
5678	2117	1072	8193	3086	1060	11122	3458	1287
4977	2213	891	8814	2931	1202	*1931*		
6114	2253	1086	8771	2876	1218	5522	1845	1197
5523	2232	990	10309	3308	1244	7026	2119	1326
1896			7273	2348	1237	7941	2491	1275
5688	2186	1039	*1916*			8426	2644	1275
6805	2141	1273	8241	2671	1234	7162	2162	1325
5307	1615	1311	8772	2700	1299	*1936*		
5385	1952	1106	6912	2470	1049	9515	2855	1333
6493	2083	1248	8412	2800	1201	8559	2847	1203
1901			5857	2473	949	6753	3118	866
7431	2253	1321	*1921*			9648	3115	1239
6544	2133	1228	3974	1505	1052	13006	5506	928
7191	2252	1278	5356	1778	1204	*1941*		
7364	2870	1026	8330	2753	1210	5383	2084	1027
8088	3128	1034	7988	2738	1167	8953	3281	1091
1906			8861	3079	1151	6926	2604	1066
9128	3483	1049	*1926*			6135	2074	1186
9736	3942	989	12001	3798	1264	7730	2392	1294
6471	2835	911	10129	3341	1213	*1946*		
7174	2857	1024				5366	2103	1023

Notes

Above data very close to that given in *Estimates*. Slight deduction made to exclude Cooch Behar up to 1901/02. Greater Bengal includes 80 to 90 percent of output, remainder from Assam.

Yield given in 000's bales of 400 lbs.; Y/A in lbs.

APPENDIX TABLE 3A

12. Tea

British India

Yield	Acres	Y/A	Yield	Acres	Y/A	Yield	Acres	Y/A
1891			*1911*			*1931*		
54	355	344	113	541	470	162	723	504
54	367	327	126	566	507	178	721	553
58	387	336	130	569	513	156	726	483
59	391	338	132	582	510	163	733	499
62	405	346	157	591	596	161	738	487
1896			*1916*			*1936*		
68	421	361	157	604	583	161	740	488
67	454	330	156	622	564	175	740	529
69	457	337	155	632	549	184	739	557
79	491	363	158	645	549	183	737	555
86	496	399	144	652	493	187	738	570
1901			*1921*			*1941*		
83	497	374	113	655	388	204	741	617
82	499	367	129	655	442	228	743	686
90	500	402	155	657	529	233	744	702
94	498	426	155	660	527	206	742	621
94	499	423	149	672	499	236	743	711
1906			*1926*			*1946*		
103	503	457	162	679	535	239	764	700
103	509	454	161	690	523			
104	520	450	166	705	529			
109	524	468	179	711	564			
111	531	469	162	723	504			

Assam

	1891			1901			1911	
1891			*1901*			*1911*		
40	242	372	60	338	399	80	354	506
38	247	341	59	340	388	89	362	550
42	257	366	65	338	429	89	368	543
42	269	353	68	338	450	93	376	554
45	276	362	68	339	448	110	383	642
1896			*1906*			*1916*		
45	292	346	72	339	478	109	389	627
48	311	344	73	342	480	110	400	615
49	326	334	74	346	480	113	406	624
57	330	388	78	348	503	107	412	581
63	337	418	78	350	500	104	420	558

12. Tea—Continued

Yield 1921	Acres	Y/A	Yield 1931	Acres	Y/A	Yield 1941	Acres	Y/A
81	417	435	108	431	564	133	440	678
89	412	485	115	428	600	140	441	709
106	412	577	98	430	510	127	443	642
106	413	574	103	436	534	123	442	624
100	416	541	101	437	518	131	441	668
1926			*1936*			*1946*		
108	420	576	100	439	509	149	454	733
105	424	556	108	440	549			
110	427	576	116	439	594			
116	430	603	133	438	680			
104	433	539	116	439	592			

Greater Bengal

1891			1911			1931		
12	91	302	29	149	436	40	202	442
14	93	326	32	153	463	49	202	542
14	111	282	36	158	509	44	204	478
14	98	326	34	161	470	44	206	483
16	104	335	40	163	551	43	206	473
1896			*1916*			*1936*		
16	106	346	41	168	552	45	207	486
17	119	328	41	170	542	49	206	533
18	130	313	40	171	527	48	205	525
20	133	338	45	175	571	48	204	525
21	135	344	32	174	414	50	205	546
1901			*1921*			*1941*		
21	135	342	26	179	329	51	205	556
20	135	341	32	182	395	66	206	718
23	136	374	39	183	482	79	204	868
24	135	399	39	184	474	57	204	623
24	136	394	38	190	447	80	205	873
1906			*1926*			*1946*		
27	137	443	42	191	499	70	213	732
27	139	433	43	192	507			
27	142	423	43	198	483			
27	143	426	50	199	557			
29	146	443	44	203	482			

Notes

Above data are as given in *Estimates,* except that for 1939–46 adjustments were made because of changes in provincial boundaries as between
Bengal and Assam, as explained in Chapter III, 1.3.

APPENDIX TABLE 3A

13. Tobacco

British India

Yield	Acres	Y/A	Yield	Acres	Y/A	Yield	Acres	Y/A
1891			*1911*			*1931*		
299	964	695	368	910	906	424	1057	898
398	1147	777	358	877	914	420	1023	921
482	1207	894	304	916	743	374	982	851
323	1158	625	411	967	952	462	1149	900
337	1094	690	385	948	910	418	1101	851
1896			*1916*			*1936*		
379	985	862	398	957	931	422	1047	903
428	1027	933	352	926	851	449	1147	876
435	1083	900	398	937	952	431	1155	836
301	881	765	395	974	907	431	1180	818
279	956	654	318	831	858	409	1125	815
1901			*1921*			*1941*		
339	946	803	418	963	972	436	1196	818
378	938	902	371	922	900	403	1055	856
373	977	855	352	906	871	350	909	862
328	938	783	376	946	889	380	975	874
334	1002	747	344	983	784	376	1035	813
1906			*1926*			*1946*		
354	1012	784	337	948	795	332	913	815
274	911	674	401	1022	878			
347	895	868	417	1023	914			
390	931	938	423	1046	905			
405	971	934	387	995	871			

Madras

1891			*1901*			*1911*		
25	100	567	77	176	982	79	192	925
51	151	760	81	204	889	77	206	836
60	181	746	83	211	882	87	208	939
50	158	703	72	161	1009	95	227	939
51	163	703	68	192	799	87	216	899
1896			*1906*			*1916*		
51	126	899	88	228	869	93	208	1002
59	150	879	74	192	859	94	208	1009
77	172	1009	67	173	872	100	236	949
44	119	826	79	201	879	89	228	878
42	170	554	89	222	902	86	201	959

13. Tobacco—Continued

Yield	Acres	Y/A	Yield	Acres	Y/A	Yield	Acres	Y/A
1921			*1931*			*1941*		
86	203	950	119	269	989	137	357	865
90	214	946	115	256	1009	122	308	896
94	220	876	108	248	974	102	262	885
117	265	989	128	292	981	142	352	907
105	249	940	110	280	882	141	387	820
1926			*1936*			*1946*		
94	232	912	120	277	985	116	328	795
123	276	998	133	318	952			
112	255	983	130	344	853			
114	257	991	138	332	948			
102	243	940	135	335	914			

Greater Bengal

1891			*1911*			*1931*		
214	650	737	190	423	1010	185	434	954
267	775	773	193	420	1030	197	442	997
336	731	1030	134	435	691	176	426	925
193	726	597	196	428	1030	203	441	1030
221	696	710	201	438	1030	181	447	907
1896			*1916*			*1936*		
266	642	931	189	430	987	196	439	927
295	648	1020	159	411	871	192	444	918
267	657	910	218	476	1027	182	427	905
204	587	778	203	462	986	170	435	827
168	551	683	165	375	989	155	437	753
1901			*1921*			*1941*		
200	531	845	191	416	1030	185	439	896
193	502	861	181	418	968	176	427	874
195	539	810	162	405	894	172	420	867
190	547	781	167	393	954	126	299	874
160	530	674	146	425	768	122	306	829
1906			*1926*			*1946*		
163	508	719	151	432	784	123	295	865
138	502	617	185	437	948			
200	482	930	187	437	959			
202	440	1030	191	437	979			
201	438	1030	185	420	986			

Notes

Madras. Y/a up to 1918/19 based on relationship with sesamum y/a; agreement in signs of first differences of the two series, 17 out of possible 27. Relative mean deviation of predicted yields per acre from actual is 3.9% for 1919/20–33/34. Discontinuity in y/a trends before and after 1937/38 adjusted by lowering earlier yields per acre, as explained in Chapter III, 2.2. Zamindari lands included up to 1906/07 by raising *Estimates* acreage 45% based on proportion of zamindari acreage to other, ryotwari, acreage, and tobacco grown, in each district, according to data available for later years.

Greater Bengal. Y/a up to 1924/25 based on wheat y/a, asfd 14/21, rmd 7.1% for 1925/26–33/36.

APPENDIX TABLE 3A

14. Groundnut

British India

Yield	Acres	Y/A	Yield	Acres	Y/A	Yield	Acres	Y/A
1891			*1911*			*1931*		
129	399	724	428	1021	939	1777	3816	1043
168	399	943	465	1119	931	2373	4946	1074
149	399	836	538	1821	662	2491	5306	1051
149	399	836	741	2101	790	1355	3419	888
144	399	808	693	1369	1134	1697	3644	1043
1896			*1916*			*1936*		
115	304	847	959	2031	1058	2161	4750	1019
77	202	854	824	1654	1116	2710	6406	948
104	209	1115	487	1154	946	2345	5694	922
53	171	694	647	1291	1123	2394	5532	949
88	307	642	825	1822	1014	2736	5951	1030
1901			*1921*			*1941*		
225	454	1110	775	1755	989	1795	4461	901
251	519	1083	997	2109	1059	1933	5088	856
243	499	1091	918	2195	939	2330	5403	966
242	481	1127	1167	2291	1141	2730	6644	920
261	511	1144	1560	3269	1068	2302	6414	804
1906			*1926*			*1946*		
304	657	1036	1537	3339	1031	2450	6511	843
321	773	930	2094	4159	1128			
408	907	1008	2398	4802	1118			
394	953	926	1994	4441	1005			
422	881	1073	2308	4741	1090			

Madras

Yield	Acres	Y/A	Yield	Acres	Y/A	Yield	Acres	Y/A
1891			*1901*			*1911*		
80	270	666	194	376	1154	306	806	1062
108	270	893	218	468	1044	341	924	1034
106	270	876	197	427	1036	411	1605	718
100	270	826	211	407	1164	580	1866	870
100	270	826	243	437	1248	633	1136	1248
1896			*1906*			*1916*		
82	175	1056	262	568	1035	825	1793	1031
49	106	1033	281	669	940	680	1415	1076
69	129	1196	344	800	963	442	1001	989
49	113	970	309	823	840	569	1144	1114
74	256	651	353	742	1066	740	1600	1036

14. Groundnut—Continued

Yield	Acres	Y/A	Yield	Acres	Y/A	Yield	Acres	Y/A
1921			*1931*			*1941*		
678	1459	1041	1234	2635	1049	1187	2793	952
823	1754	1051	1729	3517	1101	1306	3387	864
744	1807	922	1777	3779	1053	1605	3554	1011
948	1904	1115	920	2351	877	1954	4308	1016
1264	2599	1089	1202	2520	1068	1568	4175	841
1926			*1936*			*1946*		
1207	2680	1009	1657	3495	1062	1694	4132	919
1671	3337	1122	2059	4658	990			
1830	3679	1114	1618	3785	958			
1522	3209	1062	1709	3633	1054			
1765	3572	1107	1930	3936	1099			

Bombay-Sind

1891			*1911*			*1931*		
49	129	859	122	215	1266	498	989	1128
60	129	1037	123	191	1355	579	1195	1085
43	129	741	123	202	1348	643	1292	1115
49	129	846	155	222	1378	375	862	974
44	129	771	151	213	1595	418	892	1050
1896			*1916*			*1936*		
33	129	573	128	220	1293	407	987	924
28	96	641	137	215	1373	523	1344	872
35	80	956	42	136	744	582	1436	908
4	58	172	74	136	1280	553	1516	817
14	51	622	82	205	1024	663	1580	940
1901			*1921*			*1941*		
31	78	891	86	273	1090	500	1309	856
31	56	1216	164	330	1111	465	1264	824
46	72	1434	165	359	1030	560	1363	920
31	74	930	204	344	1328	532	1526	781
18	74	546	275	596	1034	465	1417	735
1906			*1926*			*1946*		
42	89	1051	313	602	1165	508	1518	756
40	104	866	398	740	1205			
64	107	1332	526	1000	1178			
85	130	1466	426	1068	893			
69	139	1639	487	999	1092			

Notes

Madras. Y/a up to 1903/04 based on relationship with sesamum y/a; agreement in signs of first differences of the two series is 26 out 42 possible. Relative mean deviation of predicted yields per acre from actual is 8.2% for 1904/05–12/13. Y/a trend discontinuity up to 1914/15 and starting with 1915/16 adjusted by raising all yields per acre prior to 1915/16 by 25%, which brings highest yields per acre in earlier period up to highest in later period; also see Chapter III, 2.2. Zamindari acreage added to *Estimates* up to 1910/11 on basis of proportion of zamindari to other, ryotwari, reported acreage, and area under groundnut, in each district, according to data available for later years. Groundnut acreage for the region as a whole up to 1894/95 taken as that for the first reported year, 1895/96; this relatively high acreage for the first four years corresponds to the much higher level of exports for those years as compared with the several years after 1895/96.

Bombay-Sind. Y/a up to 1896/97 based on sesamum y/a, asfd 39/49, rmd 27% for 1897/98–1905/06. Y/a up to 1922/23 lowered by 39% according to average reduction for same years in later issues of *Estimates* as compared with earlier issues.

Yield is given in shell.

Appendix Table 3a

15. Rape and Mustard Seed

British India

Yield	Acres	Y/A	Yield	Acres	Y/A	Yield	Acres	Y/A
1891			*1911*			*1931*		
855	4927	389	1337	7182	417	1012	6126	370
1001	5253	427	1275	6082	470	1029	5978	386
788	5245	337	1073	6212	387	934	5907	354
754	5362	315	1212	6466	420	894	5278	379
846	4367	434	1102	6443	383	941	5242	403
1896			*1916*			*1936*		
798	4515	396	1195	6486	413	847	5801	367
1153	5464	473	1150	7095	363	1005	5369	420
991	4712	471	762	4857	351	912	5458	376
886	4204	472	1154	5870	440	1102	6029	411
1027	5736	402	855	4987	384	1090	6159	397
1901			*1921*			*1941*		
981	4720	465	1167	6316	414	1074	6119	394
1059	5926	400	1216	6223	432	1195	5820	460
1212	6220	436	1144	6147	416	906	5275	386
890	6311	316	1222	6410	420	1015	5444	418
997	6208	359	912	5152	369	894	5366	374
1906			*1926*			*1946*		
1097	6728	365	999	5491	407	978	5275	416
693	5317	292	822	5826	315			
1037	6371	365	913	6937	294			
1293	6781	427	1093	5873	416			
1360	6470	471	991	6494	341			

United Provinces

Yield	Acres	Y/A	Yield	Acres	Y/A	Yield	Acres	Y/A
1891			*1901*			*1911*		
392	1726	509	468	1581	663	646	3018	475
394	1630	541	547	2475	495	585	2519	520
261	1688	346	572	2560	501	350	2304	340
232	1722	302	355	2649	301	575	2540	505
397	1386	642	428	2181	440	484	2581	420
1896			*1906*			*1916*		
360	1609	501	454	2363	430	496	2653	419
464	1548	671	228	1967	260	426	2964	322
434	1602	607	450	2290	440	297	1939	343
446	1457	686	502	2446	460	535	2583	464
396	1543	575	595	2517	530	385	2220	388

15. Rape and Mustard Seed—Continued

Yield	Acres	Y/A	Yield	Acres	Y/A	Yield	Acres	Y/A
1921			*1931*			*1941*		
476	2287	466	467	2932	357	586	3097	424
548	2586	475	496	2811	395	518	2630	441
558	2715	460	403	2813	321	452	2644	383
534	2660	450	387	2650	327	560	2736	458
428	2593	370	479	2578	416	460	2786	369
1926			*1936*			*1946*		
449	2390	421	399	2779	322	534	2821	424
296	2751	241	516	2584	447			
350	3009	261	433	2744	353			
523	2556	458	588	2803	470			
455	3470	294	570	2738	468			

Greater Bengal

Yield	Acres	Y/A	Yield	Acres	Y/A	Yield	Acres	Y/A
1891			*1911*			*1931*		
323	2200	329	399	2098	426	275	1415	435
372	2256	369	410	2048	448	294	1343	490
334	2209	339	431	2064	468	299	1291	519
344	2222	347	328	1984	370	317	1324	536
332	2148	346	370	2047	405	267	1268	470
1896			*1916*			*1936*		
312	2004	349	413	2017	459	290	1284	506
439	2240	439	397	1959	454	276	1301	476
448	2167	463	282	1808	349	262	1287	456
372	2033	410	337	1739	434	254	1291	441
338	2043	371	298	1659	402	238	1261	423
1901			*1921*			*1941*		
373	1922	435	323	1682	430	246	1251	441
342	1914	400	291	1571	415	269	1386	434
366	1974	415	274	1538	399	251	1342	418
360	1977	408	334	1557	480	206	1083	425
287	1862	345	246	1479	373	193	1056	411
1906			*1926*			*1946*		
337	2026	372	292	1490	439	207	1066	434
276	1889	327	269	1440	418			
232	1855	280	301	1428	472			
440	2278	433	296	1370	484			
491	2137	514	286	1426	449			

Greater Punjab

Yield	Acres	Y/A	Yield	Acres	Y/A	Yield	Acres	Y/A
1891			*1896*			*1901*		
70	610	255	54	526	231	75	755	223
138	871	356	144	1128	287	106	1061	224
114	913	280	58	599	215	178	1182	337
99	818	271	28	406	152	128	1278	224
53	491	240	232	1666	340	197	1716	257

Rape and Mustard Seed — Continued

Yield	Acres	Y/A	Yield	Acres	Y/A	Yield	Acres	Y/A
1906			*1921*			*1936*		
193	1640	264	253	1663	341	171	1094	350
124	979	283	259	1437	404	120	835	322
222	1439	346	208	1269	367	118	752	351
243	1463	372	220	1408	350	163	1216	300
168	1197	314	136	875	348	192	1478	291
1911			*1926*			*1941*		
213	1537	310	156	1006	347	165	1150	321
167	980	382	160	1078	332	139	975	319
181	1144	354	172	1868	206	89	655	304
191	1161	369	159	1212	294	138	1006	307
165	1239	298	150	980	343	136	900	338
1916			*1931*			*1946*		
174	1179	331	194	1265	344	130	769	379
213	1397	342	158	1292	274			
120	712	378	140	1215	258			
187	965	434	108	743	326			
102	648	353	121	802	338			

Notes

United Provinces acreage for 1891/92–92/93 adjusted for apparent error in printed source. Greater Bengal acreage and yield per acre for 1891/92 approximated on basis of other series. Greater Punjab minor districts added to 1912/13 as explained in Chapter III, 1.1.

APPENDIX TABLE 3A

16. Sesamum

British India

Yield	Acres	Y/A	Yield	Acres	Y/A	Yield	Acres	Y/A
1891			*1911*			*1931*		
194	2783	156	420	3785	249	356	3221	248
328	3374	218	404	3819	237	397	3421	260
344	3662	210	311	3867	180	376	3431	245
306	3312	207	432	4133	235	286	2714	236
349	3708	211	427	4030	237	313	3014	233
1896			*1916*			*1936*		
306	3532	194	396	3813	233	334	3004	249
410	3769	244	305	3048	224	356	3329	240
417	3655	256	227	2572	198	323	3039	238
326	3701	197	382	3242	264	339	3135	242
302	4209	161	327	3293	222	348	3174	246
1901			*1921*			*1941*		
365	3796	215	416	3592	259	296	3210	207
499	4481	250	332	3100	240	357	3427	233
519	4700	247	332	3070	242	320	2773	258
346	3772	205	360	3206	252	307	2864	240
364	3884	210	305	2839	241	298	2874	232
1906			*1926*			*1946*		
450	3757	268	307	2755	250	279	2906	215
284	4135	154	360	3208	251			
436	4117	237	349	3323	235			
511	4443	258	329	3160	233			
454	4111	247	348	3104	251			

United Provinces

1891			*1901*			*1911*		
40	558	161	83	864	215	129	1175	245
55	692	178	115	1033	249	134	1217	247
70	710	221	104	1122	208	60	1228	109
56	625	201	49	904	121	116	1372	189
70	708	221	63	978	144	126	1399	202
1896			*1906*			*1916*		
57	850	150	126	1084	260	108	1278	189
75	732	230	40	1230	73	82	1038	177
85	868	219	134	1322	227	46	1132	91
83	721	257	139	1381	225	115	1143	225
103	860	268	135	1339	226	103	1151	200

16. Sesamum—Continued

Yield	Acres	Y/A	Yield	Acres	Y/A	Yield	Acres	Y/A
1921			*1931*			*1941*		
128	1225	234	123	1212	227	113	1362	186
98	1073	205	133	1227	243	132	1437	206
112	1122	224	128	1340	214	114	1305	195
103	1095	211	93	1057	197	118	1279	207
91	921	221	103	1179	196	126	1342	210
1926			*1936*			*1946*		
100	936	239	104	1065	219	92	1244	166
105	1043	226	115	1323	195			
93	1192	175	101	1301	174			
101	1182	191	126	1285	220			
112	1104	227	122	1280	213			

Madras

Yield	Acres	Y/A	Yield	Acres	Y/A	Yield	Acres	Y/A
1891			*1911*			*1931*		
55	723	171	110	887	279	97	747	291
101	988	229	93	824	252	112	836	300
108	1081	225	102	809	283	106	836	284
87	918	212	109	861	283	79	653	271
120	1262	212	100	823	271	89	764	261
1896			*1916*			*1936*		
109	899	271	105	779	302	104	840	277
136	1148	265	114	832	307	101	835	271
132	960	307	87	681	286	99	915	242
103	925	249	117	881	297	95	768	277
88	1181	167	91	753	271	107	819	293
1901			*1921*			*1941*		
133	1010	296	92	778	265	88	726	272
130	1088	268	96	733	293	102	877	261
141	1189	266	86	696	277	85	730	261
128	936	307	105	789	298	80	646	277
108	1004	241	106	791	300	71	636	250
1906			*1926*			*1946*		
91	775	262	85	682	279	83	714	260
109	941	259	107	837	286			
110	936	263	99	760	292			
115	974	265	101	773	293			
99	818	272	98	746	294			

Greater Bengal

Yield	Acres	Y/A	Yield	Acres	Y/A	Yield	Acres	Y/A
1891			*1896*			*1901*		
40	418	217	31	333	209	55	411	300
53	415	285	50	367	305	45	385	262
56	520	241	52	367	317	58	428	304
43	356	271	50	388	289	59	494	268
36	369	219	45	396	255	62	515	270

16. Sesamum—Continued

Yield	Acres	Y/A	Yield	Acres	Y/A	Yield	Acres	Y/A
1906			*1921*			*1936*		
72	496	325	66	401	368	63	354	399
46	419	246	54	348	348	70	379	414
59	453	292	56	350	359	54	351	345
89	495	403	54	349	347	57	337	379
79	489	362	50	343	327	52	356	327
1911			*1926*			*1941*		
76	387	440	52	363	321	57	362	353
60	489	275	55	358	344	54	364	332
60	461	292	58	360	361	58	373	348
55	457	270	56	345	364	59	369	358
57	444	288	55	342	360	55	341	361
1916			*1931*			*1946*		
55	412	299	56	361	347	45	298	338
48	369	291	65	361	403			
52	412	283	66	363	407			
67	402	373	65	360	404			
55	366	337	57	352	363			

Notes

United Provinces. Acreage for 1891/92–92/93 approximated from relative change between these years and 1893/94 for sesamum in Central Provinces. Y/a for same two years gotten by dividing this acreage into the reported output.

Madras. Zamindari lands added up to 1910/11 as explained in Chapter III, 2.1; acreage reported up to 1906/07 raised by 39%. Discontinuity in y/a trends up to and after 1915/16 adjusted as indicated in Chapter III, 2.2. Yield per acre, and output, for 1899/00 obtained by approximating the y/a for that year on the basis of the percentage change from 1898/99 to 1899/00 for cotton.

Greater Bengal. Data for 1891/92–94/95 obtained by estimating sesamum acreage as a percentage of "other oilseeds" or "total oilseeds" for which data were available in *Agricultural Statistics,* and estimating the y/a by the percentage change in cotton y/a between those years and 1895/96.

APPENDIX TABLE 3A

17. Linseed

British India

Yield	Acres	Y/A	Yield	Acres	Y/A	Yield	Acres	Y/A
1891			*1911*			*1931*		
478	3914	254	625	4522	310	375	2811	299
579	3590	363	535	3649	328	370	2757	297
521	4877	239	373	2514	332	329	2626	277
333	4482	166	392	2974	295	363	2724	296
378	3604	235	468	3040	345	344	2643	270
1896			*1916*			*1936*		
214	2092	229	514	3237	356	357	2911	272
439	2755	357	499	3442	325	392	3180	281
423	2911	325	211	1747	271	379	3099	272
301	1949	346	415	2775	335	404	3034	295
327	2642	277	265	1948	305	367	2877	283
1901			*1921*			*1941*		
345	2788	277	428	2684	357	312	2628	266
479	2968	362	511	3078	370	351	2697	292
568	3837	332	436	3304	293	332	2851	261
323	3754	193	463	3200	321	339	2799	271
339	2785	273	376	3197	262	303	2564	265
1906			*1926*			*1946*		
409	3211	285	386	2966	289	290	2518	258
155	1679	207	343	2807	254			
287	2503	257	306	2615	259			
418	2713	345	356	2401	329			
540	3180	380	350	2616	297			

United Provinces

1891			*1901*			*1911*		
207	1173	395	176	871	453	300	1596	421
268	741	810	237	1157	459	224	1161	431
166	1245	299	250	1374	408	98	608	361
123	1357	203	101	1281	177	158	888	399
138	964	321	121	778	348	189	945	448
1896			*1906*			*1916*		
99	580	382	169	948	399	205	1005	457
203	944	482	37	327	253	177	1054	376
179	879	456	108	694	348	72	390	414
162	767	473	182	907	449	149	790	422
155	914	380	245	1129	486	105	597	394

17. Linseed—Continued

Yield	Acres	Y/A	Yield	Acres	Y/A	Yield	Acres	Y/A
1921			*1931*			*1941*		
162	943	385	158	910	389	137	825	372
198	1019	435	147	852	386	152	858	397
188	1030	409	106	806	322	143	922	347
205	1105	416	139	862	361	154	866	398
168	1083	347	147	745	365	135	875	346
1926			*1936*			*1946*		
181	1061	382	148	908	370	145	859	378
137	1053	291	157	1040	358			
105	760	309	148	925	358			
147	731	450	171	912	420			
154	954	362	161	840	429			

Greater Bengal

Yield	Acres	Y/A	Yield	Acres	Y/A	Yield	Acres	Y/A
1891			*1911*			*1931*		
97	650	335	159	775	460	112	788	318
122	806	339	142	728	437	122	766	357
132	777	381	184	747	552	116	755	344
121	733	370	128	706	406	120	725	371
96	713	302	164	844	435	92	647	319
1896			*1916*			*1936*		
85	588	324	180	861	468	108	690	351
125	663	422	192	880	489	115	732	352
145	678	479	113	739	343	109	740	330
127	653	436	176	854	462	108	725	334
133	807	369	137	773	397	94	697	302
1901			*1921*			*1941*		
111	784	317	181	834	486	107	712	337
160	864	415	176	873	452	115	730	353
169	923	410	159	846	421	99	715	310
114	829	308	142	852	373	95	716	297
128	830	345	121	821	330	86	678	284
1906			*1926*			*1946*		
115	806	320	118	780	339	88	677	291
86	589	327	97	719	302			
73	635	258	127	790	360			
124	673	413	126	768	368			
133	707	421	113	770	329			

Central Provinces

Yield	Acres	Y/A	Yield	Acres	Y/A	Yield	Acres	Y/A
1891			*1896*			*1901*		
147	1752	188	24	715	75	42	795	118
155	1738	200	80	864	207	50	615	182
161	2366	152	67	1009	149	96	993	216
57	1885	68	4	329	27	81	960	189
74	1232	135	26	650	90	77	912	189

17. Linseed—Continued

Yield	Acres	Y/A	Yield	Acres	Y/A	Yield	Acres	Y/A
1906			*1921*			*1936*		
106	1158	205	65	767	189	88	1182	167
24	548	98	123	1019	270	106	1287	184
91	955	213	77	1299	133	106	1298	183
90	926	218	100	1094	205	109	1263	193
124	1080	257	72	1148	140	97	1218	178
1911			*1926*			*1941*		
139	1859	167	75	1001	168	54	966	125
142	1509	210	72	917	176	74	1033	160
71	952	166	54	930	130	80	1136	158
80	1224	146	65	754	193	79	1130	157
83	1048	177	65	739	197	74	947	175
1916			*1931*			*1946*		
99	1176	189	87	937	208	48	913	118
93	1257	166	83	1008	184			
16	509	70	80	933	192			
68	978	155	88	997	198			
16	447	79	80	1131	158			

Notes

United Provinces. Area of mixed and pure crop totalled under acreage given here. For 1891/92–92/93 acreage of mixed crop obtained by dividing reported output for mixed crop by y/a of pure crop.

Greater Bengal. For 1891/92 acreage and yield per acre estimated from relationship of linseed and wheat in this region from 1892/93 to 1902/93; for y/a agreement in signs of first differences of the two series is 24 out of possible 55, relative mean deviation of predicted yields per acre from actual, 17.5%; or acreage, asfd 40/55, rmd 10.4%.

Central Provinces. Combined States-Province *Estimates* reports separated per Chapter III, 1.3, 1919/20–21/22.

APPENDIX TABLE 3A

18. Indigo

British India

Yield	Acres	Y/A	Yield	Acres	Y/A	Yield	Acres	Y/A
1891			*1911*			*1931*		
110	1096	11	50	272	21	10	52	22
192	1277	17	43	220	22	11	59	21
197	1639	13	28	167	19	7	43	18
257	1792	16	27	149	20	10	59	19
210	1499	16	57	352	18	6	39	17
1896			*1916*			*1936*		
186	1699	12	99	765	14	7	42	19
184	1407	15	130	702	21	6	38	18
148	1055	16	49	286	19	6	39	17
122	1071	13	45	243	21	5	38	15
164	1043	18	45	240	21	10	65	17
1901			*1921*			*1941*		
123	839	16	69	334	23	10	60	19
89	688	14	55	283	22	10	60	19
115	753	17	37	180	23	10	60	19
65	504	14	22	112	22	9	52	19
54	409	15	28	137	23	8	47	19
1906			*1926*			*1946*		
73	458	18	19	105	20	5	30	19
56	401	16	10	61	18			
41	289	16	16	82	22			
40	293	15	14	71	22			
46	282	18	13	64	23			

Madras

1891			*1901*			*1911*		
22	194	14	44	279	19	21	90	28
58	351	20	47	247	23	15	62	27
68	515	16	54	282	23	12	55	23
78	601	16	20	147	16	14	72	21
75	484	19	20	133	18	41	222	20
1896			*1906*			*1916*		
59	531	13	37	211	21	59	460	14
71	378	23	20	142	17	81	324	28
35	246	17	12	82	18	33	144	26
38	290	16	14	96	18	24	101	26
54	294	22	20	83	29	28	112	28

18. Indigo — Continued

Yield 1921	Acres	Y/A	Yield 1931	Acres	Y/A	Yield 1941	Acres	Y/A
49	197	28	8	37	24	9	52	19
33	141	26	9	46	22	9	52	19
21	89	26	5	30	19	9	52	19
17	70	27	9	54	19	8	48	19
19	78	28	4	26	17	7	42	19
1926			1936			1946		
11	54	23	5	30	19	4	27	17
7	33	25	4	23	19			
11	49	25	4	29	15			
12	53	24	4	30	15			
10	47	24	9	55	18			

Notes

Yield in 000's cwts. (120 lbs.).

British India. No *Estimates* reports were issued for indigo during 1941/42–46/47. Indian Union acreages available for 1944/45–46/47; 1941/42–43/44 approximated between 1940/41 and 1944/45. Y/a for 1941/42 to 1946/47 set at average for recent previous years.

Madras. Zamindari lands added to *Estimates* reports up to 1906/07 on basis of proportion of zamindari area to other, ryotwari, area, and indigo area, in each district on basis of later data.

APPENDIX TABLE 3B

ANNUAL CROP OUTPUT ESTIMATED WITH YIELDS PER ACRE ORIGINATED IN
THIS STUDY, AS A PROPORTION OF ALL-CROP OUTPUT IN BRITISH INDIA
AND SIX REGIONS

(Percent)

	Madras	Bombay-Sind	Greater Punjab	United Prov.	Central Prov.	Greater Bengal	British India
1891/92	44.9	73.4	54.3	63.9	53.2	18.4	38.8
	48.9	68.9	50.3	67.6	54.4	14.2	36.4
	42.7	63.2	44.6	69.1	60.5	13.5	36.8
	42.8	69.3	43.5	80.7	63.7	10.8	34.6
	36.4	68.4	44.2	74.5	65.5	12.6	37.6
1896/97	26.8	72.0	43.8	68.7	67.3	17.9	30.9
	26.8	69.5	46.6	69.8	62.3	12.6	35.7
	39.5	64.7	43.3	53.2	62.6	7.9	30.4
	41.4	51.9	30.5	53.7	77.8	7.4	27.9
	37.6	67.6	32.5	54.9	53.8	7.9	30.8
1901/02	38.9	69.4	30.4	54.6	59.3	9.1	32.1
	35.2	66.2	33.2	53.7	61.2	7.5	30.6
	33.7	59.7	33.7	51.7	51.7	8.3	29.6
	37.3	61.6	31.8	50.4	46.8	7.5	27.0
	34.1	63.3	30.3	50.6	49.5	8.1	29.3
1906/07	34.4	58.5	5.9	53.3	53.3	8.2	28.0
	31.7	61.8	7.2	54.8	55.8	8.3	26.8
	33.8	65.5	5.5	56.1	58.6	8.4	29.6
	31.2	60.1	6.0	53.7	54.3	7.2	26.2
	30.0	61.1	6.0	51.9	54.9	7.2	25.5
1911/12	26.2	30.2	5.5	12.7	35.0	3.6	13.0
	10.1	3.5	6.2	11.2	31.3	4.0	9.0
	10.6	3.6	6.2	1.3	3.1	2.5	3.7
	11.7	3.7	5.8	1.2	2.8	4.3	4.6
	11.0	3.5	7.3	1.0	2.8	3.5	4.3
1916/17	10.0	3.7	7.8	1.1	3.1	3.2	4.2
	10.4	3.6	6.6	1.0	3.5	2.8	4.0
	11.2	3.4	7.4	1.3	3.1	5.0	5.3
	7.6	3.2	6.7	1.0	0.7	3.7	3.6
	8.3	4.9	8.1	0.8	0.5	3.8	4.2
1921/22	7.6	4.8	6.9	1.1	0.8	3.7	3.9
	7.8	4.8	6.0	1.0	0.7	3.3	3.7
	7.9	4.0	5.9	0.8	0.6	3.6	3.6
	7.6	4.2	5.4	0.8	1.4	3.2	3.6
	6.7	3.6	7.1	0.9	1.0	0.6	2.7
1926/27	6.9	4.1	4.8	0.1	0.8	0.7	2.3
	6.2	2.2	5.6	0.1	0.8	0.9	2.3
	6.2	2.4	5.0	0.1	1.2	0.6	2.2
	6.3	2.5	5.0	0.1	1.2	0.8	2.2
	6.0	2.5	5.3	0.2	1.5	0.8	2.2

APPENDIX TABLE 3B—*Continued*

	Madras	Bombay-Sind	Greater Punjab	United Prov.	Central Prov.	Greater Bengal	British India
1931/32	6.5	2.2	4.4	0.2	0.0	0.7	2.0
	6.2	2.3	5.0	0.2		0.7	2.1
	5.9	2.3	5.4	0.2		0.6	2.0
	6.0	2.3	5.4	0.2		0.6	2.0
	5.9	2.4	4.6	0.4		0.0	1.9
1936/37	0.0	0.0	4.1	0.4			0.6
			5.0	0.6			0.7
			5.6	0.8			0.8
			0.0	0.6			0.1
				0.0			0.0

Source : Computed from data in Table 2.2, Appendix Tables 3A and 4C.

APPENDIX TABLE 4A

BRITISH INDIA : VILLAGE LEVEL CROP PRICES, AND EXPORT VALUE PER UNIT
FOR CERTAIN CROPS, AVERAGES FOR 1924/25–28/29 AND 1934/35–38/39
(Rupees)

	Average for 1924/25–28/29 Village Level	Export Level	Average for 1934/35–38/39 Village Level	Export Value
Rice	170.96		94.43	
Wheat	142.92		80.90	
Jowar	121.14		69.38	
Gram	117.33		68.81	
Bajra	128.22		72.19	
Barley	102.63		56.13	
Maize	113.52		57.82	
Ragi	121.14			
Sugarcane	213.42		113.37	
Cotton	164.79		87.29	
Jute	54.40		23.48	
Tea	1587.20	1917.60	1255.29	1541.30
Tobacco	543.90		307.75	
Groundnut	214.12	258.69	117.50	141.95
Rapeseed	220.77		128.37	
Sesamum	250.72	291.36	147.91	
Linseed	195.46	237.36	116.17	
Indigo	241.55	291.83		

Note: Prices are per ton unit, except for cotton and jute which are for 400 pound bales, and indigo which is for a hundredweight of 112 pounds. Sugarcane price is for raw sugar, gur.

Source : For the 1920's most prices are from Thomas and Sastry, *op. cit.,* Appendix A, which are weighted averages of the provincial average Harvest Prices given in *Agricultural Statistics;* for other crops see Chapter IV, 1. For the 1930's British India average prices were obtained by weighting the provincial Harvest Prices by average output during that period according to data given in Appendix Table 3A.

APPENDIX TABLE 4B

COMPOSITION OF INDUSTRIAL WORKERS' FOOD EXPENDITURES IN THIRTEEN
AREAS OF INDIA DURING 1943–47
(Percent)

Locality; Survey Yr.; No. of Families in Survey	C&P	Milk	Meat	Oil	Veg.	Cond.	Sugar	Tea
Tea Workers, 1947: Surma Valley, Assam; 200	85.0	0.4	5.4	8.3	8.5	7.2	1.5	
Assam Valley and Brahmaputra Valley; 560	76.1	0.1	5.1	8.8	7.9	5.7	2.7	
North Bengal; 297	74.3	0.2	7.0	6.6	6.1	4.5	1.1	
Howrah and Bally, Bengal; 1943/44; 1,435	59.8	4.9	7.3	5.9	9.5	3.4	2.6	2.9
Jharia Coal Workers, Bihar; 1945/46; 999	72.6	1.3	8.9	5.1	8.0	4.1	2.4	0.4
Monghyr and Jamalpur, Bihar; 1944; 578	77.9	5.3	2.5	4.7	4.5	2.3	1.9	0.3
Jamshedpur, Bihar; 1945; 691	55.4	10.1	6.9	5.1	11.6	3.3	4.2	1.5
Cuttack, Orissa; 1944/45; 168	58.6	4.4	6.2	5.4	10.4	4.7	4.0	1.7
Jubbulpore City, Central Provinces; 1944/45; 482	54.6	12.2	4.2	5.4	8.6	4.1	3.4	3.8
Delhi; 1943/44; 139	54.1	19.3	3.8	4.1	9.8	2.5	4.0	0.4
Sholapur, Bombay; 1944/45; 778	49.3	9.1	10.0	5.0	6.1	6.4	6.4	2.8
Bombay City; 1944/45; 2,030	41.9	7.7	11.9	5.0	11.8	7.2	4.7	5.1
Ludhiana, Punjab; 1944/45; 213	41.7	35.4	3.2	0.5	8.4	3.7	6.9	0.6

Note: C&P—cereals and pulses; cond.—condiments; veg.—vegetables.
Source: Reports of S. R. Deshpande, Director, Cost of Living Index
Scheme, Government of India, for the localities cited above.

APPENDIX 4c

AGGREGATE ANNUAL OUTPUT, ACREAGE, AND YIELD PER ACRE OF ALL-CROPS (AC), FOODGRAIN (FG) AND NONFOODGRAIN (NFG) CROPS IN BRITISH INDIA AND REGIONS, 1891/92–1946/47 (OUTPUT—MILLION RUPEES; ACRES—MILLIONS; Y/A—RUPEES)

British India

	AC	FG	NFG	AC	FG	NFG	AC	FG	NFG
		Yield			Acreage			Yield per Acre	
1891/92	7490	5844	1646	168	140	27.9	44.6	41.7	59.0
	8827	6842	2045	177	148	29.2	49.9	46.2	70.0
	9026	7234	1792	178	145	33.0	50.7	49.9	54.3
	9630	7665	1965	186	154	32.0	51.8	49.8	61.4
	9017	6969	2048	176	146	30.1	51.2	47.7	68.0
1896/97	7288	5384	1904	165	137	28.1	44.2	39.3	67.8
	10404	8147	2257	182	153	29.3	57.1	53.2	77.0
	10396	8204	2192	179	151	27.9	58.1	54.3	78.6
	8371	6702	1669	163	137	25.8	51.4	48.9	64.7
	9375	7206	2169	181	151	29.9	51.8	47.7	72.5
1901/02	8900	6716	2184	174	146	28.3	51.1	46.0	77.2
	10426	8128	2298	182	152	29.9	57.3	53.5	76.9
	10112	7765	2347	186	152	34.2	54.4	51.1	68.6
	9453	7142	2311	187	152	34.8	50.6	47.0	66.4
	9001	6788	2213	185	151	33.8	48.7	45.0	65.5
1906/07	10135	7467	2668	193	157	36.3	52.5	47.6	73.5
	8100	5930	2170	180	146	34.0	45.0	40.6	63.8
	9044	6842	2202	186	153	33.4	48.6	44.7	65.9
	11458	8859	2599	195	160	34.7	58.8	55.4	74.9
	11349	8768	2581	196	160	35.7	57.9	54.8	72.3
1911/12	10706	8128	2578	191	153	38.1	56.1	53.1	67.7
	10488	7730	2758	193	157	35.7	54.3	49.2	77.3
	9776	7119	2657	188	151	37.1	52.0	47.1	71.6
	10606	7616	2990	199	161	38.0	53.3	47.3	78.7
	11053	8414	2639	193	160	32.7	57.3	52.6	80.7
1916/17	11533	8682	2851	200	164	36.5	57.7	52.9	78.1
	11466	8646	2820	201	163	38.1	57.0	53.0	74.0
	8188	5869	2319	172	140	31.6	47.6	41.9	73.4
	11284	8283	3001	196	158	37.5	57.6	52.4	80.0
	8742	6449	2293	178	146	32.4	49.1	44.2	70.8
1921/22	10668	8252	2416	194	162	31.5	55.0	50.9	76.7
	10937	8276	2661	196	162	34.2	55.8	51.1	77.8
	10148	7211	2937	192	155	37.2	52.9	46.5	79.0
	10273	7318	2955	199	158	41.4	51.6	46.3	71.4
	10245	7188	3057	194	154	39.7	52.8	46.7	77.0

APPENDIX TABLE 4c—*Continued*

	Yield			Acreage			Yield per Acre		
	AC	FG	NFG	AC	FG	NFG	AC	FG	NFG
1926/27	10249	7106	3143	190	152	38.2	53.9	46.8	82.3
	9936	6695	3241	192	154	38.5	51.8	43.5	84.2
	10668	7376	3292	198	157	41.2	53.9	47.0	79.9
	10849	7590	3259	196	156	40.3	53.4	48.7	80.9
	10948	7604	3344	198	159	38.8	55.3	47.8	86.2
1931/32	10616	7705	2911	198	161	36.8	53.6	47.9	79.1
	10720	7313	3407	194	157	37.0	55.3	46.6	92.1
	11280	7752	3528	200	161	38.7	56.4	48.1	91.1
	10558	7218	3340	191	155	35.9	55.3	46.6	93.0
	10406	6776	3630	192	158	34.4	54.2	42.9	105.5
1936/37	11355	7550	3805	200	160	40.2	56.8	47.2	94.7
	11128	7338	3790	199	157	42.0	55.9	46.7	90.2
	9823	6666	3157	197	158	39.2	49.9	42.2	80.5
	10831	7176	3655	197	158	39.4	54.9	45.4	92.8
	10883	6578	4305	203	159	44.3	53.6	41.4	97.2
1941/42	10420	7009	3411	201	162	38.6	51.8	43.3	88.3
	10833	7195	3638	205	168	37.4	52.8	42.8	97.3
	11708	7988	3720	207	170	37.1	56.6	47.0	100.3
	10930	7671	3259	210	175	35.0	52.0	43.8	93.1
	10499	7093	3406	206	172	34.3	51.0	41.2	99.3
1946/47	10526	7127	3399	203	169	34.2	51.9	42.2	99.4

Greater Bengal

	Yield			Acreage			Yield per Acre		
	AC	FG	NFG	AC	FG	NFG	AC	FG	NFG
1891/92	3258	2650	608	53.9	46.5	7.36	60.4	57.0	82.6
	3995	3138	857	53.3	44.9	8.42	75.0	69.9	101.8
	4260	3454	806	53.5	45.1	8.45	79.6	76.6	95.3
	4673	3866	807	54.1	45.9	8.19	86.4	84.2	98.5
	3674	2943	731	52.6	44.6	7.96	69.8	66.0	91.8
1896/97	2487	1759	728	50.6	43.2	7.43	49.2	40.7	98.0
	4640	3714	926	55.1	47.2	7.85	84.2	78.7	118.0
	4588	3781	807	54.3	47.2	7.10	84.5	80.1	113.7
	4069	3332	737	53.5	46.4	7.13	76.1	71.8	103.4
	3716	2934	782	50.5	43.2	7.31	73.6	67.9	107.0
1901/02	3409	2584	825	49.0	41.9	7.09	69.6	61.7	116.4
	4111	3343	768	51.7	44.8	6.93	79.5	74.6	110.8
	3809	2991	818	49.2	42.0	7.21	77.4	71.2	113.5
	4046	3241	805	53.4	45.6	7.81	75.8	71.1	103.1
	3670	2870	800	52.0	44.2	7.82	70.6	64.9	102.3
1905/07	3641	2775	866	52.1	43.8	8.25	69.9	63.4	105.0
	3174	2319	855	50.6	42.4	8.24	62.7	54.7	103.8
	3250	2386	864	47.1	40.0	7.14	69.0	59.7	121.0
	4469	3683	786	53.1	45.6	7.53	84.2	80.8	104.4
	4587	3731	856	53.0	45.5	7.50	86.5	82.0	114.1

APPENDIX TABLE 4c—*Continued*

	Yield			Acreage			Yield per Acre		
	AC	*FG*	*NFG*	*AC*	*FG*	*NFG*	*AC*	*FG*	*NFG*
1911/12	4165	3311	854	52.4	44.8	7.59	79.5	73.9	112.5
	3677	2741	936	51.1	43.7	7.39	72.0	62.7	126.7
	3815	2950	865	50.6	43.3	7.34	75.4	68.1	117.8
	3291	2350	941	51.1	43.5	7.63	64.4	54.0	123.3
	4027	3218	809	51.5	44.6	6.89	78.2	72.2	117.4
1916/17	4067	3203	864	51.7	44.5	7.16	78.7	72.0	120.7
	4202	3325	877	51.2	44.1	7.07	82.1	75.4	124.0
	3005	2237	768	49.8	43.1	6.68	60.3	51.9	115.0
	3804	2924	880	50.6	43.6	6.98	75.2	67.1	126.1
	3222	2542	680	49.2	42.8	6.38	65.5	59.4	106.6
1921/22	3641	3032	609	50.0	44.4	5.64	72.8	68.3	108.0
	3729	3076	653	50.2	44.4	5.77	74.3	69.3	113.2
	3215	2405	810	48.0	41.4	6.64	67.0	58.1	122.0
	3388	2595	793	49.0	42.4	6.59	69.1	61.2	120.3
	3339	2513	826	49.2	42.3	6.87	67.9	59.4	120.2
1926/27	3346	2356	990	48.2	40.7	7.50	69.4	57.9	132.0
	3028	2117	911	45.9	38.9	6.96	66.0	54.4	130.9
	3778	2881	897	49.3	42.5	6.75	76.6	67.8	132.9
	3685	2740	945	48.6	41.6	6.96	75.8	65.9	92.7
	3793	2828	965	48.6	41.6	7.04	78.0	68.0	137.1
1931/32	3575	2893	682	48.9	43.3	5.61	73.1	66.8	121.6
	3460	2618	842	48.2	42.4	5.76	71.8	61.7	146.2
	3404	2488	916	48.2	42.1	6.14	70.6	59.1	149.1
	3493	2506	987	48.1	41.7	6.38	72.6	60.0	154.7
	2937	2037	900	46.9	41.0	5.86	62.6	49.7	153.6
1936/37	3711	2690	1021	48.5	41.9	6.60	76.5	64.2	154.7
	3426	2513	913	48.2	41.7	6.47	71.1	60.3	141.1
	2931	2140	791	48.5	41.8	6.65	60.4	51.2	118.9
	3313	2339	974	48.5	41.8	6.69	68.3	56.0	145.6
	2907	1761	1146	49.1	39.9	9.20	59.2	44.1	124.6
1941/42	3216	2497	719	48.5	42.9	5.60	66.3	58.3	128.4
	3052	2106	946	49.8	42.8	6.95	61.3	49.2	136.1
	3782	2915	867	53.5	46.9	5.58	70.7	62.2	153.5
	3376	2654	722	55.1	49.7	5.35	61.3	53.4	135.0
	3289	2427	862	51.5	46.5	4.97	63.9	52.2	173.4
1946/47	3214	2527	687	52.4	47.4	5.01	61.3	53.3	137.1

United Provinces

1891/92	1323	928	395	28.5	22.6	5.87	46.4	41.1	67.3
	1436	1026	410	28.2	23.0	5.16	50.9	44.6	79.5
	1450	976	474	29.2	23.1	6.13	49.7	42.3	77.3
	1489	1104	385	36.9	30.7	6.23	40.4	36.0	61.8
	1689	1185	504	34.4	28.8	5.56	49.1	41.1	90.6

APPENDIX TABLE 4G—*Continued*

	Yield			Acreage			Yield per Acre		
	AC	FG	NFG	AC	FG	NFG	AC	FG	NFG
1896/97	1412	1051	361	30.9	25.4	5.46	45.7	41.4	66.1
	1792	1289	503	34.1	28.6	5.45	52.6	45.1	92.3
	1771	1263	508	34.4	28.8	5.56	51.5	43.9	91.4
	1638	1217	421	31.5	26.2	5.26	52.0	46.4	80.0
	1859	1357	502	35.7	30.1	5.63	52.1	45.1	89.2
1901/02	1819	1329	490	36.0	30.2	5.75	50.5	44.0	85.2
	1983	1480	503	37.4	30.3	7.13	53.0	48.8	70.6
	1909	1440	469	38.2	31.2	7.03	50.0	46.1	66.7
	1507	1024	483	38.3	31.0	7.32	39.3	33.0	66.0
	1608	1143	465	35.5	38.9	6.63	45.3	40.0	70.1
1906/07	1991	1364	627	39.4	32.1	7.32	50.3	42.5	85.7
	1304	943	361	32.3	25.8	6.51	40.4	36.6	55.5
	1742	1275	467	36.1	29.2	6.87	48.3	43.7	68.0
	2004	1487	517	37.9	30.8	7.09	52.9	48.3	72.9
	2009	1443	566	39.1	31.6	7.47	51.4	45.7	75.8
1911/12	2093	1481	612	39.7	31.5	8.16	52.7	47.0	75.0
	2081	1452	629	39.0	31.5	7.53	53.4	46.1	83.5
	1386	919	467	33.8	26.6	7.17	41.0	34.5	65.1
	2117	1479	638	38.8	31.2	7.63	54.6	47.4	83.6
	2105	1549	556	39.3	32.2	7.11	53.6	48.1	78.2
1916/17	2215	1636	579	40.3	32.9	7.42	55.0	49.7	78.0
	2074	1538	536	40.8	32.8	7.95	50.8	46.9	67.4
	1339	980	359	31.5	25.6	5.94	42.5	38.3	60.4
	2098	1494	604	37.8	30.5	7.27	55.5	49.0	83.1
	1531	1092	439	34.8	28.3	6.48	44.0	38.6	67.7
1921/22	1969	1485	484	38.3	31.8	6.52	51.4	46.7	74.2
	1961	1431	530	38.9	32.1	6.78	50.4	44.6	78.2
	2003	1402	601	38.7	31.6	7.13	51.8	44.4	84.3
	1790	1305	485	38.5	31.2	7.28	46.5	41.8	66.6
	1794	1266	528	37.5	30.4	7.09	47.8	41.6	74.5
1926/27	1928	1337	591	37.0	30.1	6.89	52.1	44.4	85.8
	1731	1229	502	38.5	31.4	7.14	45.0	39.1	70.3
	1442	989	453	37.5	30.4	7.10	38.5	32.5	63.8
	1785	1252	533	36.5	29.6	6.86	48.9	42.3	77.7
	1815	1231	584	38.7	30.8	7.92	46.9	40.0	73.7
1931/32	1970	1270	700	38.7	31.2	7.47	50.9	40.7	93.7
	1922	1141	781	37.2	29.9	7.31	51.7	38.2	106.8
	1939	1178	761	38.6	31.0	7.60	50.2	38.0	100.1
	2035	1251	784	37.6	30.3	7.25	54.1	41.3	108.1
	2203	1274	929	37.6	30.1	7.48	58.6	42.3	124.2
1936/37	2246	1232	1014	39.0	30.9	8.10	57.6	39.9	125.1
	2173	1252	921	42.6	34.7	7.92	51.0	36.1	116,3
	1730	1198	532	39.8	32.3	7.51	43.5	37.1	70.8
	2130	1414	716	39.7	32.1	7.55	53.7	44.0	94.8
	2128	1268	860	39.0	31.0	8.00	54.6	40.9	107.5

APPENDIX TABLE 4c—*Continued*

	Yield			Acreage			Yield per Acre		
	AC	*FG*	*NFG*	*AC*	*FG*	*NFG*	*AC*	*FG*	*NFG*
1941/42	1731	1107	624	38.7	31.0	7.68	44.7	35.7	81.3
	2116	1341	775	40.3	33.0	7.31	52.5	40.6	106.0
	2054	1239	815	41.0	33.3	7.65	50.1	37.2	106.5
	1986	1242	744	40.5	33.0	7.47	49.0	37.6	99.6
	1903	1223	680	41.0	33.7	7.27	46.4	36.3	93.5
1946/47	1913	1189	724	40.5	33.1	7.41	47.2	35.9	97.7

Madras

	AC	*FG*	*NFG*	*AC*	*FG*	*NFG*	*AC*	*FG*	*NFG*
1891/92	869	729	140	22.2	19.3	2.93	39.1	37.8	47.8
	931	749	182	24.3	20.8	3.51	38.3	36.0	51.9
	1078	875	203	25.4	21.1	4.30	42.4	41.5	47.2
	1032	843	189	24.5	20.5	3.96	42.1	41.1	47.7
	1413	1200	213	25.4	21.1	4.30	55.6	56.8	49.5
1896/97	1290	1100	190	24.6	21.0	3.58	52.4	52.4	53.1
	1286	1082	204	25.0	21.2	3.77	51.4	51.0	54.1
	1448	1242	206	25.4	22.1	3.25	57.0	56.2	56.3
	1090	923	167	23.3	20.0	3.29	46.8	46.2	50.8
	1254	1075	179	25.1	21.4	3.71	49.9	50.2	48.2
1901/02	1457	1216	241	26.1	22.5	3.63	55.8	54.0	66.4
	1515	1261	254	27.3	23.2	4.06	55.5	54.3	62.6
	1498	1247	251	26.9	22.6	4.27	55.7	55.2	58.8
	1219	994	225	24.6	20.7	3.94	49.6	48.0	57.1
	1306	1062	244	25.4	21.5	3.86	51.4	49.4	63.2
1906/07	1413	1157	256	26.2	22.2	4.00	53.9	52.1	64.0
	1396	1142	254	26.4	22.2	4.22	52.9	51.4	60.2
	1268	1014	254	26.3	22.2	4.07	48.2	45.7	62.4
	1462	1200	262	26.3	22.1	4.21	55.6	54.3	62.2
	1631	1334	297	26.9	22.6	4.28	60.6	59.0	69.4
1911/12	1731	1434	297	26.3	21.5	4.77	65.8	66.7	62.3
	1545	1263	282	27.0	22.5	4.50	57.2	56.1	62.7
	1537	1231	306	28.1	22.6	5.47	54.7	54.5	55.9
	1630	1308	321	27.4	22.2	5.19	59.5	58.9	61.8
	1755	1405	350	27.8	23.2	4.56	63.1	60.6	76.8
1916/17	1868	1465	403	27.9	22.4	5.52	67.0	65.4	73.0
	1806	1371	435	28.1	22.6	5.61	64.3	60.7	77.5
	1465	1088	377	26.5	21.2	5.31	55.3	51.3	71.0
	1694	1344	350	27.9	23.1	4.78	60.7	58.2	73.2
	1647	1275	372	26.9	22.0	4.88	61.2	60.0	76.2
1921/22	1692	1322	370	27.3	22.8	4.54	62.0	58.0	81.5
	1751	1321	430	27.8	22.5	5.28	63.0	58.7	81.4
	1556	1143	413	26.1	20.5	5.57	59.6	55.8	74.1
	1751	1260	491	27.4	21.4	6.01	63.9	58.9	81.7
	1861	1307	554	28.1	21.4	6.72	66.2	61.1	82.4

APPENDIX TABLE 4c—*Continued*

	Yield			Acreage			Yield per Acre		
	AC	FG	NFG	AC	FG	NFG	AC	FG	NFG
1926/27	1663	1178	485	27.1	21.1	5.95	61.4	55.8	81.5
	1879	1265	614	28.2	21.5	6.70	66.6	58.8	91.6
	1938	1288	650	28.5	21.2	7.31	68.0	60.8	88.9
	1893	1303	590	28.8	21.9	6.87	65.7	59.5	85.9
	1911	1296	615	28.7	21.9	6.77	66.6	59.2	90.8
1931/32	1826	1308	518	27.6	21.6	6.02	66.2	60.6	86.0
	1934	1308	626	27.9	21.2	6.74	69.3	61.7	92.9
	1918	1274	644	27.2	21.0	7.18	70.5	60.7	89.7
	1662	1192	470	27.1	21.3	5.77	61.3	56.0	81.5
	1780	1241	539	27.7	21.3	6.38	64.3	58.3	84.5
1936/37	1907	1272	635	29.0	21.7	7.28	65.8	58.6	87.2
	1956	1237	719	29.4	20.9	8.50	66.5	59.2	84.6
	1696	1105	591	28.2	21.1	7.12	60.1	52.4	83.0
	1861	1200	661	28.5	21.4	7.11	65.3	56.1	93.0
	2064	1319	745	29.5	21.7	7.75	70.0	60.8	96.1
1941/42	1797	1246	551	27.6	21.0	6.59	65.1	59.3	83.6
	1724	1169	555	28.7	21.7	6.98	60.1	53.9	79.5
	1862	1233	629	29.2	22.2	6.95	63.8	55.5	90.5
	1962	1254	708	28.9	21.7	7.20	67.9	57.8	98.3
	1651	1038	613	27.2	20.2	7.04	60.7	51.4	87.1
1946/47	1916	1262	654	28.4	21.4	6.98	67.5	59.0	93.7

Greater Punjab

1891/92	540	432	108	17.2	15.6	1.60	31.4	27.7	67.5
	770	645	125	22.1	20.0	2.05	34.8	32.3	61.0
	792	655	137	21.6	19.2	2.44	36.7	34.1	56.1
	745	601	144	21.0	18.4	2.59	35.5	32.7	55.6
	554	439	115	15.6	13.4	2.18	35.5	32.8	52.8
1896/97	587	457	130	15.2	13.0	2.20	38.6	35.2	59.1
	792	641	151	22.3	19.6	2.72	35.5	32.7	55.5
	573	481	92	17.5	15.5	2.02	32.7	31.0	45.5
	499	398	101	12.8	11.0	1.81	39.0	36.2	55.8
	873	692	181	24.6	21.2	3.40	35.5	32.6	53.2
1901/02	592	458	134	17.2	14.8	2.35	34.4	30.9	57.0
	737	594	143	19.4	16.6	2.82	38.0	35.8	50.7
	970	792	178	21.6	18.6	2.97	44.9	42.6	59.9
	890	711	179	21.0	17.8	3.22	42.4	40.0	55.6
	904	793	111	20.5	17.6	2.90	44.1	45.1	38.2
1906/07	1059	868	191	26.8	23.4	3.44	39.5	37.1	55.5
	745	572	173	21.4	18.5	2.94	34.8	30.9	58.8
	1032	823	209	26.6	23.0	3.57	38.8	35.8	58.5
	1111	875	236	26.3	22.8	3.48	42.2	38.4	67.8
	1064	874	190	25.6	22.4	3.14	41.6	39.1	60.5

APPENDIX TABLE 4C—*Continued*

	Yield			Acreage			Yield per Acre		
	AC	FG	NFG	AC	FG	NFG	AC	FG	NFG
1911/12	993	826	167	24.3	20.7	3.56	40.9	39.9	46.9
	939	738	201	24.2	21.1	3.10	38.8	35.0	64.8
	1006	750	256	24.4	20.7	3.67	41.2	36.2	69.8
	1143	904	239	28.7	25.1	3.60	39.8	36.0	63.8
	762	602	160	23.4	20.7	2.67	32.6	29.1	59.9
1916/17	1000	786	214	28.3	25.3	3.04	35.3	31.1	70.4
	1122	892	230	29.4	25.6	3.80	38.2	34.8	60.5
	864	645	219	20.7	17.9	2.81	41.7	36.0	77.9
	1141	858	283	26.2	22.4	3.78	43.5	38.3	74.9
	762	529	233	21.2	17.9	3.28	35.9	29.6	71.0
1921/22	1172	947	225	27.8	24.3	3.50	42.2	39.0	64.3
	1201	939	262	28.5	25.0	3.50	42.1	37.6	74.9
	1213	914	299	27.2	23.4	3.78	44.6	39.1	79.1
	1074	747	327	28.2	23.8	4.40	38.1	31.4	74.3
	1064	752	312	26.2	21.9	4.28	40.6	34.3	72.9
1926/27	1077	817	260	26.8	22.6	4.24	40.2	36.2	61.3
	952	686	266	25.9	22.2	3.68	36.8	30.9	72.3
	1015	764	251	28.5	23.4	5.06	35.6	32.6	49.6
	1160	888	272	27.2	23.2	3.99	42.6	38.3	68.2
	1097	812	285	26.4	22.5	3.85	41.6	36.1	74.0
1931/32	1058	776	282	26.9	22.7	4.23	39.3	34.2	66.7
	1031	745	286	26.1	22.1	4.04	39.5	33.7	70.8
	1150	807	343	30.3	25.9	4.36	38.0	31.2	78.7
	1132	787	345	23.4	19.6	3.83	48.4	40.2	90.1
	1226	805	421	27.4	23.0	4.35	44.7	35.0	96.8
1936/37	1376	871	505	27.0	22.2	4.83	51.0	39.2	104.6
	1247	859	388	27.2	22.4	4.78	45.8	38.3	81.2
	1095	735	360	25.5	21.2	4.28	42.9	34.7	84.1
	1213	837	376	25.2	20.6	4.56	48.1	40.6	82.5
	1307	847	460	28.3	23.3	4.97	46.2	36.4	92.6
1941/42	1347	904	443	27.9	23.2	4.70	48.3	39.0	94.3
	1478	1071	407	29.5	25.5	4.02	50.1	42.0	101.2
	1315	902	413	28.2	24.2	4.04	46.6	37.3	102.2
	1446	1011	435	31.3	27.0	4.29	46.2	37.4	101.4
	1382	930	452	31.0	26.9	4.06	44.6	34.6	111.3
1946/47	1318	868	450	26.9	23.0	3.89	49.0	37.7	115.7

Bombay-Sind

1891/92	698	531	167	24.0	20.3	3.73	29.1	26.2	44.7
	856	634	222	24.3	20.3	3.97	35.2	31.2	55.9
	941	619	322	23.8	19.2	4.62	39.5	32.2	69.7
	851	633	218	24.1	19.6	4.47	35.3	32.3	48.8
	721	509	212	23.1	18.7	4.40	31.2	27.2	48.2

APPENDIX TABLE 4c—*Continued*

	Yield			Acreage			Yield per Acre		
	AC	FG	NFG	AC	FG	NFG	AC	FG	NFG
1896/97	593	432	161	19.6	16.0	3.64	30.3	27.0	44.2
	872	678	194	23.9	20.3	3.58	36.5	33.4	54.2
	895	649	246	23.4	19.5	3.88	38.2	33.3	63.4
	418	234	184	19.2	16.3	2.93	21.8	14.4	62.8
	655	478	177	21.4	18.0	3.42	30.6	26.6	51.8
1901/02	530	390	140	22.8	18.7	4.11	23.2	20.9	34.1
	825	593	232	23.4	19.2	4.24	36.8	30.9	54.7
	852	578	274	23.7	18.4	5.30	35.9	31.4	51.7
	597	435	162	23.4	18.4	4.95	25.5	23.6	32.7
	752	521	231	22.6	17.6	5.04	33.3	29.6	45.8
1906/07	885	564	321	24.4	18.9	5.50	36.3	29.8	58.4
	680	468	212	23.9	18.7	5.22	28.5	25.0	40.6
	808	578	230	25.3	20.4	4.87	31.9	28.3	47.2
	977	639	338	25.1	19.9	5.20	38.9	32.1	65.0
	936	631	305	25.5	19.7	5.83	36.7	32.0	52.3
1911/12	620	412	208	22.4	16.8	5.57	27.7	24.5	37.3
	954	652	302	25.0	19.8	5.24	38.2	32.9	57.6
	954	633	321	25.4	19.7	5.71	37.6	32.1	56.2
	1075	725	350	25.9	20.0	5.93	41.5	36.3	59.0
	995	728	267	24.6	20.3	4.33	40.4	35.9	61.7
1916/17	1100	742	358	26.5	20.8	5.70	41.5	35.7	62.8
	967	647	320	26.4	20.4	6.05	36.6	31.7	52.9
	522	344	178	21.8	16.9	4.86	23.9	20.4	36.6
	1040	719	321	25.6	20.4	5.21	40.6	35.2	61.6
	675	466	209	23.2	18.5	4.65	29.1	25.2	44.9
1921/22	904	649	255	25.3	21.1	4.15	35.7	30.8	61.4
	949	650	299	25.4	20.3	5.10	37.4	32.0	58.6
	833	526	307	25.3	19.3	5.99	32.9	27.3	51.3
	989	642	347	26.5	19.9	6.56	37.3	32.3	52.9
	913	558	355	25.8	19.0	6.75	35.4	29.4	52.6
1926/27	900	600	300	25.9	20.0	5.90	34.7	30.0	50.8
	1025	648	377	26.4	20.1	6.35	38.8	32.2	59.4
	1090	659	431	26.7	19.7	6.97	40.8	33.4	61.8
	946	603	343	27.5	20.7	6.81	34.4	29.1	50.4
	1012	668	344	27.2	21.6	5.59	37.2	30.9	61.5
1931/32	986	635	351	26.5	20.4	6.06	37.2	31.1	57.9
	1060	661	399	27.1	20.9	6.22	39.1	31.6	64.1
	1054	646	408	27.5	21.2	6.27	38.3	30.5	65.1
	985	647	338	26.9	21.0	5.89	36.6	30.8	57.4
	1050	631	419	27.3	20.8	6.53	38.5	30.3	64.2
1936/37	1004	582	422	27.1	20.8	6.30	37.0	28.0	34.9
	1051	614	437	28.4	21.5	6.91	37.0	28.6	63.2
	1038	618	420	28.0	21.2	6.77	37.1	29.2	62.0
	968	548	420	28.0	21.1	6.93	34.8	26.0	60.6
	1133	608	525	28.8	21.6	7.21	39.3	28.1	72.8

APPENDIX TABLE 4c—*Continued*

	Yield			Acreage			Yield per Acre		
	AC	FG	NFG	AC	FG	NFG	AC	FG	NFG
1941/42	1051	562	489	28.6	21.5	7.09	36.7	26.1	68.9
	1079	643	436	27.5	21.8	5.72	39.2	29.5	76.2
	1194	706	488	28.2	22.2	5.97	42.3	31.8	81.7
	1011	616	395	27.3	22.8	4.49	37.0	27.0	88.0
	930	574	356	26.4	22.2	4.17	35.2	25.9	85.4
1946/47	933	564	369	27.2	22.7	4.47	34.3	24.8	82.5

Central Provinces

	AC	FG	NFG	AC	FG	NFG	AC	FG	NFG
1891/92	543	400	143	19.1	13.6	5.50	28.4	29.4	26.0
	551	416	135	19.8	14.4	5.35	29.6	28.9	25.2
	564	424	140	20.1	14.1	6.03	28.1	30.0	23.2
	518	407	111	18.5	13.2	5.32	28.0	30.8	20.9
	638	468	170	18.7	14.1	4.62	34.1	33.2	36.8
1896/97	499	375	124	17.6	13.0	4.60	28.4	28.8	27.0
	647	474	173	17.6	12.9	4.65	36.8	36.7	37.2
	732	516	216	18.8	13.8	5.02	38.9	37.4	43.0
	432	358	74	16.3	12.1	4.23	26.5	29.6	17.5
1900/01	693	430	263	18.1	12.7	5.39	38.3	33.9	48.8
	745	516	229	19.0	13.6	5.39	39.2	37.9	42.5
	849	583	266	19.5	13.7	5.81	43.5	42.6	45.8
	677	455	222	19.2	12.9	6.30	35.3	35.3	35.2
	806	488	318	19.9	13.4	6.48	40.5	36.4	49.1
	664	438	226	19.9	13.3	6.64	33.4	32.9	34.0
1906/07	783	533	250	20.4	13.7	6.74	38.4	38.9	37.1
	493	331	162	19.0	13.0	5.99	25.9	25.5	27.1
	713	498	215	19.6	13.6	6.02	36.4	36.6	35.7
	915	622	293	20.4	14.3	6.13	44.9	43.5	47.8
	719	522	197	20.7	14.1	6.56	34.7	37.0	30.0
1911/12	803	543	260	20.9	13.4	7.50	38.4	40.5	34.7
	793	534	259	20.7	13.8	6.88	38.3	38.7	37.6
	639	385	254	20.0	13.3	6.65	32.0	28.9	38.2
	878	582	296	20.6	13.7	6.91	42.6	42.5	42.8
	981	680	301	21.0	14.8	6.15	46.7	45.9	48.9
1916/17	773	572	201	20.8	14.3	6.45	37.2	40.0	31.2
	691	518	173	20.5	14.0	6.46	33.7	37.0	26.8
	541	341	200	18.9	13.7	5.19	28.6	24.9	38.5
	922	597	325	19.9	13.7	6.16	46.3	43.6	52.8
	405	267	138	18.8	13.1	5.69	21.5	20.4	24.3
1921/22	883	584	299	19.6	13.5	6.05	45.1	43.3	49.4
	870	590	280	20.3	13.7	6.57	42.9	43.1	42.6
	824	556	268	21.1	14.2	6.91	39.1	39.2	38.8
	796	518	278	21.1	14.0	7.12	37.7	37.0	39.0
	766	512	254	21.1	14.0	7.13	36.3	36.6	35.6

APPENDIX TABLE 4c—*Continued*

	Yield			Acreage			Yield per Acre		
	AC	FG	NFG	AC	FG	NFG	AC	FG	NFG
1926/27	796	540	256	21.0	14.5	6.45	37.9	37.2	39.7
	830	507	323	21.3	14.8	6.45	39.0	34.3	50.1
	839	493	346	21.3	14.4	6.86	39.4	34.2	50.4
	881	557	324	21.0	14.3	6.66	42.0	39.0	48.6
	818	517	301	21.2	14.9	6.32	38.6	34.7	47.6
1931/32	683	538	145	21.2	14.9	6.34	32.2	36.1	22.9
	773	538	235	21.0	15.1	5.92	36.8	35.6	40.0
	772	549	223	20.9	14.8	6.07	36.9	37.1	36.7
	754	569	185	20.9	15.0	5.81	36.1	37.9	31.8
	683	497	186	20.9	15.0	5.87	32.7	33.1	31.7
1936/37	812	567	245	21.2	15.3	5.87	38.3	37.1	41.7
	767	549	218	21.4	15.2	6.18	35.8	36.1	35.3
	733	553	180	21.0	15.2	5.80	34.9	36.4	31.0
	747	528	219	20.9	15.5	5.40	35.7	34.1	40.6
	711	450	261	21.0	15.4	5.63	33.9	29.2	46.4
1941/42	637	370	267	20.7	15.1	5.59	30.8	24.5	47.8
	759	568	173	20.3	15.2	5.10	37.4	37.4	33.9
	771	574	197	21.3	16.1	5.17	36.2	35.7	38.1
	723	546	177	21.0	16.0	5.03	34.4	34.1	35.2
	707	513	194	21.7	16.7	4.96	32.6	30.7	39.1
1946/47	565	399	166	21.0	16.0	4.95	26.9	24.9	33.5

Sources: Computed from adjusted crop data, as in Appendix 3A, and average 1924/25–28/29 prices given in Appendix Table 4A, as explained in Chapter IV, 1. For British India and Greater Bengal, see also modified series in Appendix Tables 9B and 9c.

APPENDIX TABLE 4D

DECENNIAL POPULATION OF BRITISH INDIA AND REGIONS, 1891–1951
(Millions)

	1891	1901	1911	1921	1931	1941	1951
British India	212.97	220.60	231.60	233.56	256.76	289.21[a] 389.00[b]	437.13
Bengal	39.10	42.15	45.49	46.70	50.12	60.31	
Bihar	28.20	28.25	29.35	29.02	32.37	36.34	
Orissa	6.71	7.13	7.58	7.35	8.03	8.73	
Greater Bengal	74.01	77.53	82.42	83.08	90.51	100.00[a] c108.60[a]	121.77
United Provinces	46.50	47.31	46.81	45.38	48.41	55.02	63.22
Madras	33.73	36.26	39.13	40.13	44.20	49.34 49.84[c]	57.02
Punjab	18.65	19.94	19.58	20.68	23.58	28.42	
N. W. Frontier	1.86	2.04	2.20	2.25	2.42	3.04	
Delhi	0.37	0.41	0.41	0.49	0.64	0.92	
Greater Punjab	20.88	22.39	22.19	23.42	26.64	31.18[a] c31.15[a]	36.44
Bombay	15.98	15.32	16.14	16.01	17.99	20.85	
Sind	2.88	3.21	3.51	3.28	3.89	4.54	
Bombay-Sind	18.86	18.53	19.65	19.29	21.88	25.38 34.04[c]	40.56
Central Provinces	12.95	11.84	13.76	13.74	15.32	16.81	18.05
Assam	5.36	5.73	6.58	7.46	6.62	10.20 7.59[c]	9.04

Notes: [a] Reduced from total of 1941 Census reports in accord with view in 1951 Census, cited below, which points out overestimates in 1941 Census. [b] India and Pakistan. [c] As of the 1951 boundaries.

Source: *Census of India 1941*, V, 1, Part I, Table II – Variations in Population over 50 Years (for provinces as of 1941 boundaries); *Census of India, 1951*, V. 1, Part 1B, pp. 104–105.

APPENDIX TABLE 5A

BRITISH INDIA : TREND RATES OF CHANGE IN POPULATION AND THE OUTPUT, ACREAGE, AND YIELD PER ACRE OF INDIVIDUAL CROPS AND CROP AGGREGATES FOR EACH REFERENCE DECADE

(Percent per Year)

Output

	91–01	*96–06*	*01–11*	*06–16*	*11–21*	*16–26*	*21–31*	*26–36*	*31–41*	*36–46*
Pop.	0.35	0.42	0.49	0.49	–0.01	0.45	0.95	1.07	1.19	1.27
Rice:	0.37	–0.57	0.49	1.12	–0.79	–1.02	–0.09	–0.15	–1.00	0.76
Wheat:	1.63	2.35	2.03	1.56	–0.98	–0.43	0.07	0.74	1.38	0.08
Jowar:	1.48	–0.17	–0.42	1.09	–0.29	0.17	0.24	–0.29	–0.82	–0.49
Gram:	1.04	2.11	2.54	1.26	0.42	–0.17	–3.23	–1.06	–1.02	0.72
Bajra:	2.47	1.96	1.74	0.46	–1.73	–0.01	–0.45	–0.96	0.75	3.03
Barley:	4.90	0.73	2.15	0.55	–0.61	–2.20	–2.63	–0.51	–1.75	–0.46
Maize:	2.20	1.31	1.05	1.63	–0.36	–2.49	0.86	–0.40	–0.47	1.75
Ragi:	1.17	0.25	–0.16	–0.30	0.28	–1.02	–0.49	–1.03	–1.22	–1.17
FG	0.88	0.01	1.24	0.30	–0.63	–0.79	–0.17	0.06	–0.51	0.75
Sugarcane:	–0.28	–1.48	0.50	2.13	–0.37	0.50	1.01	7.62	2.92	0.44
Cotton:	2.17	4.85	2.90	1.43	–0.40	2.14	0.33	0.13	1.87	–2.39
Jute:	2.61	4.03	1.07	0.81	–3.23	0.36	1.66	–2.96	0.55	–2.17
Tea:	4.94	4.23	3.45	4.33	1.68	0.44	1.54	0.40	2.28	4.11
Tobacco:	–1.51	–1.26	0.85	1.17	0.30	–0.56	1.37	1.27	0.48	–1.85
Groundnut:	0.34	15.40	9.18	10.03	4.60	10.14	10.09	0.71	1.33	0.79
Rape and Mustard:	2.78	–2.72	2.19	0.22	–1.23	–0.61	–1.42	–0.57	1.02	1.07
Sesamum:	2.83	3.08	0.54	–1.57	–2.31	–0.10	0.12	–0.31	–0.72	–0.61
Linseed:	–1.45	–0.31	1.33	2.52	–1.80	0.14	–1.88	0.04	0.19	–3.44

APPENDIX TABLE 5A—*Continued*

	91–01	96–06	01–11	06–16	11–21	16–26	21–31	26–36	31–41	36–46
Indigo:										
	−6.38	−10.62	−11.11	2.02	0.85	−11.56	−16.21	−9.79	−2.89	3.80
NFG	1.28	1.90	1.51	1.96	0.74	1.44	2.31	1.40	1.25	−0.66
AC	0.97	0.35	1.34	0.69	−0.60	−0.40	0.53	0.46	0.00	0.39

Acreage

	91–01	96–06	01–11	06–16	11–21	16–26	21–31	26–36	31–41	36–46
Rice:										
	−0.21	−0.36	0.31	0.38	0.11	−0.32	−0.12	0.24	0.52	1.23
Wheat:										
	−0.96	2.29	0.60	0.88	−0.85	0.82	0.81	0.64	0.39	0.29
Jowar:										
	0.70	−0.17	−0.76	−0.17	0.82	−0.50	−0.11	0.36	0.28	0.43
Gram:										
	−0.66	1.89	1.93	1.34	0.11	1.61	−0.57	0.01	−1.44	0.90
Bajra:										
	1.82	1.94	1.52	−0.18	−1.31	−0.74	−0.03	−0.14	0.92	2.73
Barley:										
	2.95	0.93	1.46	0.04	−1.12	−1.39	−0.53	−0.96	−0.33	0.82
Maize:										
	1.72	0.73	0.13	0.10	0.14	−1.72	0.52	0.17	−0.32	1.49
Ragi:										
	0.15	−0.12	0.09	−0.50	−0.50	−0.62	−0.83	−1.14	−1.37	−0.60
FG	0.21	0.48	0.37	0.43	−0.09	0.13	0.06	0.21	0.18	1.10
Sugarcane:										
	−1.78	−1.73	−0.40	0.45	1.03	0.49	0.44	3.96	2.99	0.51
Cotton:										
	−0.33	4.25	3.11	0.57	−0.47	1.67	−0.10	−1.73	−0.27	−3.27
Jute:										
	−0.55	5.49	2.16	−1.85	−2.97	0.65	0.73	−3.22	2.85	−1.48
Tea:										
	3.52	1.66	1.01	1.74	1.92	1.12	1.05	0.51	0.26	0.13
Tobacco:										
	−3.37	−0.80	−0.40	−0.20	−0.03	0.02	1.31	1.09	1.33	−1.62
Groundnut:										
	−1.98	12.99	11.06	10.69	2.34	9.52	9.89	1.90	2.55	2.05
Rape and Mustard:										
	0.57	−1.17	1.63	−0.27	−1.02	0.19	0.65	−1.33	−0.07	0.05
Sesamum:										
	2.34	1.87	−0.31	−1.69	−2.78	−0.66	0.12	−0.21	−0.11	−0.30
Linseed:										
	−5.72	2.50	0.05	0.61	−1.76	2.00	0.13	0.07	0.74	−1.36

Appendix Table 5a — *Continued*

	91–01	96–06	01–11	06–16	11–21	16–26	21–31	26–36	31–41	36–46
Indigo:	–6.93	–11.68	–12.26	0.49	–0.64	–13.74	–15.26	–8.34	–0.84	2.82
NFG	–0.24	1.73	1.33	0.62	–0.06	0.67	0.48	–0.11	0.84	–1.05
AC	0.87	0.77	0.62	0.42	–0.31	0.23	0.26	0.05	0.33	0.76

Yield per Acre

	91–01	96–06	01–11	06–16	11–21	16–26	21–31	26–36	31–41	36–46
Rice:	0.52	0.07	0.21	0.74	–0.97	–0.70	0.04	–0.35	–1.51	–0.48
Wheat:	2.53	0.34	1.35	0.76	–0.02	–1.22	–0.76	0.17	0.87	–0.20
Jowar:	0.80	0.16	0.41	1.17	–0.92	0.93	0.18	–0.80	–0.97	–0.95
Gram:	1.55	0.16	0.40	–0.05	0.33	–1.51	–2.56	–1.11	0.34	–0.18
Bajra:	0.78	–0.26	0.22	0.64	0.08	0.11	–0.62	–0.41	–0.20	0.28
Barley:	1.88	–0.25	0.60	0.62	1.40	–1.03	–2.03	0.35	–1.55	–2.21
Maize:	0.46	0.63	0.91	1.52	–0.82	–1.01	0.76	–0.48	–0.15	0.28
Ragi:	1.25	0.40	–0.26	–0.23	0.77	–0.40	0.37	–0.08	–0.06	–0.61
FG	0.64	–0.21	–0.02	0.76	–0.54	–0.71	–0.22	–0.08	–0.98	–0.47
Sugarcane:	1.53	0.25	0.77	1.58	–1.09	–0.10	0.58	3.51	0.20	0.10
Cotton:	2.44	0.87	–0.35	0.95	0.19	0.36	0.33	1.93	2.02	0.80
Jute:	3.22	–1.05	–1.40	2.61	–0.55	–0.25	1.11	0.34	–1.96	–0.67
Tea:	1.44	2.59	2.34	2.42	0.12	–0.78	0.53	–0.11	2.00	3.95
Tobacco:	0.81	–0.47	1.25	1.31	0.31	–0.56	0.05	0.11	–0.81	–0.31
Groundnut:	1.23	3.34	–0.77	–0.89	1.89	–0.10	0.40	–1.15	–1.09	–0.61
Rape and Mustard:	2.23	–1.15	0.28	0.56	–0.37	–0.91	–1.66	1.11	1.08	0.69
Sesamum:	0.55	1.04	0.62	0.11	0.06	0.84	0.38	0.11	–0.54	–0.28
Linseed:	4.02	–2.92	0.97	2.12	–0.17	–1.85	–2.15	–0.03	–0.59	–0.42

APPENDIX TABLE 5A—*Continued*

	91–01	96–06	01–11	06–16	11–21	16–26	21–31	26–36	31–41	36–46
Indigo:	0.89	0.89	1.72	1.63	1.52	1.63	−0.56	−1.70	−1.75	0.46
NFG	2.06	−0.16	0.14	1.21	0.38	0.30	1.24	2.21	0.40	0.77
AC	0.87	−0.03	0.09	0.95	−0.36	−0.36	0.28	0.39	−0.34	−0.42

Notes

Years in the column headings are for crop years, i.e. 91–01 for 1891/92–1901/02. Trends calculated as described in Chapter IV, 3. Pop., FG, NFG, AC, represent population, foodgrains, nonfoodgrains, all-crops.

Source: Computed from data in Appendix 3A.

Appendix Table (5b)

ONAL TREND RATES OF CHANGE IN POPULATION (P), AND THE OUTPUT (Y), ACREAGE (A),
YIELD PER ACRE (Y/A), OF ALL-CROPS (AC), FOODGRAIN (FG) AND NONFOODGRAIN (NFG)
CROPS FOR EACH REFERENCE DECADE
(Percent per Year)

Greater Bengal

	91–01	96–06	01–11	06–16	11–21	16–26	21–31	26–36	31–41	36–46
	0.47	0.54	0.61	0.61	0.05	0.25	0.86	0.93	1.00	1.15
C	0.02	−0.98	0.02	−0.67	−1.39	−0.54	0.50	−0.47	−1.22	0.27
G	−0.04	−1.28	−0.13	−0.81	−1.20	−1.43	−0.06	−0.61	−1.93	0.17
FG	0.25	0.37	0.87	0.46	−2.04	0.23	2.28	0.10	0.75	−0.93
C	−0.33	−0.45	0.05	0.03	−0.42	−0.61	−0.23	−0.06	0.21	1.20
G	−0.05	−0.58	−0.01	0.19	−0.21	−0.65	−0.33	0.13	−0.01	1.56
FG	−1.29	−0.21	0.52	−0.95	−1.78	−0.29	−0.27	−0.08	0.98	−0.60
:AC	0.56	−0.61	0.07	0.29	−0.97	−0.81	0.73	−0.30	−1.44	−0.90
G	0.23	−0.75	−0.02	0.10	−1.00	−1.10	0.29	−0.73	−1.92	−0.59
FG	1.54	0.07	0.49	0.84	−0.67	0.49	1.06	2.33	−0.52	0.24

United Provinces

	91–01	96–06	01–11	06–16	11–21	16–26	21–31	26–36	31–41	36–46
	0.17	0.03	−0.11	−0.11	−0.45	0.25	0.65	0.97	1.29	1.35
C	2.20	0.50	0.57	0.81	−0.65	−0.34	−0.52	1.92	0.33	−0.67
G	2.53	1.25	0.22	0.92	0.34	−0.92	−1.30	0.21	0.40	−0.20
FG	1.51	0.73	1.37	1.55	−1.88	0.26	1.91	5.25	0.02	−1.50
C	1.40	1.06	0.34	0.58	−0.39	0.18	−0.05	0.38	0.58	0.29
G	1.63	0.71	0.05	0.55	−0.16	0.21	−0.24	0.25	0.65	0.44
FG	0.38	2.96	1.47	0.91	−1.29	−0.02	0.79	0.85	0.34	−0.40
:AC	1.42	−0.64	0.09	0.66	−0.32	−0.32	−0.56	1.63	0.60	−1.03
G	1.72	−0.68	0.17	1.08	−0.18	−1.06	−0.47	−0.03	−0.02	−0.73
FG	−0.06	−1.25	−0.50	0.45	−0.51	0.59	1.08	4.40	−0.35	−1.49

Madras

	91–01	96–06	01–11	06–16	11–21	16–26	21–31	26–36	31–41	36–46
	0.72	0.75	0.77	0.77	0.20	0.42	0.97	1.04	1.10	1.22
C	2.64	0.58	1.31	2.32	0.33	0.90	1.49	0.10	0.17	−0.07
G	2.87	0.02	1.06	1.91	−0.31	−0.69	0.27	−0.33	−0.45	−0.16
FG	1.38	3.35	2.48	4.21	2.99	4.02	3.16	0.73	1.11	0.30

APPENDIX TABLE 5B—*Continued*

	91–01	96–06	01–11	06–16	11–21	16–26	21–31	26–36	31–41	36–4
A:AC	0.45	0.56	0.38	0.74	0.06	0.01	0.52	–0.06	0.41	–0.0
FG	0.49	0.43	0.13	0.29	–0.16	–0.64	–0.20	–0.09	0.02	0.1
NFG	–0.44	2.03	1.97	2.76	0.92	2.29	2.03	0.90	0.47	–0.5
Y/A:AC	2.14	0.17	0.97	1.68	0.31	0.46	1.02	0.12	–0.33	–0.0
FG	2.13	–0.14	0.99	0.96	–0.21	–0.09	0.40	–0.03	–0.61	0.1
NFG	1.97	1.90	0.94	1.51	2.47	1.41	1.57	0.22	0.00	0.5

Greater Punjab

	91–01	96–06	01–11	06–16	11–21	16–26	21–31	26–36	31–41	36–4
P	0.70	0.30	–0.09	–0.09	0.37	1.58	1.29	1.94	1.59	1.5
Y:AC	1.20	3.89	3.08	0.52	0.56	1.26	–0.39	1.73	1.86	1.9
FG	1.06	4.12	2.92	–0.16	–0.05	–0.60	–0.61	0.56	1.23	2.5
NFG	2.07	3.72	3.68	1.88	2.15	3.34	0.26	3.02	3.24	0.6
A:AC	0.36	2.81	2.88	0.94	0.07	0.82	0.17	–0.02	0.13	1.4
FG	0.00	2.74	2.98	1.08	–0.10	0.45	–0.03	–0.08	–0.14	1.8
NFG	1.92	3.35	1.85	–0.11	0.32	2.71	1.35	0.72	1.12	–1.1
Y/A:AC	0.57	1.71	0.21	–0.63	0.34	0.45	–0.29	1.97	1.64	0.2
FG	0.77	1.72	–0.01	–1.28	–0.18	0.17	–0.39	0.84	1.21	0.2
NFG	–0.87	–0.14	1.43	1.65	1.92	0.55	0.20	3.37	1.03	2.2

Bombay-Sind

	91–01	96–06	01–11	06–16	11–21	16–26	21–31	26–36	31–41	36–4
P	–0.17	0.21	0.59	0.59	–0.32	0.42	1.26	1.40	1.55	1.5
Y:AC	–3.04	0.49	2.75	2.59	–0.10	0.71	1.84	0.51	0.42	0.4
FG	–3.35	–0.16	2.21	2.66	0.09	–0.17	0.97	0.04	–0.07	0.4
NFG	–2.25	2.14	3.96	2.41	–1.55	2.50	2.85	1.33	2.71	0.3
A:AC	–0.60	0.88	1.03	0.52	–0.13	0.61	0.85	0.39	0.52	–0.1
FG	–0.59	0.11	0.64	0.51	0.14	0.08	0.57	0.63	0.29	0.7
NFG	0.48	4.20	1.95	0.68	–1.14	2.31	1.87	0.02	1.12	–2.8
Y/A:AC	–1.58	0.42	1.59	1.71	–1.03	0.25	0.84	0.10	0.00	0.4
FG	–1.82	0.31	1.51	1.73	–1.10	–0.08	0.43	–0.56	–1.19	–0.3
NFG	–0.19	–2.11	1.29	1.42	0.29	0.18	0.96	0.34	1.54	5.4

Central Provinces

	91–01	96–06	01–11	06–16	11–21	16–26	21–31	26–36	31–41	36–4
P	–0.89	0.31	1.51	1.51	–0.19	–0.25	1.09	1.01	0.93	0.8
Y:AC	2.82	2.08	0.65	1.37	–0.99	1.17	0.23	–1.09	–0.65	–0.7
FG	1.55	0.73	0.97	1.22	–1.05	0.49	0.13	0.63	–1.00	–0.7
NFG	6.31	5.06	–0.02	1.09	–0.85	1.53	0.44	–3.70	0.96	–1.0

APPENDIX TABLE 5B—*Continued*

	91–01	96–06	01–11	06–16	11–21	16–26	21–31	26–36	31–41	36–46
	0.12	1.25	0.85	0.39	−0.57	0.62	0.52	−0.07	−0.09	−0.07
	−0.45	0.19	0.53	0.40	−0.19	0.25	0.86	0.54	0.40	0.67
	1.53	3.66	1.55	−0.68	−0.61	1.01	−0.61	−1.55	−1.22	−2.02
AC	3.31	0.91	−0.67	0.73	−1.19	0.63	−1.37	−1.04	−0.58	−0.65
	2.31	0.59	0.62	0.97	−0.91	0.32	−0.70	0.07	−1.38	−1.37
	5.43	1.54	−1.38	0.80	0.45	0.93	1.29	−2.76	0.58	0.81

Source: Computed from data in Appendix Table *4C*.

APPENDIX TABLE 5c

ANNUAL GROSS FOODGRAIN AVAILABILITY, OUTPUT PLUS NET TRADE FLOW
IN BRITISH INDIA
(Thousand Tons)

	Foodgrain Output	Net Trade Flow	Gross Availability		Foodgrain Output	Net Trade Flow	Gross Availability
1891/92	38566	−2111	36455	1921/22	55777	1095	56872
	45397	−1178	44219		55755	−22	55733
	47322	−785	46537		48999	−991	48008
	50257	−677	49580		49234	−1752	47572
	45945	−1005	44940		48192	304	48496
1896/97	36519	240	36759	1926/27	47921	144	48065
	54258	22	54280		45210	389	45599
	54317	−1474	52843		49125	1285	50410
	43930	−360	43570		51415	1094	52464
	48075	483	48556		50988	634	51622
1901/02	48081	−178	47903	1931/32	51394	963	52357
	54303	−1343	52960		49046	788	49834
	52330	−1978	50352		48329	1629	49958
	47589	−2803	44786		48474	2306	50780
	45497	−1266	44231		45867	1770	47637
1906/07	50316	−622	49694	1936/37	50418	1232	51650
	39736	−598	39138		48891	455	49346
	46607	632	47239		44559	856	45415
	59318	−707	58611		48091	2036	50127
	59089	−1493	57596		44723	893	45616
1911/12	54478	−2933	51545	1941/42	46877	366	47243
	52018	−3279	48739		48776	−342	48434
	47441	−1425	46016		53035	−86	52949
	51948	−140	51808		51318	264	51582
	56651	−710	55941		47325	302	47627
1916/17	58312	−629	57683	1946/47	47297	890	48187
	57786	−2394	58392				
	39427	−545	38782				
	55341	1760	57101				
	43100	502	43602				

Notes

Overland net foreign trade, which averaged only 18,000 tons inflow during 1925/26–39/40, is not included. Output is at the gross level, no deduction is made for seed or waste. Flow=imports−exports.

Source: Output aggregated from Appendix 3A Tables 1−8. Net trade flow from tonnage of "Grain, Pulse, and Flour" in *Annual Statement of Seaborne Foreign Trade of British India*, to and from foreign countries, excluding exports and imports of Burma Province; *Annual Statement of the Coasting Trade and Navigation of British India*, for coastal shipments to and from Burma up to 1936/37; *Statistical Abstract for British India* for overland shipments.

Appendix Table 5d

ANNUAL GROSS FOODGRAIN AVAILABILITY, OUTPUT PLUS NET TRADE FLOW
IN GREATER BENGAL
(Thousand Tons)

	Output	Net Sea Trade Flow	Gross Availability with Sea Trade	Inland Trade Flow	Gross Availability with Sea and Land Trade
1891/92	16053	−929	15124	318	15442
	19068	−682	18386	419	18805
	20834	−385	20449	−382	20077
	23330	−452	22878	−432	22428
	17823	−531	17292	−673	16619
1896/97	10875	−106	10769	−681	10088
	22484	15	22499	−271	22228
	22885	−741	22144	−610	21534
	20154	−827	19327	−878	18449
	17884	−580	17304	−1089	16215
1901/02	15785	−279	15506	−343	15163
	20261	−508	19753	−158	19595
	18218	−707	17511	−49	17412
	19663	−1048	18615	−54	18561
	17507	−680	16827	−395	16432
1906/07	16933	24	16957	482	17439
	14182	278	14460	242	14702
	14507	353	14860	101	14961
	22276	−301	21975	−29	21946
	22591	−676	21915	−543	21372
1911/12	20144	−1197	18947	−481	18466
	16755	−655	16100	778	16878
	17994	21	18015	478	18493
	14365	496	14861	84	14945
	19569	533	20102	338	20540
1916/17	19549	464	20013	218	20231
	20240	27	20267	18	20285
	13715	−38	13677	−702	12975
	17923	419	18342	−190	18152
	15671	200	15871	−69	15802
1921/22	18649	72	18721		
	18708	−337	18371		
	14797	−584	14213		
	15803	−551	15252		
	15401	32	15433		
1926/27	14496	−22	14474		
	13039	265	13305		
	17513	839	18352		
	16811	221	17032		
	17297	82	17379		

APPENDIX TABLE 5D—*Continued*

	Output	Net Sea Trade Flow	Gross Availability with Sea Trade	Inland Trade Flow	Gross Availability with Sea and Land Trade
1931/32	17658	265	17923		
	16087	31	16118		
	15226	404	15630	−51	15579
	15405	919	16324	−117	16207
	12529	267	12796	−306	12490
1936/37	16392	−137	16255	−498	15757
	15383	−43	15340	−130	15210
	13122	191	13313	−172	13141
	14325	627	14952	−211	14741
	10940	298	11238	−568	10670
1941/43	15317	277	15594		
	13061	−64	12997		
	17707	2	17709	−738	16971
	16192	140	16332	−263	16069
	14771	253	15024		
1946/47	15345	176	15521		

Notes

Availability measured at the gross output level, with no allowance for seed or waste.

Inland trade data unavailable for certain years.

Trade flow by sea, incoming minus outgoing shipments, includes trade with foreign countries and coastal trade with other parts of British India. Inland trade covers movements by rail and river between Greater Bengal and other regions.

Sea trade for the last six years refers only to foreign trade, including Burma. Coastal trade data unavailable. Coastal trade for 1931/32 refers only to Burma, trade with other provinces by sea for that year was unavailable.

Sources: *Annual Statement of the Seaborne Trade of British India, Annual Statement of the Coasting Trade of British India* (ceased publication with 1921/22), *Annual Statement of the Seaborne Trade and Navigation of the Bengal Presidency* (ceased publication with 1931/32), *Annual Statement of the Inland Trade of India* (ceased publication with 1920/21), *Accounts of the Trade by Rail and River in India* (monthly from 1932 on), *Accounts Relating to the Coasting Trade and Navigation of India* (monthly from 1932 on), and *Annual Statement of the Seaborne Trade and Navigation of Burma.*

APPENDIX TABLE 5E

BRITISH INDIA AND GREATER BENGAL REFERENCE DECADE TREND RATES OF CHANGE
AGGREGATE TONNAGE OF FOODGRAIN OUTPUT AND FOODGRAINS AVAILABLE AFTER
ALLOWING FOR TRADE

(Percent Per Year)

REFERENCE DECADES	BRITISH INDIA		GREATER BENGAL		
	Output	Output Plus Net Foreign Sea Trade	Output	Output Plus Net Foreign Sea Trade	Output Plus Net Foreign Sea Trade and Inland Trade
1891/92–1901/02	1.19	1.33	−0.33	−0.11	−0.57
1896/97–1906/07	0.11	−0.03	−1.04	−0.90	−0.39
1901/02–1911/12	0.79	0.90	−0.01	0.13	0.55
1906/07–1916/17	1.10	1.11	0.56	0.92	1.04
1911/12–1921/22	−0.67	−0.16	−0.72	−0.39	
1916/17–1926/27	−0.80	−0.70	−0.76	−1.08	
1921/22–1931/32	−0.30	−0.03	−0.37	0.07	
1926/27–1936–37	−0.11	0.02	0.04	0.09	
1931/32–1941/42	−0.58	−0.55	−0.11	−0.23	
1936/37–1946/47	0.28	−0.05	1.04	0.96	

Source: Computed from Appendix Tables 5c and 5d. Burma treated as a foreign country over the whole period.

APPENDIX TABLE 5F

INDEX NUMBERS OF PER CAPITA ALL-CROP OUTPUT COMPUTED FROM OUTPUT AND
POPULATION TREND RATES OF CHANGE, 1891 = 100 FOR EACH REGION

	1901	1911	1921	1931	1941	1946
I	100.9	100.0	99.7	93.2	87.6	84.2
B	90.4	81.3	72.8	64.9	57.6	54.1
	107.9	113.4	116.0	115.6	112.2	108.1
P	107.5	112.0	112.9	110.3	104.4	99.9
P	112.8	123.9	132.6	138.4	137.6	137.0
S	101.4	104.3	111.4	100.5	98.5	97.2
P	108.2	111.7	110.0	103.4	92.7	85.7

Source: Based on rates of change, and change in rates of change, Table 5.8.

APPENDIX TABLE 7A

RAINFALL AT PATNA, BIHAR, AND RICE YIELD PER ACRE IN SUBDIVISIONS OF THE
GREATER BENGAL REGION, FOR SELECTED YEARS

	Patna Rainfall		Rice Yield per Acre, lbs.					
	June–July	Annual[a]	Bengal	Bihar-	Bihar	Orissa[c]	West	Ecst
	Inches		Prov.	Orissa			Bengal	Bengal[b]
1891/92	13.00	35.90						
	34.77	46.63						
	22.57	52.82						
	19.80	62.13						
	23.94	43.89						
1896/97	17.97	34.55						
	38.67	60.05						
	17.98	61.97						
	31.14	53.31						
	22.59	48.88						
1901/02	10.12	29.41						
	12.67	45.50						
	6.04	25.29						
	29.35	65.01						
	15.16	62.17						
1906/07	20.67	40.92						
	16.71	37.41						
	10.62	26.00						
	26.03	51.71						
	26.75	63.51						
1911/12	17.53	51.90	946	1149				
	17.53	35.43	907	826				
	28.29	71.61	837	1121				
	10.60	50.53	702	826				
	26.75	61.72	886	1209				
1916/17	17.85	54.80	851	1214				
	23.23	58.05	924	1275				
	20.97	77.14	725	709				
	22.22	41.88	883	1024				
	15.08	32.26	882	727				
1921/22	11.74	43.53	951	943				
	25.12	51.29	931	1062				
	16.86	32.09	827	784				
	24.72	54.67	829	921				
	16.22	31.62	871	767				

APPENDIX TABLE 7A

	Patna Rainfall June–July Annual[a] Inhes		Bengal Prov.	Bihar-Orissa	Rice Yield per Acre, lbs. Bihar	Orissa[c]	West Bengal	East Bengal[b]
926/27	12.06	34.58	829	770				
	16.14	34.41	779	728				
	15.00	33.27	1014	872				
	18.58	55.75	908	946				
	12.32	34.51	1002	903				
931/32	19.59	38.83	961	912				
	7.98	31.31	963	720				
	15.30	50.20	897	727				
	16.66	36.01	894	765			868	831
	13.75	36.81	765	562	567	559	661	661
1936/37	25.95	64.46	999	742	756	711		
	5.30	50.06	911	729	740	697		
	22.64	56.88	771	641	621	613		
	20.99	53.54	851	648	743	613	868	831
	15.88	46.15	652	519	519	605	661	661
1941/42	11.47	42.87	915	612	606	620	966	889
	17.32	54.41	672	649	683	556	571	717
	13.88	30.99	980	649	668	591	1017	945
	10.74	39.17	798	602	616	580	845	778
	12.14	41.78	809	565	566	562	755	829
1946/47	11.35	38.67	809	616	627	595		

Notes

a. Annual rainfall is given for calendar years, i.e. for January–December 1891, where given above for 1891/92.

b. Includes part of Sylhet District, Assam.

c. As of 1935 includes parts of Madras and Central Provinces.

Source: Rainfall—Smithsonian Miscellaneous Collection, *World Weather Records;* yield per acre—given or computed from *Estimates.*

AGRICULTURAL TRENDS IN INDIA, 1891–1947

APPENDIX TABLE 8A

ANNUAL PERCENTAGE OF NET AREA IRRIGATED/NET AREA SOWN FOR BRITISH
INDIA AND REGIONS

	BI	GB	M	UP	GP	BS	CP
1891/92			24.3	29.3	38.2	12.8	3.3
			24.0	27.1	29.7	14.1	3.2
			24.2	25.9	31.0	13.8	3.1
			23.8	18.0	30.7	15.1	3.0
			23.6	26.3	45.9	11.7	3.6
1896/97			24.3	31.5	53.8	17.6	4.0
			24.2	30.0	41.8	15.5	2.9
		1.3	25.0	28.7	49.2	13.9	3.2
		1.4	24.9	33.2	72.0	17.5	1.6
		1.5	24.2	25.1	38.9	17.1	2.1
1901/02		1.8	25.1	29.5	41.2	15.6	3.4
		1.7	25.1	29.8	41.8	13.8	2.5
		1.6	25.5	31.0	38.4	16.0	1.4
		1.8	25.9	22.4	40.7	16.0	2.6
		1.6	26.5	36.3	40.7	17.5	2.5
1906/07		2.5	26.9	29.5	40.7	16.9	2.3
		2.2	30.0	35.1	48.0	14.7	3.9
	20.3	11.8	27.9	28.1	40.0	16.5	3.3
	19.4	10.2	28.6	27.5	39.6	15.1	3.6
	19.0	10.2	29.3	24.1	41.3	15.7	2.6
1911/12	19.6	10.5	28.9	22.3	49.6	16.7	2.2
	21.1	13.2	28.6	26.7	47.3	16.0	3.8
	22.3	12.3	28.8	34.8	47.5	16.0	4.0
	21.6	13.5	28.0	30.7	43.8	17.1	3.0
	22.0	15.4	28.9	30.9	53.5	15.4	2.1
1916/17	21.8	13.5	29.0	30.0	45.8	16.2	2.2
	21.0	13.7	27.9	29.8	42.0	14.3	2.2
	24.6	16.2	28.3	35.6	62.5	15.5	5.5
	23.2	15.3	29.3	28.2	50.5	14.7	4.1
	24.2	16.1	28.3	32.6	60.4	15.0	5.1
1921/22	22.4	14.8	28.9	27.5	51.3	13.8	4.8
	22.3	14.3	28.8	27.7	50.3	14.2	4.4
	21.1	14.4	27.9	22.4	48.9	14.0	4.5
	20.8	13.2	27.4	24.2	48.9	14.6	4.1
	22.2	13.4	27.4	27.9	49.1	13.5	4.7

ANNUAL PERCENTAGE OF NET AREA IRRIGATED/NET AREA SOWN FOR BRITISH
INDIA AND REGIONS

	BI	GB	M	UP	GP	BS	CP
1926/27	22.2	13.7	27.1	29.6	51.4	13.7	4.0
	20.3	14.3	26.8	15.8	50.2	13.1	4.4
	22.9	13.8	26.7	30.2	56.3	13.8	4.2
	23.5	13.9	26.8	32.1	56.4	14.9	4.2
	22.8	14.6	26.8	28.9	55.8	13.8	4.4
1931/32	22.4	14.0	27.5	28.2	52.0	14.3	3.8
	23.1	14.5	27.0	28.1	53.0	16.9	5.0
	22.8	14.1	28.0	28.4	50.0	18.4	4.5
	23.5	14.3	28.1	29.9	55.0	17.0	4.2
	23.3	14.7	27.8	30.0	55.2	17.6	5.4
1936/37	23.4	14.8	27.5	28.2	57.8	17.9	4.3
	23.5	15.2	27.3	32.0	59.2	18.6	5.2
	25.2	14.8	26.9	33.0	66.4	18.4	4.3
	25.1	17.3	27.2	32.8	63.9	17.4	5.7
	26.1	17.0	29.0	31.9	58.7	16.5	7.3
1941/42	26.7	17.2	28.4	34.2	59.6	19.0	6.1
	25.8	16.9	29.0	30.4	55.1	20.1	6.7
	26.1	15.6	29.8	30.9	59.8	19.9	6.1
	26.0	16.0	30.5	30.6	57.5	20.2	6.2
	25.9	17.0	30.3	31.2	58.9	20.3	6.6

Source: Computed from data in *Agricultural Statistics*.

APPENDIX TABLE 8B

ANNUAL PERCENTAGE OF AREA DOUBLECROPPED/NET AREA SOWN FOR BRITISH INDIA AND REGIONS

	BI	GB	M	UP	GP	BS	CP
1891/92	12.8	15.9	9.8	23.1	11.4	2.4	6.9
	13.4	17.7	11.2	21.6	12.2	3.6	7.8
	14.8	19.5	13.8	25.0	12.3	3.6	7.8
	14.3	17.7	10.7	26.5	15.2	3.7	7.2
	13.7	18.5	12.3	25.9	11.7	3.0	4.6
1896/97	12.8	17.4	12.8	21.7	14.2	3.7	2.3
	13.9	19.4	12.2	23.8	13.7	3.7	5.2
	14.4	18.6	13.3	23.7	13.7	3.5	5.3
	13.8	19.9	11.6	20.8	15.4	2.4	0.8
	14.8	19.3	13.6	21.5	16.3	3.0	4.4
1901/02	14.5	21.4	13.7	21.9	15.1	3.4	3.4
	14.7	21.3	14.1	22.2	15.7	3.3	4.2
	15.4	22.1	14.8	24.0	14.3	3.7	6.2
	15.6	21.2	12.6	23.9	16.3	3.1	6.7
	15.7	22.2	13.5	23.1	16.7	3.1	6.1
1906/07	16.0	23.5	13.1	24.2	15.1	3.6	6.8
	13.3	22.2	12.6	17.3	14.2	3.0	3.4
	13.4	21.3	12.6	17.8	13.8	3.2	7.0
	14.6	21.5	12.9	21.1	16.1	3.9	6.4
	15.3	21.1	13.2	24.7	15.4	3.9	8.3
	BI	GB	M	UP	GP	BS	CP
1911/12	16.0	20.7	13.0	25.9	18.3	3.5	9.3
	14.7	20.0	13.0	23.2	14.4	4.3	7.2
	13.3	20.5	12.2	18.9	13.1	3.6	5.5
	15.3	19.7	12.7	23.0	19.6	3.9	8.6
	15.7	20.7	13.8	25.5	16.4	4.2	9.3
1916/17	16.1	20.6	13.8	26.8	17.9	3.8	10.1
	17.1	21.1	14.0	28.3	20.7	3.8	10.4
	13.6	22.1	13.8	18.4	15.2	2.9	5.0
	15.3	21.1	15.5	22.4	13.6	3.9	9.4
	12.8	20.9	13.7	17.9	13.5	2.9	4.1
1921/22	15.8	21.8	13.7	23.1	20.0	3.5	8.6
	16.0	21.1	14.4	24.0	18.0	4.6	9.9
	14.9	20.2	12.8	23.9	14.7	3.2	10.3
	15.3	20.1	13.7	24.1	17.7	3.4	9.8
	14.6	20.2	14.6	22.5	14.4	2.6	9.0

APPENDIX TABLE 8B—*Continued*

ANNUAL PERCENTAGE OF AREA DOUBLECROPPED/NET AREA SOWN FOR BRITISH
INDIA AND REGIONS

	BI	GB	M	UP	GP	BS	GP
1926/27	14.0	19.9	12.3	21.3	13.8	3.3	9.5
	15.1	20.5	14.1	23.9	14.9	4.1	9.9
	15.8	21.0	13.8	24.6	19.6	4.1	9.5
	15.1	20.4	14.2	23.1	16.1	3.9	9.1
	15.1	21.3	14.5	23.1	13.8	4.3	9.0
1931/32	15.7	21.5	14.4	22.6	16.7	4.5	10.4
	14.8	21.1	14.5	20.5	14.6	4.1	10.6
	15.8	19.9	14.9	22.0	19.8	4.4	11.0
	14.9	21.1	14.4	21.7	12.9	4.0	11.5
	15.3	20.9	15.1	21.3	16.2	3.9	11.0
1936/37	16.1	19.9	15.4	24.7	18.1	4.7	12.0
	15.6	19.9	15.2	23.7	16.2	4.5	11.2
	16.3	22.7	14.5	24.5	15.2	4.4	12.5
	16.5	22.2	15.3	23.7	16.5	4.6	12.1
	15.9	21.5	16.8	21.1	16.3	5.2	9.5
1941/42	14.9	21.7	15.2	20.3	16.0	4.1	6.9
	17.2	23.0	17.3	23.9	18.4	4.0	10.7
	17.7	25.4	20.1	23.8	15.2	4.8	12.5
	18.2	26.5	17.4	23.5	17.8	5.0	12.7
	17.3	24.8	15.5	25.2	20.5	4.9	12.2

Source : Computed from *Agricultural Statistics*.

APPENDIX TABLE 8c

ANNUAL PERCENTAGE OF FALLOWED/GENERALLY CULTIVATED LAND FOR
BRITISH INDIA AND REGIONS

	BI	GB	M	UP	GP	BS	CP
1891/92	16.1		30.0	8.1	34.1	33.4	13.2
	12.6		23.6	6.4	12.8	30.4	12.5
	13.2		21.3	4.8	16.0	34.1	13.8
	14.7		21.0	9.7	24.2	34.3	9.3
	19.2		21.2	12.4	57.0	40.1	18.6
1896/97	25.2		27.0	19.6	65.0	66.0	24.3
	18.2	7.4	24.3	11.8	22.9	38.2	21.9
	21.0	7.8	23.1	9.2	53.6	39.8	18.9
	32.7	11.2	30.0	10.8	11.5	71.1	34.0
	21.8	14.9	23.5	8.3	18.6	53.6	22.9
1901/02	21.1	16.1	21.9	6.7	27.4	45.2	17.4
	17.7	11.6	20.7	6.0	18.7	41.9	14.8
	17.2	13.9	22.6	5.7	10.3	41.2	13.3
	18.8	9.9	31.2	5.7	19.7	45.8	12.2
	19.6	11.1	27.9	8.9	15.3	51.4	12.3
1906/07	17.3	13.9	25.0	6.1	8.9	39.6	11.7
	25.5	16.2	24.2	17.9	29.3	48.2	18.5
	22.9	25.5	26.1	9.1	11.1	43.6	15.7
	20.0	14.8	29.7	13.1	12.4	43.7	12.4
	20.0	15.5	24.9	7.5	15.2	42.8	12.6
1911/12	24.5	15.8	27.0	9.1	26.1	64.2	12.2
	20.9	15.7	23.8	7.6	16.3	46.4	15.3
	23.3	18.5	25.4	16.4	16.0	44.8	14.8
	19.3	17.4	24.4	6.7	8.6	40.3	13.7
	22.5	19.9	24.5	6.9	31.0	39.8	13.0
1916/17	21.3	19.8	24.7	5.7	9.5	33.6	14.3
	20.5	20.3	26.6	6.9	10.8	34.7	19.4
	36.3	25.5	33.2	23.1	59.0	67.8	23.3
	22.8	19.9	29.5	9.0	16.1	38.0	20.0
	28.4	22.4	29.8	12.5	37.9	51.5	20.9
1921/22	22.5	21.3	30.4	7.3	14.9	38.6	17.4
	20.6	19.3	31.0	7.9	13.6	39.2	14.3
	22.2	22.6	34.3	7.7	15.7	38.4	14.0
	20.7	21.0	30.2	9.0	13.4	34.6	12.4
	21.8	20.9	30.0	9.7	17.1	37.1	13.1

Appendix Table 8c—*Continued*

ANNUAL PERCENTAGE OF FALLOWED/GENERALLY CULTIVATED LAND FOR
BRITISH INDIA AND REGIONS

	BI	GB	M	UP	GP	BS	CP
1926/27	22.0	22.2	32.7	9.2	15.0	35.0	14.0
	21.6	26.4	29.8	8.2	18.3	33.3	13.8
	20.4	22.9	29.7	9.6	14.4	33.7	13.3
	21.4	23.1	29.5	10.4	16.1	31.4	14.3
	21.7	24.4	30.2	7.3	17.2	32.2	13.2
1931/32	21.1	23.8	31.8	6.9	14.8	33.4	14.0
	22.3	26.0	29.6	7.5	20.3	31.0	16.8
	20.5	24.3	30.6	6.9	10.0	30.9	15.1
	23.2	26.1	34.1	8.2	19.0	31.7	16.2
	23.2	29.4	31.9	7.6	14.2	31.1	16.3
1936/37	22.1	25.4	29.9	7.2	12.8	32.5	15.3
	21.0	26.6	29.5	7.3	15.1	29.2	15.5
	21.7	27.2	31.3	7.7	25.2	29.4	16.2
	22.5	26.1	31.0	6.8	20.3	31.0	16.9
	21.1	28.0	29.1	6.9	11.3	29.5	25.2
1941/42	22.1	27.2	30.9	8.2	14.3	32.6	14.3
	21.3	26.1	29.8	6.4	9.2	34.4	17.0
	21.3	21.8	27.8	6.1	13.9	33.0	14.6
	19.7	21.3	29.4	6.3	17.8	32.4	16.4
	20.6	24.7	32.0	6.3	11.4	35.3	17.6

Source: Computed from data in *Agricultural Statistics*. Generally
cultivated land = net area sown + fallow land.

APPENDIX TABLE 9A

MODIFIED ANNUAL SERIES OF GREATER BENGAL RICE OUTPUT AND YIELD PER ACRE BASED ON CONSTANT LEVEL OF RICE YIELD PER ACRE STARTING WITH 1912/13

(Output in 000's tons, y/a in pounds)

	Output	Yield Per Acre		Output	Yield Per Acre
1891/92	11114	628	1921/22	12968	783
	12989	804		13554	817
	14563	868		10303	673
	16211	604		11466	723
	12309	727		10980	694
1896/97	6985	434	1926/27	10209	677
	15533	876		9197	640
	15783	893		12979	813
	13921	793		12162	791
	12114	755		12768	829
1901/02	10585	680	1931/32	13257	819
	13960	836		11919	766
	12314	793		11482	736
	13503	793		11583	752
	11611	715		9450	619
1906/07	11398	697	1936/37	12927	825
	9489	591		12181	781
	9895	659		10439	670
	15422	900		11566	739
	15572	908		8517	576
1911/12	13643	810	1941/42	12735	797
	11971	728		10514	666
	12949	804		15792	889
	10242	628		14511	768
	14125	851		13638	774
1916/17	13942	835	1946/47	14595	810
	14559	888			
	9648	593			
	12597	779			
	10818	676			

Source : See Chapter IX, 1.3.

Appendix Table 9b

MODIFIED ANNUAL SERIES OF GREATER BENGAL ALL-CROP AND FOODGRAIN
OUTPUT AND YIELD PER ACRE BASED ON MODIFIED GREATER BENGAL RICE
YIELD PER ACRE SERIES

(Output in million rupees, y/a in rupees)

	Output		Yield per Acre	
	All-Crop	Foodgrain	All-Crop	Foodgrain
1891/92	2715	2107	50.4	45.3
	3361	2504	63.1	55.8
	3549	2743	66.3	60.8
	3881	3074	71.7	67.0
	3072	2341	58.4	52.5
1896/97	2146	1418	42.4	32.8
	3882	2956	70.5	62.6
	3817	3010	70.3	63.8
	3389	2652	63.3	57.2
	3124	2342	61.9	54.2
1901/02	2892	2067	59.0	49.3
	3429	2661	66.3	59.4
	3207	2389	65.2	56.9
	3386	2581	63.4	56.6
	3093	2293	59.5	51.9
1906/07	3085	2219	59.2	50.7
	2710	1855	53.6	43.8
	2767	1903	58.7	47.6
	3716	2930	70.0	64.3
	3826	2970	72.2	65.3
1911/12	3498	2644	66.8	59.0
	3275	2339	64.1	53.5
	3374	2509	66.7	57.9
	2929	1988	57.3	45.7
	3528	2719	68.5	61.0
1916/17	3573	2709	69.1	60.9
	3675	2798	71.8	63.4
	2659	1891	53.4	43.9
	3354	2474	66.3	56.7
	2837	2157	57.7	50.4
1921/22	3178	2569	63.6	57.9
	3254	2601	64.8	58.6
	2855	2045	59.5	49.4
	3000	2207	61.2	52.1
	2975	2149	60.5	50.8

APPENDIX TABLE 9B—*Continued*

	Output		Yield per Acre	
	All-Crop	Foodgrain	All-Crop	Foodgrain
1926/27	3015	2025	62.6	49.8
	2741	1830	59.7	47.0
	3386	2489	68.7	58.6
	3334	2389	68.6	57.4
	3442	2477	70.8	59.5
1931/32	3237	2555	66.2	59.0
	3179	2337	66.0	55.1
	3149	2233	65.3	53.0
	3257	2270	67.7	54.4
	2756	1856	58.8	45.3
1936/37	3497	2476	72.1	59.1
	3256	2343	67.6	56.2
	2812	2021	58.0	48.3
	3209	2235	66.2	53.5
	2852	1706	58.1	42.8
1941/42	3175	2456	65.5	57.2
	3046	2100	61.2	49.1
	3826	2959	71.5	63.1
	3465	2743	62.9	55.2
	3420	2558	66.4	55.0
1946/47	3404	2717	65.0	57.3

Source : See Chapter IX, 1.3.

Appendix Table 9c

MODIFIED ANNUAL SERIES OF BRITISH INDIA ALL-CROP AND FOODGRAIN
OUTPUT AND YIELD PER ACRE BASED ON MODIFIED GREATER BENGAL RICE
YIELD PER ACRE SERIES
(Output in million rupees, y/a in rupees)

	Output		Yield per Acre	
	All-Crop	Foodgrain	All-Crop	Foodgrain
1891/92	6947	5301	41.4	37.9
	8193	6208	46.3	41.9
	8315	6523	46.7	45.0
	8838	6873	47.5	44.6
	8415	6367	47.8	43.6
1896/97	6947	5043	42.1	36.8
	9646	7389	53.0	48.3
	9625	7433	53.7	49.2
	7691	6022	47.2	44.0
	8783	6614	48.5	43.8
1901/02	8383	6199	48.2	42.5
	9744	7446	53.5	49.0
	9510	7163	51.1	47.1
	8793	6482	47.0	42.6
	8424	6211	45.5	41.1
1906/07	9579	6911	49.6	44.0
	7636	5466	42.4	37.4
	8561	6359	46.0	41.6
	10705	8106	54.8	50.7
	10588	8007	54.0	50.0
1911/12	10039	7461	52.6	48.8
	10086	7328	52.3	46.7
	9335	6678	49.7	44.2
	10244	7254	51.5	45.1
	10554	7915	54.7	49.5
1916/17	11009	8188	55.0	49.9
	10939	8119	54.4	49.8
	7842	5523	45.6	39.5
	10834	7833	55.3	49.6
	8357	6064	46.9	41.5
1921/22	10205	7789	52.6	48.1
	10462	7801	53.4	48.2
	9788	6851	51.0	44.2
	9885	6930	49.7	43.9
	9881	6824	50.9	44.3

APPENDIX TABLE 9c—*Continued*

	Output		Yield per Acre	
	All-Crop	Foodgrain	All-Crop	Foodgrain
1926/27	9918	6775	52.2	44.6
	9649	6408	50.3	41.6
	10276	6984	51.9	44.5
	10498	7239	53.5	46.4
	10597	7253	53.5	45.6
1931/32	10278	7367	51.9	45.8
	10439	7032	53.8	44.8
	11025	7497	55.1	46.6
	10322	6982	54.0	45.0
	10225	6595	53.3	41.7
1936/37	11141	7336	55.7	45.9
	10958	7168	55.1	45.7
	9704	6547	49.3	41.4
	10727	7072	54.5	44.8
	10828	6523	53.3	41.0
1941/42	10379	6968	51.6	43.0
	10827	7189	52.8	42.8
	11752	8032	56.8	47.2
	11019	7760	52.5	44.3
	10630	7224	51.6	42.0
1946/47	10716	7317	52.8	43.3

Source : See Chapter IX, 1.3.

Bibliography

GOVERNMENT OF INDIA PUBLICATIONS

British India

Board of Agriculture. *Proceedings of the Board of Agriculture.*
Census Commissioner. *Census of India,* Vol. I, 1911–1941.
Department of Commercial Intelligence and Statistics. *Accounts of Trade Carried by Rail and River in India* (Quarterly).
———. *Accounts Relating to the Coasting Trade and Navigation of India.*
———. *Agricultural Statistics of India.*
———. *Annual Statement of the Coasting Trade and Navigation of British India.*
———. *Annual Statement of the Sea-Borne Trade of British India.*
———. *Crop Atlas of India.* (Rev. ed.) Delhi : Manager of Publications, 1939.
———. *Estimates of Area and Yield of the Principal Crops in India.*
———. *Index Numbers of Indian Prices.*
———. *Indian Tea Statistics.*
———. *Livestock Census,* 1st (1919) to 5th (1940).
———. *Note on the Production of Coffee* (Annual).
———. *Quinquennial Report on the Average Yield per Acre of Principal Crops.*
———. *Statistical Abstract of British India* (Annual).
Famine Inquiry Commission. *Report.* Delhi : Manager of of Publications, 1945.

Foodgrain Policy Committee. *Report*. Delhi: Manager of Publications, 1943.

Imperial Council of Agricultural Research. *Review of Agricultural Operations*.

Imperial Gazetteer of India, Vol. XV, "Khulna"; Vol. XVIII, "Murshidabad."

Leather, J. W. "Notes on the Value of Indian Cattle Dung," *Agricultural Ledger*, No. 3, 1894 (issued by Department of Agriculture).

Meteorological Department. *Rainfall of India, 1891–1939*.

Office of the Agricultural Marketing Advisor. *Report on the Marketing of Linseed in India*. Delhi: Manager of Publications, 1938.

————. *Report on the Marketing of Rice in India and Burma*. Delhi: Manager of Publications, 1941.

Rao, V. K. R. V. *The Food Statistics of India*. Issued by the Department of Food, 1946.

Sovani, N. V. (ed.). *Reports of the Commodity Prices Board*. Gokhale Institute of Politics and Economics, Publication No. 20, 1948.

Statistics Department. *Prices and Wages in India*.

————. *Report on the Trade Carried by Rail and River in Bengal*.

Subramanian, S. *Guide to Current Official Statistics:* Vol. I, "Production and Prices." (2nd ed.) Delhi: Manager of Publications, 1943. Vol. II, "Trade Transport, Communication, and Finance." Lucknow: 1945.

Unakar, R. S. M. V. "Correlation between Weather and Crops, with Special Reference to Punjab Wheat," *Memoirs of the Indian Meteorological Department*, Vol. XXV, Part IV (1929).

Republic of India

Census Commissioner. *Census of India, 1951*. Vol. I, Part IB— "Appendices to the Census Report."

Deshpande, S. R., Director, Cost of Living Index Scheme.

Reports on *Family Budgets of Industrial Workers in Ludhiana (Punjab), Bombay, Sholapur City (Bombay), Delhi City, Jubbulpore (C.P.), Jamshedpur (Bihar), Cuttack (Orissa), Monghyr and Jamalpur (Bihar), Howrah and Bally (Bengal), Jharia (Bihar), Plantation Workers in Assam and Bengal.*

Indian Council on Agricultural Research. *Indian Farming.*

———. *Sample Surveys for the Estimation of Yield of Food Crops,* 1951.

Ministry of Agriculture. *Coordination of Agricultural Statistics,* 1949.

———. *Livestock Census,* 6th (1945).

———. Directorate of Economics and Statistics. *Abstract of Agricultural Statistics,* 1949.

———. *Indian Agricultural Price Statistics,* 1950.

———. Economic and Statistical Advisor. *The Indian Crop Calendar,* 1950.

Ministry of Finance, Department of Economic Affairs. *Final Report of the National Income Committee,* February 1954.

OTHER GOVERNMENT PUBLICATIONS

Bengal, Customs Department. *Report of the Maritime Trade.*

———. Department of Agriculture. *Agricultural Statistics of Bengal.*

———. *Annual Report.*

———. *Survey and Census of Livestock of Bengal,* 1915.

Great Britain, Royal Commission on Agriculture. *Report of the Royal Commission on Agriculture in India.* London : H. M. Stationary Office, 1928.

Madras. *Report of the Economic Inquiry Conducted for the Government of Madras,* 1931.

———. *Report of the Special Officer for the Investigation of Land Tenure System on the Proposals on Land Revenue Reform,* 1950.

———. Department of Agriculture. *Season and Crop Report.*

Pakistan, Commercial Intelligence and Statistics Department. *Statistical Digest of Pakistan,* 1st issue.

Punjab Board of Inquiry. *Village Surveys, 1928–1940.*

OTHER PUBLICATIONS

Agarwal, S. N. *The Ghandian Plan.* Bombay : Padma Publications, 1944.

Anstey, Vera. "Economic Development," *Modern Indian and Pakistan.* Edited by L. L. O'Malley. London : Oxford University Press, 1941.

Barger, Harold and Hans H. Landsberg. *American Agriculture, 1899–1939: A Study of Output, Employment, and Productivity.* New York : National Bureau of Economic Research, 1942.

Bennett, Merrill K. *The World's Food.* New York : Harper and Bros., 1954.

Biswas, A. K. "A Note on the Trend of Agricultural Production in India, 1893–1946." *Memorandum of the Center for International Studies.* Massachusetts Institute of Technology, 1953.

Blyn, George. *The Agricultural Crops of India, 1893–1946: A Statistical Study of Output and Trends.* Bachelor's thesis, South Asia Regional Studies Department, University of Pennsylvania, 1951. Published in India by the National Income Unit, Government of India, 1954.

———. "Crop Production and Population Trends in Twelve Punjab Villages, 1900–1931." Unpublished MS, South Asia Regional Studies Department, University of Pennsylvania, 1953.

———. "Crop Production and Population Growth in India," *The Business Whirl.* Commerce and Finance School of Villanova University, Vol. VII, No. 2, (May 1960).

———. "Irrigation in Ancient India." Unpublished MS, South Asia Regional Studies Department, University of Pennsylvania, 1950.

Bowley, A. L. and D. H. Robertson. *A Scheme for an Economic Census of India.* New Delhi : Government of India Press, 1934.

A Brief Memoir Outlining a Plan of Economic Development for India. Sponsored by Tata, Birla, and other industrialists. Bombay, 1944.

Buchanan, Daniel H. *The Development of Capitalistic Enterprise in India.* New York : The MacMillan Company, 1934.

Burns, Arthur F. "Measurement of Physical Volume of Production," *Quarterly Journal of Economics,* Vol. XLIV, No. 1 (February 1930).

————. *Production Trends in the United States Since 1870.* New York : National Bureau of Economic Research, 1934.

Burns, William. *Technological Possibilities of Agricultural Development in India.* Lahore : Superintendent of Government Printing, 1944.

Callander, William F. "Crop and Livestock Reporting," *Encyclopaedia of the Social Sciences,* III, 607–611. New York : MacMillan Co., 1937.

Chatterjee, S. P. *Bengal in Maps.* Calcutta : Orient Longmans Ltd., 1949.

Croxton, F. E. and D. J. Crowden. *Applied General Statistics.* (2nd ed.) New York : Prentice Hall, 1955.

Davis, J. S. "Some Observations on Federal Agricultural Statistics," *Supplement to Proceedings of the American Statistical Association, March 1928.*

Davis, Kingsley. *The Population of India and Pakistan.* Princeton : Princeton University Press, 1951.

Desai, R. C. "Consumer Expenditure in India, 1931/32 to 1940/41," *Journal of the Royal Statistical Society,* CXI, Part IV (1948).

————. *Standard of Living in India and Pakistan.* Bombay : Popular Book Depot, 1953.

Dubey, Daya Shankar. "A Study of the Indian Food Problem," *Indian Journal of Economics,* Vol. III, Parts 1, II (1920/21).

Dutt R. Palme. *India Today.* (2nd rev. ed.) Bombay : People's Publishing House, 1949.

Ezekiel, Mordecai. *Methods of Correlation Analysis.* New York : John Wiley and Sons, Inc., 1930.

Fabricant, Solomon. *The Output of Manufacturing Industries, 1899–1937.* New York : National Bureau of Economic Research, 1940.

Farmer, B. H. "On Not Controlling Subdivision in Paddy Lands." *Institute of British Geographers, Transactions and Papers, 1960.*

Gandhi, M. P. *The Indian Sugar Industry.* Calcutta : G. N. Mitra, 1934.

Geddes, Arthur. *Au Pays de Tagore: la civilization rurale du Bengale occidentale et ses facteurs geographiques.* Paris : Libraire Arman Colin, 1937.

——. "Half a century of population trends in India, a regional study of net change and variability, 1881–1931," *Geographical Journal,* XCVIII.

——. "The Alluvial Morphology of the Indo-Gangetic Plain," *Institute of British Geographers, Transactions and Papers,* Publication No. 28, 1960.

——. "The Population of Bengal, Its Distribution and Changes," *Geographical Journal,* Vol. 89, No. 4 (1937).

——. "The Population of India," *Geographical Review,* Vol. XXXII (1942).

——. "Variability in Change of Population and Its Significance with Examples from India-Pakistan and North America, to 1941," *Proceedings of the International Population Conference,* Vienna, 1959.

Ghandi, M. K. *Food Shortage and Agriculture.* Edited by B. Kumarappa. Ahmedabad : Navijivan Publishing House, 1949.

——. *The India of My Dreams.* Edited by R. K. Prabhu. Bombay : Hind Kitabs, 1947.

Goldsmith, Raymond. "The Economic Growth of Tsarist Russia, 1860-1913," *Economic Development and Cultural Change,* IX, 3 (April 1961).

Hunter, W. W. *The Annals of Rural Bengal.* London : Smith, Elder & Co., 1868.

Indian National Congress, Central Elections Board. *27 Months of Service.* Bombay, n.d.

Iyengar, K. R. R. and H. C. Arora. "Long Term Growth of National Income in India, 1901–1956," *Indian Conference on Research in National Income, Papers on National Income and Allied Topics,* Vol. I. Edited by V. K. R. V. Rao et al. Bombay : Asia Publishing House, 1960.

Jathar, G. B. and S. G. Beri. *Indian Economics.* (9th ed.) Madras : Oxford University Press, 1949.

Johnston, B. F. and J. W. Mellor. "Agriculture in Economic Development," *American Economic Review,* LI, 4 (September 1961).

Khambata, K. J. and K. T. Shah. *Wealth and Taxable Capacity of India.* Bombay : D. B. Taraporeval Sons and Co., 1924.

Lamb, Helen B. *Economic Development of India.* Allahabad : Friends Book Depot, 1954.

Majumdar, S. C. *Rivers of the Bengal Delta.* University of Calcutta, 1942.

Mann, Harold H. "The Economic Results and Possibilities of Irrigation," *Indian Journal of Agricultural Economics,* Vol. XIII, No. 2 (1958).

Meek, D. B. "Some Measures of Economic Activity in India," *Journal of the Royal Statistical Society,* XCVI, 1933.

Meston, Lord, of Agra and Dunottar. "Statistics in India," *Journal of the Royal Statistical Society,* XCVI, 1933.

Mills, Frederick C. *Statistical Methods.* (3rd ed.) New York : Henry Holt and Co., 1955.

Mitra, N. N. (ed.) *The Indian Annual Register.*

Mukerjee, Radhakamal. *Food Planning for Four Hundred Millions.* London : MacMillan Co., 1938.

———. *The Food Supply.* (2nd ed.) London : Oxford University Press, 1944.

Mukerji, Kshiti Mohon. "Planning and the Public Sector in an Underdeveloped Economy." Unpublished Ph.D. dissertation, Department of Economics, University of Calcutta, 1958.

Naidu, B. V. N. and S. Hariharan. *Groundnut.* Madras : Annamali University, 1941.

Nanavati, Manilal B. and J. J. Anjaria. *The Indian Rural Problem*. (3rd ed.) Bombay : The Indian Society of Agricultural Economics, 1947.

Nehru, J. *Discovery of India*. New York : The John Day Co., 1946.

O'Malley, L. S. S. *Bengal District Gazeteers: Murshidabad*. Calcutta, 1914. Jessore, 1912.

———. *Bengal, Bihar and Orissa, Sikkim*. Cambridge : University Press, 1917.

Patel, Surendra J. "Agricultural Labourers in Modern India and Pakistan," *Indian Journal of Economics,* Vol. XXXIII, Part 1 (July 1952).

———. "Long-Term Changes in Output and Income in India : 1896–1960," *Indian Economic Journal,* Vol. V, No. 3 (January 1958).

Patil, B. A. *Agricultural Price Problems in India*. Bombay : The Bombay State Cooperative Union, 1959.

Pesek, Boris P. "Economic Growth and Its Measurement," *Economic Development and Cultural Change,* IX, 3 (April 1961).

Rao, V. K. R. V. *The National Income of British India, 1931/32*. London : MacMillan and Co., Ltd., 1940.

Roy, M. N. *People's Plan for Economic Development of India*. Written for the Radical Democratic Party. Delhi : 1944.

Singh, D. Bright. *Inflationary Price Trends in India Since 1939*. Bombay : Asia Publishing House, 1957.

Smithsonian Miscellaneous Collection. *World Weather Records*.

Sovani, N. V. *Post-War Inflation in India—a Survey*. Gokhale Institute of Politics and Economics, Publication No. 21, 1949.

Spate, O. H. K. *India and Pakistan*. New York : H. P. Dutton and Co., 1954.

Stamp, L. Dudley. *Asia, a Regional and Economic Geography*. (8th ed.) London : Methuen and Co., Ltd., 1950.

Thomas, P. J. and N. S. Sastry. *Commodity Prices in South India, 1918–1938*. Madras : University of Madras, 1940.

————. *Indian Agricultural Statistics.* Madras : University of Madras, 1939.

Thorner, Daniel and Alice. *Land and Labour in India.* Bombay : Asia Publishing House, 1962.

————. *India and Pakistan, Most of the World.* Edited by Ralph Linton. New York : Columbia University Press, 1949.

————. *Comparability of Census Economic Data, 1881–1951.* Bombay : Indian Statistical Institute, 1958.

————. *The Working Force in India, 1881–1951.* Bombay : Census of 1961 Project, Indian Statistical Institute.

Thorner, Daniel : "Long-term Trends in Output in India," *Economic Growth: Brazil, India, Japan.* Edited by S. Kuznets *et al.* Duke University, 1955.

Wade, C. P. G. *Mechanical Cultivation in India, a History of the Large Scale Experiments Carried Out by Burmah-Shell Oil Storage and Distribution Company of India,* Delhi : Imperial Council on Agricultural Research, 1935.

Wickizer, V. D. and M. K. Bennett. *The Rice Economy of Monsoon Asia.* Stanford : Food Research Institute, 1941.

Woytinsky, W. W. and E. S. *World Population and Production: Trends and Outlooks.* New York : The Twentieth Century Fund, 1953.

Zobler, Leonard. "A New Areal Measure of Food Production Efficiency," *Geographical Review,* LI, 4 (October 1961).

Index

A (*see* acreage)
AC (*see* all-crop)
acreage
  and population change, 208–209
  and y/a changes, compared by crops and regions, 226–231
  annual, AC, FG, NFG: by regions, 316–325; by crops, regional, 253–311
  change and climate, 231
  change and influence on y/a, 164, 179, 236–237; for Greater Bengal crops, 174–175
  change for foodgrains compared with nonfoodgrains, 233
  changes in land use: B.I., 127–130, 231–232; regional, 131–141, 231–232
  expansion, and irrigation, 135–138
  irrigated, minor foodgrains, 160–161
  irrigated/sown, annually, by regions, 340–341
  NFG/AC, regional 181
  NFG/FG, regional, 167–168 n
  RD trend rates, AC, FG, NFG, regional, 331–333
  total sown, by provinces, 252
  trends, B.I., by crops: foodgrains, 140–144; nonfoodgrains, 144–147
adjustments of crop data, 57–73
Agricultural Statistics, 39–40

aggregation of crops
  by nutritive value, 74
  price weights, 75–78
  with alternate price weights, 213-216
Ajmer-Merwara, and geographical coverage, 35
all-crop Y, A, Y/A
  annual, by regions, 316–325
  RD trend rates, B.I., 327–330; regionally, 331–333
all-crop Y and Y/A, modified annual series based on zero rice y/a trend in Greater Bengal
  Greater Bengal, 347–348
  B.I., 349–350
Anjaria, J. J., 45 n
Anstey, V., on agricultural trends, 22–23 n
Argentina, and linseed exports, 107
Arora, H. C., 21 n
asfd (agreement of signs of first differences), 67
Assam, and geographical coverage, 35
availability
  all-crop, 123–124, 247–248
  and output: foodgrains, 103–107, 240–244; nonfoodgrains, 115–118, 244–245
  foodgrain: annual, B.I., 334, Greater Bengal, 335–336; RD trend rates, B.I., and Greater Bengal, 337

DATE DUE

MAY 4			
GAYLORD			PRINTED IN U.S.A.